Loved by Choice

Loved by Choice

True Stories That Celebrate Adoption

Susan Horner
Kelly Fordyce Martindale

Fleming H. Revell
A Division of Baker Book House Co
Grand Rapids, Michigan 49516

Published by Fleming H. Revell
a division of Baker Book House Company
P.O. Box 6287, Grand Rapids, MI 49516-6287

Printed in the United States of America

Library of Congress Cataloging-in-Publication Data

Horner, Susan E.
    Loved by choice : true stories that celebrate adoption / Susan E. Horner, Kelly Fordyce Martindale.
        p.   cm.
    ISBN 0-8007-1786-4
    1. Adoption—United States—Case studies. 2. Adoptive parents—United States—Biography. 3. Birthparents—United States—Biography. 4. Adopted children—United States—Biography. I. Martindale, Kelly Fordyce. II. Title.
HV875.55 .H674 2002
306.874—dc21   2002001190

For current information about all releases from Baker Book House, visit our web site:
http://www.bakerbooks.com

Contents

Acknowledgments

I am grateful to every contributor. You openly shared your lives with us, making the book possible. Special thanks to my husband, Marc, and daughters, Anneli and Amy, for your encouragement and advice. And to my dear, sweet mother, who helped us with the laundry and meals. And thank you, friends, for your prayers.

Susan Horner

I dedicate this book to my dad, Jack Fordyce, my greatest encourager, and to my father-in-law, Dick Martindale, for adopting my husband, Mike, and my sister-in-law, Lori.

I am deeply grateful to my husband; my kids—Jason, Robert, and Audrey; and Ruth Moxness, Carma Hedrick, Peggy Blewett, and Joseph Coenen; and especially to all of you who shared your lives with us and opened old wounds so others could be healed.

Kelly Fordyce Martindale

Introduction

Loved by Choice grew from one consuming vision—that more people would consider adoption. We found it disturbing that with unwed moms adoption is the least considered option and that potential adopting parents negated the option because of extreme fear of loving and then losing an adopted child due to some legality. Our vision for *Loved by Choice* is not unique. Nearly five years ago, Dave Thomas, founder of Wendy's Old Fashioned Hamburgers, challenged our country to share the positive side of adoption. He expressed his concern that adoption stories in the news are not always good.

We are saddened by the death of Mr. Thomas. But we know he has left a legacy that will affect adoption for years to come because of the significant work he and the Dave Thomas Foundation for Adoption have already accomplished. *Loved by Choice* builds on the principles set forth by Dave Thomas and others affected by adoption.

Thankfully, in the last year our country is seeing a positive surge in adoption stories, both in special programs and with adopted characters in television shows. These programs not only encourage adoption, but they support and validate everybody affected by an adoption. In writing *Loved by Choice* we discovered that each individual, whether adoptee or adopted, grandparent or sibling, has a unique perspective on the very personal and loving act of adoption.

We know others will celebrate with the men and women who labored emotionally and spiritually until the joyful moment their child was permanently placed in their arms and their home. And for the mothers who have placed their babies, we hope this book will crown them with the honor and dignity they deserve. We found these mothers to be incredible women who love and care in such a sacrificial way that they were willing to suffer loss so their child could have more. Through the trials of giving up a baby or accepting one with special needs, even a baby infected with HIV as in "The Year of Jubilee," every story ultimately shows that adoption is the perfect choice.

We, the compilers and our literary agent, have been touched personally by adoption. Susan E. Horner has emotionally and prayerfully supported families during their decisions to adopt. Susan was asked to attend child-birthing classes with a woman who had made the choice to place her baby for adoption. Susan's admiration and compassion for mothers who choose adoption was kindled through their friendship. Kelly Fordyce Martindale has worked with crisis pregnancy centers for many years and has family members who are adopted, including her husband. Our literary agent, William D. Watkins, was adopted from birth, as were his brother and sister.

Loved by Choice not only makes you feel good about the choice for adoption but it

- encourages the choice for life because adoption works
- provides evidence that adoption influences personal growth and wholeness
- brings awareness of the positive impact adoption has on society
- inspires families during the lengthy process to adopt
- answers questions regarding the true meaning of "family"
- breaks down cultural boundaries and unites human hearts through these real-life adoption stories

You'll laugh and certainly cry as you read each individual's story. But the candor in which the stories have been written will instigate conversations promising to initiate change, both personal and societal. Why? Because the first-person accounts of adoption from different viewpoints are delivered in a straight-forward manner and with poignant honesty. They answer the difficult, often unasked questions about adoption. The stories build a bridge between those adopting and those supporting. They help each one involved in an adoption to have under-standing, respect, and compassion for the other. Readers will find usable and up-to-date adoption resources from around the country and a basic and personal guide to the complete adop-tion process.

In short, *Loved by Choice* is an all-inclusive, clear, practical guide through the adoption process that also touches the heart with personal stories. We are confident that readers will con-nect with the families in *Loved by Choice*. It is our belief that for every negative adoption story portrayed by the media, there are hundreds of positive stories. We've provided about sixty of them. Janie Roos, mother of three adopted children, said, "I have never seen a book that covers so many points of view and emotions of those involved in adoption."

This book encourages understanding and compassion between birth parents and adoptive parents. Through these sto-ries we know there will be fewer tears shed from fear and mis-trust and more tears of joy and mutual gratefulness.

We liken adoption to tree grafting. The tree is both real and symbolic of the family. People have been grafting trees for thou-sands of years, and family trees and histories will continue to grow strong and beautiful through adoption.

Take the story of Mr. Jones, who had grown up on an orchard and knew all about tree grafting. He brought home three ten-der buds, each from a different kind of apple tree. Each slen-der slip represented one of his adopted children.

Mr. Jones made the proper cuts into the bark of the trunk and set a tiny branch into each slit. Then he tightly wrapped each branch to the trunk until a union of living cells formed between them. The branches drew their water and nutrients from the tree's roots, sprouted leaves, and made food for the well-being of the whole tree.

One perfect spring the family apple tree burst with beautiful blossoms. His oldest daughter's branch was loaded with dark pink, while his son's branch was smothered in creamy white blossoms. The baby's branch was full of dewy pink flowers.

People would stop and take in the beauty of the Joneses' family tree. And in the fall each branch provided the family with a different variety of apple. For though the branches were nourished from the tree's roots, they still carried within the beauty and flavor from which they came.

There's a saying that blood is thicker than water, but *Loved by Choice* proves that blood has nothing to do with *family*— unconditional love and acceptance make the difference.

Part 1

Connected through Adoption
Branches of a Family Tree

No Regrets

Tanya Corn

In January 1985, I was sixteen years old and had just found out I was pregnant. I was devastated because I knew I couldn't have a baby. How was a sixteen-year-old girl supposed to raise a child? I still needed to grow up. When I told my boyfriend, Dave, he was shocked. Neither of us thought it could happen the first time having sex. Boy, were we wrong. For a while we tried to ignore the truth, but eventually we had to make some decisions.

Dave and I decided that we could not go through with this pregnancy. I had to have an abortion. I wasn't comfortable with this decision, but I didn't feel I had a choice.

In April we made an appointment to go to an abortion clinic. I was very nervous. What if someone found out we were here? What if something happened to me? And how could I kill this baby? Finally a nurse took me to a room and asked if I was sure of this decision. I said yes, despite my fears.

They did an exam to see how far along I was and discovered I was four months pregnant, not three. As a result they would not perform the abortion. I was too far along and it would be more complicated. I was scared, relieved, and angry all at the same time. Looking back, I feel like the baby and I had been protected.

Dave and I left the clinic not knowing what to do. It wouldn't be long before I started showing and my mom was already suspicious. She kept asking me if I was pregnant, and every time I told her no.

A couple of weeks after we had gone to the clinic I finally told my mom. I knew I had broken my mom's heart. She cried so much. I felt so bad that I had done this to her and the rest of my family. As I left for school that day, I couldn't believe this was real.

When Dave met me for our usual walk to school, he could see I had been crying and asked what was wrong. When I told him he got angry for having told my mom without him. I think he was also angry because he wanted to wait longer before we told. We both kept thinking we would wake up from this nightmare we had created for ourselves.

That evening I had to tell my dad and that was even harder than telling my mom. Daddy insisted I not get married, and I strongly agreed. I did not want to be married at sixteen and raise a baby. My dad also said that I could no longer see Dave outside of school.

Dave's mother, however, insisted we get married. His parents had an apartment we could live in, and Dave could quit school and work to support us. But by then I had already decided to give the baby up for adoption. Then the accusations started flying. Everyone was crying. It was a mess.

It was hard to keep going to school since I was starting to show. Friends and teachers asked me about the pregnancy, and many were supportive when I told them I wasn't keeping the baby. I was too young to raise a child and I couldn't quit school. Nor were my parents going to raise this child. They would have, but I didn't feel that was right.

My mom made arrangements for me to go to a doctor and also to get counseling. I didn't feel that I needed counseling, but I went anyway. When I first met Pam at the adoption agency, I told her that I didn't need any help. She just smiled and started talking to me about the choice I was making—how it would affect the baby, my family members, and myself.

Pam wanted to make sure that I felt I was doing the right thing. While I never faltered in my decision to give the baby up, I came to realize how hard it would be. Pam and I eventually became friends through my private and group sessions. It helped to know there were other girls in my position going through the same ups and downs.

Dave and I would sneak visits when we could. Eventually he lost interest in me and decided he didn't want any part of the baby. So it all fell on me. I had to be responsible, but Dave didn't.

I began to hope this baby would be a boy. I thought if he looked like Dave, then it would be easier to give him up. I would always insist that it was a boy.

It took a long time for me to get over the hurt and forgive him for not sticking with me till the baby came. Years later Dave realized that he had missed out by not seeing or holding his baby.

Eventually, through counseling, I started to accept that no matter what, this was my baby and I would love it. I'm not sure when it happened, but I began to love my child growing inside me.

I started thinking of the adoptive parents and what a gift it would be to give my child to a couple who were longing for a baby. When it came time to choose who would raise my baby, Pam gave me letters from three couples. David and Janie's letter was the first one I read. They expressed their deep love for each other and God, and that drew me to them. They also had a dog. Being an animal lover, I wanted my child to know the joy of a family pet.

Finally I wanted to choose a couple that could financially support my child. I felt their deep love for my child and knew they were the right people for my baby.

The adoption would be semi-open. We would know first names and would meet at the agency, but that was all. About two weeks before the baby was born, my mom and I met David and Janie. I fell in love with both of them instantly. They asked me a lot of questions, and I asked them questions too. I asked them to come to the birth and they were excited to know I wanted them there.

On Tuesday, September 10 at 11:49 A.M., I gave birth to a beautiful baby girl and named her Brina Ashley. David and Janie named her Rebekah Jane and called her Becky. I thought it was a very pretty name.

I could not believe the overwhelming love that filled my heart for her. I remember holding my tiny baby and being so amazed. She was a perfectly wonderful little girl.

I wondered if I could still go through with the adoption. But I also knew that no matter how hard I tried I could not give this precious little baby everything she would need. I had nothing to offer but love, and that wasn't enough.

Becky slept most of the time. In fact, the only time she seemed to wake up was when her grandpa held her. She must have felt something deep within, because she only opened her eyes when she was with him.

Our days together in the hospital were bittersweet. I held Becky and cried a lot. I told her how much I loved her and hoped she'd understand why I was giving her up for adoption. I asked my baby to forgive me, hoping that maybe someday she would understand how heartbreaking this was for me.

My last day in the hospital was very difficult. The nurses had me sit and rock Becky for a while to say good-bye. When I finally laid her down and walked out of the nursery, my heart was hurting so badly I could not stop the tears. When I got back to my room, my teddy bear of a daddy was waiting to hold me. I wondered if the hurt would ever stop.

As we were leaving the hospital, we crossed paths with David and Janie. That was hard, but I was relieved to know Becky's new parents had come for her and she would not be alone. Janie gave me a big hug and thanked me for this gift, which made me cry even more. It was a very hard day.

But time does heal. As the days went by I cried less and less. It helped knowing Becky was being well taken care of.

I continued in counseling for about a year and a half after Becky was born. What helped me the most was sharing my story with other girls who were experiencing the same emotions and hearing how they dealt with their inner turmoil.

Becky was nine months old when the adoption was finalized and I received an unexpected gift: the chance to see my little girl again. The moment I saw her I knew I had made the right choice. She was a healthy, happy, smiling, wonderful child. When she looked at me it was as if she knew who I was and loved me. My joy was indescribable.

When Becky was three I was working for Pam at the adoption agency. The agency was planning a party for adoptive parents and children. David and Janie would be there. Pam cleared with them that I would be there too. David, Janie, and Becky met me at the office a few days before the party for a visit, and Becky was very at ease with me.

When I arrived at the party, Becky took my hand, walked me around, and told everyone that I was her birth mom. What joy filled my heart! She seemed to understand I loved her very much.

After that I chose not to see Becky for a long time but was kept up-to-date through letters and pictures. I said I didn't want her to be confused, but really I needed to get on with my life. I knew she was okay, and that I was going to be okay too.

Janie continues to send me pictures and notes about what Becky is doing. This has helped me a lot. Becky has now met my husband and my two daughters and our families have had some wonderful visits together. The semi-open adoption has since grown into a trusting open relationship. I usually let Janie contact me, though, because I don't want to overstep the boundaries of our beautiful friendship.

Mother's Day Bouquet

Janie Roos

David and I met while he was in medical school. I was a nurse working in Newborn ICU and he was about to start his pediatric residency. It was a whirlwind romance, and we knew from the start we would be married. We both loved children and wanted to be parents, but David discovered he was infertile.

Three years after we were married we found a surgeon who had some success with David's type of infertility. We traveled across the country, checked into the hospital, and prayed the surgery would work. After many months it was evident that David was still infertile. It was so hard to accept that we would never become pregnant.

We began to pursue adoption and were told the average wait for an infant was three to five years. I really wanted to adopt an infant, so we put our names on a waiting list, filled out the paperwork, and asked several friends to write letters saying they thought we would be fit parents.

Then a friend in another state told us her patient was looking for an adoptive couple. We were thrilled and started putting our nursery together in hopes we would soon be parents.

While refinishing a small wooden crib that had been in David's family for years, we got a call from our lawyer. He said the adoption was off. I hung up the phone and went downstairs crying, but continued to work on the crib in faith that we would one day have a child to place in it.

Shortly after the failed adoption we heard about a new adoption agency. The woman in charge had such a loving spirit, and talking with her was just what I needed. She comforted me in my isolation from friends who were pregnant or had babies.

She also had compassion for women in crisis pregnancies. She encouraged the pregnant women who came to her to ask God what his plans were for their babies. It seemed like a revolutionary attitude at the time.

I soon realized that a girl could be carrying our child that very moment. I started praying for her and our baby. I became concerned for the difficulties she was experiencing and desired to meet this young woman who was going to make such a loving sacrifice.

At that time it was uncommon for adoptive parents to meet birth parents, but I desired to know the birth mother. I wanted to reassure her that we would be the best parents we could be. Further, the more I knew about her, the better I could answer our child's questions. And most of all, I needed to hear from her that she felt confident God was calling her to relinquish her baby. I didn't want to feel like I had snatched her baby away.

About four months after our initial contact with the agency we received a call. A teenager was looking at our file and expressed a desire to meet with us. David and I enjoyed meeting Tanya and her mother, Mary Jo. It was an incredible meeting and confirmed to me how miraculous it is for a child to be placed in a family.

Tanya chose us, and we were thrilled.

Twenty-four hours after Becky was born the agency called and said Tanya and her family were ready for us to see our baby. To say we were excited would be an understatement.

Mary Jo brought Becky in to us and lovingly placed her in our arms. She stayed with us a few minutes as we checked out our beautiful new daughter. Mary Jo was proud of her new granddaughter, and of Tanya for the difficult decision she had made. It helped me to know Tanya had such a supportive family.

We stayed about an hour in the hospital. We were thrilled to finally meet our beautiful daughter, Becky. We wanted to stay longer but understood Tanya and her family were saying their good-byes. This was their time with Becky.

Our adoption agency thought it was best for babies to be placed directly with their adoptive parents instead of going to foster care until they were relinquished. We were taking a risk in that we had no legal right to Becky when we brought her home from the hospital.

What a wonderful, incredible feeling it was to bring her home at three days old. I had taken care of newborn babies in ICU for almost nine years and thought I knew all about caring for babies; however, I didn't feel confident at all during my first few days at home with Becky. Thank God for lots of supportive friends.

When Becky was less than two weeks old I went shopping with her in the Snugli. People would ask how old she was and when I told them they would say, "Boy, you look great!"

The bittersweet part for me was while I was experiencing great joy, I knew Tanya was experiencing great loss. I did not feel I was a better mother than Tanya could have been; my circumstances were just different. I was older and had a loving husband who wanted a child as much as I did. She was a teenager, without a husband, trying to finish high school.

It took incredible strength to be able to say good-bye to her beautiful daughter, especially not knowing if she would ever see her again. I wanted to make sure Tanya and her family knew Becky was doing great, so I sent pictures to the agency to pass on to Tanya several times that first year.

The relinquishment did not go smoothly, partially because the agency was new and also because some court dates were canceled because of snow.

When Becky turned nine months old Tanya asked the agency social worker if she could see Becky. It really scared me because Tanya was still Becky's legal mother and technically could take her from us.

I prayed and called my pastor's wife. As we talked God gave me peace. I realized children do not belong to their parents, adoptive or otherwise. They belong to God. Our time with them is a gift.

When Tanya heard we preferred she see Becky after the relinquishment, she graciously agreed.

A few weeks after the papers were signed we took Becky to see Tanya. Sometimes when Becky smiles I am reminded of Tanya. She will always be a part of Becky.

As Mother's Day approached my thoughts turned to Tanya. I worried about how she was feeling. Was she regretting the decision she made to relinquish her baby? Was she feeling depressed and lonely that no one thought of her as a mother?

I talked to one of my friends who had relinquished a baby several years before. She said her child's parents had sent her a bouquet of roses on Mother's Day. I was much more comfortable with this than just sitting around wondering how Tanya was feeling.

Almost every year now David and I have sent flowers or a gift along with pictures of Becky, for Mother's Day. One year Tanya sent me flowers. I felt so honored. Now all of our kids write cards and help select gifts to send to their birth moms. I want these special women to know they have not been forgotten.

We accepted Tanya as an important person in our daughter's life and wanted a fairly open relationship with her. When Becky was young we would try to meet with Tanya at the agency about once a year. Sometimes it was at our request and other times it was at hers. This was always arranged through the agency.

As Becky got older and our adoption guidelines became more relaxed, we exchanged phone numbers. Now we call each other occasionally and arrange our own meetings. Tanya has always been gracious about scheduling visits in advance.

Tanya married a wonderful man and now has two beautiful daughters. She is a wonderful mother. Just as I always knew she would be.

Different This Time Around
Mary Jo Sattler

Ramsay and I liked each other the summer between eighth and ninth grade. Then my family moved away. Years later we met again after I was divorced with two little daughters. He said he fell in love with all three of us.

Even though Ramsay was never able to adopt them, in his heart they are his own. And Tammy and Tanya love their precious Daddy.

Our oldest daughter, Tammy, had a baby boy between her junior and senior year in high school. It was a closed adoption. I often wonder how my grandson is doing. When I worry about him, I think of Ramsay. If he could love my girls the way he does, surely an adoptive couple could do the same for our grandson.

When Tanya was sixteen, I started to panic. All the things I had seen with Tammy I was seeing with Tanya. And it was all too familiar. I kept thinking she and her boyfriend were getting entirely too close. And as it turned out they were.

When Tanya told me she was pregnant my feelings of devastation were overwhelming. My first thought was for me, *Oh my God, my Lord, I'm going to lose another grandchild!* I didn't think I could bear it.

Ramsay was angry, hurt, and totally baffled this had happened again!

Tanya decided to have her baby adopted, which we agreed with. We found a wonderful Christian adoption agency. Tanya made up her mind who she wanted, and then brought me the biography to see if we agreed on the couple.

I thought David and Janie sounded ideal because of their heartfelt need and because their beliefs so paralleled our own.

David and Janie were already there when we walked into the office. My first reaction was that Janie looked so much like Tanya she could be her sister. David was kindness itself, and my heart went out to them. What a comfort it was to meet the people who would be the parents of my grandchild. This was a totally different experience than with our grandson.

Tanya had a pretty rough labor. Ramsay was pretty shaken up by it. I ached for her, knowing how young she was. Finally we had a beautiful baby girl. So like Tanya as a newborn.

Tanya and I held and nurtured the baby as soon as she was born. The separation ritual had to begin. I loved my grandbaby from the day Tanya told me she was pregnant. When Becky was born, I cradled her in my arms and whispered how much I loved her, and that Jesus loved her even more. I told her he would take care of her, and be her best friend, because I couldn't be there. I prayed a prayer of dedication to the Lord, trying to infuse in Becky all the love I would not be able to physically show or say for the next "hundred years."

Ramsay held Becky every time we came to the hospital. He would hardly let me hold her. He would sit with her crooked in his arm, down at his lap. I finally asked him why he didn't hold her on his chest like he held all the other babies. He said he wouldn't be able to let her go if she got that close to his heart. It about broke my heart. Sometimes we forget, in our own agony, how much things can affect others.

When David and Janie came to the hospital I wanted to be the one to take Becky to them because Tanya didn't think she could. The Lord, Becky, and I walked into the room, and in my heart and mind I relinquished my granddaughter to David and Janie.

Oh, how I cried. They did too. Their crying was from pure joy; mine was from such an agony of my spirit that I could hardly stand it. And yet I knew how much better Becky's life would be with them.

The next day Tanya said good-bye to Becky. I said good-bye to Becky. Ramsay could not say good-bye.

As we were leaving the hospital David and Janie were just arriving. They seemed to exude such love for Tanya. They hugged Tanya and me while Ramsay, trying to conceal his pain, faced forward in the car.

We went to court several weeks later for a part of the adoption process. Although it hurt to have to go through the relinquishing all over again, we all had a peace about the rightness of it.

Even though Tanya said and did all the right things, I never felt that in her heart she had truly given her child to David and Janie. She always seemed to hold on to a part of Becky. I ached for Tanya; it was hard to see my daughter hurting so much.

When Becky was about five years old, Tanya came to me and said, "Mom, I've finally been able to let go of Becky." I immediately had a feeling of pure joy wash over me.

I've always appreciated David and Janie for being open with Tanya, welcoming her into their home, loving her for herself, and letting her see what a beautiful, kind, generous person her daughter has become. Not knowing what happened to Tammy's baby has always weighed on my mind.

Recently I was able to meet Becky. I could hardly wait to get home and tell Ramsay she is everything we could hope for in a granddaughter.

Doubly Loved

Becky Roos as told to Susan Horner

I just love Tanya, my birth mom. It's always fun for me when she and my family spend time together. My dad took a video of

Tanya and my grandmother, Mary Jo, visiting me at the adoption agency when I was nine months old. And we have a video of Tanya when she was twenty and I was three.

Tanya married when I was ten. We all got together so Tanya's husband and I could meet each other. We have videos of that visit too. It's cool to be able to watch how both of us have grown up and changed over the years.

I'm glad Tanya chose not to parent me, but placed me for adoption instead. I'm thankful Tanya gave me to a woman who was longing for a baby. Mom had already experienced college and a career and was at a place in her life where staying home with a baby seemed exciting.

Tanya gave me a dad who was praying for me before I was born, a dad who couldn't wait to hold me and call me his own, a dad who wanted to provide for me and give me many opportunities. When I go away to camp for a week, he sends me a note telling me he loves me, and how proud he is of me, and that he hopes I have fun while I'm away.

My parents encircle Zac, Amy, and me with their love, giving us a feeling of security and confidence. I'm thankful Tanya gave me that.

I'm fifteen years old and there's no way I will be ready in two years to be the kind of mother I hope to be someday.

I think Tanya and I both benefited from her choice. Mom has told me how painful it was for Tanya to place me for adoption. I admire Tanya for hurting so I wouldn't have to and for going on with her life by setting goals and achieving them.

I'm not saying Tanya would have resented me, but being a teenager myself, I have a lot of things I want to do and can understand how some teen moms might feel toward their kids.

I can't imagine how hard it would have been for me to have a teen mom who was still in high school, maybe working at a fast-food restaurant and dating. It doesn't seem like there would have been much time for me in her schedule.

Last Christmas Tanya suggested that her mother come visit me. Meeting my birth grandmother, Mary Jo, for the first time was really special. As soon as she saw me she smiled and said, "I can tell where you came from!" We welcomed her inside and had a fun visit together. I listened as Mary Jo and Mom reminisced.

They had not seen each other in fifteen years. Mary Jo said she knew Tanya had chosen the perfect family for me when she met Mom and Dad at the adoption agency. Mary Jo said she felt peace when she placed me in Mom's arms.

I had heard the story before, but as I listened to Mary Jo and heard her perspective, my heart was touched in a new way. Suddenly, I felt doubly loved. I have always known my parents and both of their families loved me. But it just hit me that Tanya's family loved me too.

Thank you, Tanya, for letting me feel doubly loved.

Her Selfless Sacrifice

Janie Roos

David and I dreamed of having a family with children close in age. Adopting Becky was a dream come true and we loved her dearly, but we still had a strong desire for another child.

I volunteered at the adoption agency and knew we might have to wait up to five years to adopt another infant. When Becky was one year old I asked about the possibility of a second adoption. Our agency was new and we would be their first couple to go through a second adoption.

Several weeks later the agency called to tell us Linda was studying our file and wanted more information about us. They asked if we could quickly update our profile. I could hardly believe it. If she chose us, then our children would be less than two years apart.

It was all happening so fast, so David and I began praying for Linda. We asked God to help Linda know what to do, to confirm his will with his peace.

We prayed for Linda to choose the right parents for her baby, even if her choice wasn't us. Then we got another call. Linda asked if she and the baby's father could meet with us. We had met Becky's birth mother and grandmother and it had been a wonderful experience, so we agreed.

The four of us and the director met at the agency. The meeting with Linda and Steve was much different than our first experience. We liked Linda but felt uncomfortable with Steve. I sensed Linda was anguishing over the thought of parting with her child.

David and I left the meeting concerned. As with Becky, this baby would be placed with us just one or two days after birth, before parental rights were legally relinquished. Thus, if Linda changed her mind, she could take back her baby.

We truly wanted what was best for Linda and her child, and David and I felt strongly about not wanting any mother to feel manipulated to place her baby for adoption. If Linda did not have complete peace about the adoption, then her child was not the baby God had for us.

Because we had Becky, we thought that if Linda changed her mind, we would be able to handle the disappointment, so we agreed to adopt Linda's baby.

When Amy was born we received a call from the social worker saying Linda wanted us to come visit in the hospital. We were thrilled. It was a profoundly emotional time. We experienced such joy at holding this baby for whom we had waited and prayed. At the same time, we ached for Linda.

Linda nursed Amy during their time together in the hospital. Because one of my jobs as a newborn intensive care nurse was instructing mothers about the benefits of early breast milk, I knew this was a good thing for Amy, something I was unable to provide. But I also worried. The bond that forms when a mother nurses her baby might make it even more difficult for Linda. I told God my fears and in my heart gave the baby back to him.

On Easter morning, Linda released Amy to us. We were able to take our sweet, beautiful little daughter home and then on to a celebration with family and friends.

When Amy was two weeks old, Linda stood before a judge and relinquished her rights as Amy's parent. A few hours later we met with her at the agency. She told us it was the hardest thing she had ever done. The night before, she had called the social worker and said she couldn't relinquish Amy. But after much prayer and talking with the social worker, she decided she had done the right thing.

Our hearts broke for Linda. I vowed to pray faithfully for her. I asked God to have his hand of blessing on this woman who had been through so much for her baby. I had great concern and respect for Linda and wanted to reassure her we would do the best we could for her child.

Amy's adoption was complete when she was five months old. She and I had grown so close in those few months.

With all my children, and we now have three, I felt like it was very important to spend as much time holding them as possible. They had not grown in my womb, so they needed a lot of time to get to know me.

I had worked in the Newborn ICU as a breast-feeding consultant and understood how important it was for a mother and baby to connect. I held all my children a lot when they were babies and specifically when they were eating. I put them in a Snugli when I worked around the house or went shopping. If they were right there with me I could be in tune to their needs and they could be in tune to me. When they were older I carried them in a backpack.

Each of my children were so different in their responses to my efforts to bond with them. Amy is the only one who screamed in the church nursery because she wanted just me. So I kept her with me until she was over a year and then she did fine.

Amy was a wonderful baby—so cheery and always grinning. When something excited her she had total body joy and would laugh and clap her feet.

I assumed because she was bottle-fed and not breast-fed that anyone would be able to feed her, but she wouldn't even take a bottle from her father. She was happy with her daddy only if I was around.

One time I left her with David for an hour to go grocery shopping. When I came back she was sitting in the middle of the living room floor screaming. David was glued to Monday Night Football.

I picked Amy up and calmed her down and asked angrily, "What were you doing?" David said, "Well, if I held her she screamed, if I put her down she screamed, so I put her down."

Our family visited with Linda at the adoption agency about once every year or two. As Amy grew, so did her interest in her adoption. She saw it as a strong part of who she was. I didn't feel intimidated by Amy's interest in Linda. If I were an adopted child, I would be just as curious as Amy was.

In fourth grade Amy's class was assigned to do a report on their family and cultural history. It was very important to Amy that she include Linda in her report.

I wanted to do whatever I could to help my daughter so I called the agency. They told us Linda had married a wonderful man. The director at the agency said she felt certain we could contact Linda on our own without their assistance, so I did.

Linda invited us over for lunch and talked to us about her family history. She graciously answered Amy's questions about her adoption.

When we returned home Amy informed me she was not going to put David and me in her family project. It would be only about Linda. I was taken by surprise how much that hurt me. It was like an arrow to my heart.

I called a friend who had an adopted daughter in Amy's grade at school. We talked about how our family doesn't seem different than other families until these issues come up. Even though it is hard when they do, it's good because it allows us to discuss adoption with our children and their friends.

I insisted Amy include both of her family histories. She was not amused, but I felt it was important.

After spending the afternoon in Linda's home, David and I decided it would be good for Amy if she and Linda spent more time together. So we started inviting her to our home.

Looking back, all three of our children's adoptions started out as semi open and in one way or another have turned into open adoptions.

The openness has not always been comfortable. When we would meet with our three children's different biological mothers, I would try to tell myself that it was all fine and I should be relaxed. The truth is, it was initially quite stressful. I would go home from these meetings exhausted. I would ask myself, Why? It was because I was trying to do everything within my power to assure these women that they had made the right decision; that David and I were wonderful parents and that their child would always be happy with us.

I wanted to appear perfect. The rub is that I am not perfect and neither are my children. I'm more relaxed now when we visit and don't feel like I have to prove myself.

Amy is fourteen now. She is a beautiful young lady and has done very well in school, soccer, swimming, and volleyball. She has a heart for young children and is gifted in reaching out to them.

Even with all her superb qualities there are days when she can be difficult. There are times we struggle with attitudes. I'm not one of her favorite persons on those days.

David and I ask the Lord to bring godly, loving adults into our children's lives; adults who will have a good impact on our kids. And Linda is one of our answers to prayer.

Over the years as I have gotten to know Linda, I am amazed at how unselfish she is concerning Amy. I trust Linda with Amy. When Amy was twelve she and Linda started spending time together without me. They have fun, but Linda also challenges Amy to do her best and to honor David and me as her parents.

Linda has grown tremendously through her difficulties and is a wonderful role model of how someone can turn their life around. She is sensitive and understanding of our busy life and is careful not to intrude.

Linda made a difficult choice for the sake of her child. She enriched our lives with a daughter and continues to bless us with her friendship.

Thank you, Linda, for your selfless sacrifice.

Two Moms to Love

Amy Roos as told to Susan Horner

I cannot remember a time in all of my fourteen years when I did not know about Linda. The day I was born my parents came to the hospital with their video camera. We have a movie of my mom holding me and saying how beautiful I am, and she can't believe how blessed she is to have me for her daughter. Then my dad held me. I was so calm and quiet. It's neat that my parents videotaped Linda holding me too. I can't explain it but it means a lot to me.

When I hear my mom say how incredible Linda is and how hard it must have been for her to give me up for adoption, it makes me feel good about who I am. I came from Linda, and she will always be a part of me.

When I was in the fourth grade we were given the assignment to write about our family's history. My mom said I was a part of her and my dad's family history, but I wanted to know about my biological relatives. It was important to me to discover my past. So my mom called Linda and Linda called her mom.

My school project was a big success, and I learned many interesting things about my ancestors. I am part Swedish and part German and related to the famous Chief Massasoit from Massachusetts.

In the last two years Linda and I have been spending time alone, just the two of us. She takes me out for lunch and asks me about school and sports. I was honored when Linda asked me to help name her new puppy. We came up with the name Sable.

Linda even came to a couple of my basketball games. She sat with my parents and met my friends. My friends think Linda is really cool. Most of them don't understand though. Sometimes they ask why I don't go back with Linda. I've told them when a woman gives her baby to a family, she can't just come and take the baby back. I tell my friends I have two moms.

I've tried to explain to my friends that when they think of "Mom," and all that a mom means to a kid, that is how I feel about my adopted mom. And Linda has a special place in my heart that only she can fill. Linda is like an older sister I look up to. I can tell she cares about me and likes spending time with me.

The two friends who really understand are Sarah and Natalie. Sarah has been friends with my family since kindergarten and Natalie from the time we were babies. But Natalie didn't always understand.

My mom remembers when we were six and Natalie blurted out, "You're not Amy's real mom anyway!"

Mom answered, "Natalie, I am very real. And I am Amy's mother."

If you knew my mom, then you would know that's the kind of thing she would say to anyone who gave her a hard time about not being my real mom. If my other friends knew my family, they would also understand why I feel perfectly fine with my situation. I think it was meant to be. God wanted it like this.

Another reason I wouldn't want to switch back is I couldn't imagine living without my sister, Becky, and my little brother, Zac. Even though we get on each other's nerves, I would really miss them.

Last year Linda invited me over to her house for lunch and explained to me why she placed me for adoption. My birth father, Steve, was an alcoholic and was being abusive. It was a dangerous and scary time for Linda. She wanted me to be safe and knew Mom and Dad would take good care of me.

Linda was worried I might have hard feelings toward her for putting me up for adoption. She wanted me to understand that she never rejected me. Linda asked me if I was okay with what she did. I told her I was and had no hard feelings. I'm thankful Linda gave me to a nice Christian family. And I'm thankful to my mom and dad for understanding how important it is for me to get to spend time with Linda.

When my mom and I argue I hardly ever think, Linda *wouldn't treat me this way,* or *Linda wouldn't say, "No, you can't do that."* Linda and I both see my mom as "The Mom": the one who can put me on restriction, and the one who comforts me when I'm sad or sick. My mom is always doing things for me and is really involved in whatever I am doing, like going camping with our Girl Scout troop.

One day when my mom and I were having a big argument I yelled, "Just leave me alone!" She said, "No, I can't leave you alone, Amy. You're my daughter." I don't remember if we worked out our argument, but at that moment I felt more confident about how much my mom cares for me and worries about me. I realized it's out of her love for me that she won't leave me alone and has to know what's going on in my life. She wants the very best for me.

The first few times Linda and I went places without my parents, I felt nervous and shy with her. Now it feels natural to be together.

My advice for anyone who wants to someday meet his or her biological mom is don't force it, take it slow. Give her some time to get used to you. She might be scared you're angry with her for putting you up for adoption. Even though how you feel about her is really really special and different from any other person in your whole life, you still have to be patient and let your relationship grow naturally like any other friendship.

If my adoption had been closed, I would be wondering all the time why my birth mom placed me for adoption. My biological heritage would be an unsolved mystery rolling around in my mind. Maybe because I am interested in archeology and digging up the past, or maybe it is just normal to want to know.

I'm really glad my mom and dad agreed to an open adoption. I can think about other stuff, instead of planning how to someday crack the case of my missing birth mother.

Part 2

My Heart Rejoices

Adoptive Moms Celebrate Motherhood

Daughter of My Heart

Kathryn Lay

"Your daughter is adorable," the woman at the grocery store checkout said, patting my two-year-old daughter on the head.

"Thanks, I think so too," I said.

My heart swelled each time I heard that word. Daughter. She really was my daughter—legally and emotionally. I couldn't help but share the exciting news.

"We went to court today to finalize her adoption. It's been a long day of celebrating," I explained.

The woman nodded. "Oh, congratulations." She leaned a bit closer. "How nice of you. Did you do it because you wanted to help or couldn't you have children of your own?"

I stepped back, shocked and hurt at her comment. "She *is* my own," I said. Lifting my daughter from the grocery cart, I whispered in her ear, "My sweet daughter." She bopped me on the nose with her stuffed dog and said, "My mama!" My heart swelled again. Yes, I was her mama.

For ten long years Richard and I waited, hoped, and dreamed of children in our lives. Someday, we hoped a child would jump into our arms and call us Mom and Dad. And then those painful years of waiting ended when Michelle arrived. My heart was filled with an unnamed joy when our caseworker told us her name—the very name I would have chosen for a daughter.

When at the age of six Michelle began asking questions about her birth mother, I was devastated. I had long believed I could have this conversation without pain or fear, but I was wrong. My daughter's curiosity was natural. Yet, I took it personally and felt sure that I was no longer "Mama" in her eyes. Because she was only six, I didn't feel Michelle was ready for the complete story of her mother's drug issues, emotional problems, and social services having to step in on her behalf. We explained that her birth mother had a lot of problems and sicknesses and that she couldn't raise a baby. We explained that God knew this and gave Michelle a chance to be with a family who could take care of her.

"Did she love me at all?" Michelle asked.

I struggled to respond without bursting into tears. "She must have," I said.

After that, I was extra nice, afraid to yell or be strict or force any issues. What if she hated me and wanted her "real" mother? For several weeks, questions about her birth mother, birth sisters, and birth grandparents kept popping up. We told her that when she was old enough we'd help her find her birth family. She hugged me in response. My throat ached, but I knew it was the right thing to promise.

After a while, the awkwardness wore off and I was no longer afraid of losing her love. We chased kites at the park, worked on homework, argued about chores, and life went back to normal.

When she was nine, Michelle approached me with a conversation that put all my doubts to rest. Friends she'd always thought of as buddies suddenly were potential boyfriends.

"Mom, can we talk?" Alone in her room, she struggled to explain how she "liked this boy" and what if he didn't like her? "You won't laugh at me?" she asked before she opened her heart.

"I'd never laugh at your feelings," I promised.

The talk ended with a hug, and a "Thanks, Mom."

My heart leapt. I'm Mama, mother, and Mom. She came to us as a miracle and has given me memories and joy I'll never forget. Sometimes I make her laugh or make her proud. Sometimes I embarrass her. Sometimes she is angry with me and slams the door.

But, yes, she is my *real* daughter. And all the above proves it.

Heart's Delight

Jean M. Olsen

Rag dolls, stuffed animals, doll clothes, uniforms for Sudanese schoolgirls, handcrafted gifts for missionary coworkers—I created them all cheerfully. But when it came to making newborn outfits, every stitch tugged at my heart, because they were for someone else's baby.

In Sudan, a mother was always called by the name of her firstborn child: *Mama Barry,* or *Mama Grace.* Since I wasn't a mother, I was just *Madam Olsen.*

At different times, we made long trips to consult our mission doctors in the neighboring countries of Zaire and Uganda. They thought my inability to conceive was the result of surgery I'd had as a teenager in 1947. The doctors in Zaire suggested several procedures, which we carefully followed.

Several months later, quite sure I'd conceived, I sent my temperature charts to the doctor with another missionary family who was traveling to Zaire. "She's definitely pregnant," the doctor told our coworkers. But by the time they returned six weeks later to confirm the good news, I had miscarried.

An older missionary lady encouraged me. "You're young. You have lots of time." Then she revealed her own early, heartbreaking experiences—she had had four miscarriages and a stillborn baby before God gave her four healthy children. "God will give you children, in his time," she encouraged. "I'm sure of it."

Often I reminded myself not to doubt God's love or goodness, and my spirits would rise. But when my next period came, I'd become despondent again. Repeatedly, I wrestled with the Lord, begging him to bless us: "Lord, children are a heritage from you. Please, please give us a child." Eventually I stopped holding other people's babies because I'd get so emotional.

Although I was a little ashamed of myself for not accepting my lot, I told our field director, "I don't want to come back for a second term without a baby."

In the spring of 1957, a few months before furlough, a coworker sent me the address of an agency in Chicago, Illinois, that allowed missionaries to adopt babies. By the light of a flickering kerosene lamp, I composed a letter to the Evangelical Child Welfare Agency (ECWA, now Evangelical Family Welfare Agency) and requested an application.

Their answer arrived a few weeks before we left Sudan for furlough. "We don't have nearly enough babies for everyone who wants them, but we pray that God will give you your heart's desire," they wrote.

On the application form, for our choice of age and sex, I wrote "newborn baby girl." In the blank that asked for our nationality, Dan, my husband, insisted we put "American" rather than the ethnic origin of our families.

I mailed the form to ECWA, saying we'd contact them when we got settled in the States and could meet them personally. That August I sent them our New Jersey address, and by return mail, a most amazing letter arrived.

"We believe we have a baby for you. The mother requested that her baby go to missionaries. You are missionaries. When the baby came, it was a girl. You asked for a girl. You didn't indicate your nationality on the application form. However, since your name is Olsen, spelled with an *e*, you must be Norwegian. The baby's mother and father were born in Norway. Everything fits so perfectly, we believe God wants you to have this baby. But before we can say for sure, we want to meet you. Let us know when you can come to Chicago."

In September, we borrowed a station wagon and a baby basket and headed west. Our parents said, "Don't take baby clothes—you'd be terribly disappointed if it doesn't work out."

Every mile of the way I wondered, *Will they like us? Will they let us have the baby right away, or will we have to come back later?*

A caseworker took us to lunch and then drove us to the foster mother's home, an ordinary house in the suburbs. An elderly woman invited us in, went upstairs, and then reappeared a moment later. She put a tiny bundle in my arms. "I hope you don't mind a little towhead with blue eyes," she said.

It was love at first sight. What a beautiful baby—fair complexion, rosy cheeks, the bluest eyes I'd ever seen, and a faint trace of blond fuzz. "We'd love her even if she had purple hair," I blurted.

"Are you going to take her with you now?" the woman asked.

My words stumbled over each other. "We didn't know if we'd be allowed to. All we brought was a basket. Can we get some things tonight and come back tomorrow?"

"Of course," she said.

The next morning, in a huge downpour, we returned for Karen, our miracle baby. Our African friends would have said, "This rain is a sign of God's blessing." And we would have shouted, "Amen!"

Karen was not quite three months when we began our homeward journey. I couldn't put that precious baby down. I cuddled her, talked to her, and sang to her, expecting her to fall asleep in my arms. But she cried and cried—all the way from Chicago to New Jersey. When we got home, I was nearly in tears myself and handed her to my mother. "Here. Take your granddaughter," I said.

In Granny's arms, Karen quieted down right away. I soon got over my nervousness and was tickled pink to be a mother. In no time she settled into our adoring family.

Most weekends we visited family, friends, and supporting churches. After our first tearful trip, Karen loved traveling. Before long, she'd been in fifteen states.

In the spring of 1958 we were summoned to Chicago for our court appearance to finalize the adoption. How we prayed that everything would be okay. We'd heard horrible stories about mothers changing their minds and taking their babies back. We prayed that the judge would take one look at us, know we were the perfect family, and quickly sign the final papers.

When the judge asked us to stand, my heart nearly thudded out of my chest. "Do you realize an adopted child has the same rights as a natural-born child?" he asked.

"Yes," we both said, then held our breath as he shuffled his papers around. At last, he picked up a pen and signed his name. Karen was ours—absolutely!

Three months later we began our trip back to Africa with another missionary couple. We shared a house while we studied Arabic in Khartoum, Sudan. They too had a baby daughter. The girls spent many hours each day cooling off in a plastic wading pool while we struggled to pronounce the strange, throaty sounds of Arabic. In the cool of the evening we'd push Karen in her stroller along the banks of the Nile. No wonder her first word after Mama and Dada was camel.

After Arabic study, we boarded the Nile steamer to go south to Juba. During the four-hour trip to our old station, I smiled so hard my face ached. I couldn't wait to introduce Karen to my Sudanese friends. They greeted me with the treasured words I longed to hear, "Mama Karen." It was music to my ears.

The folks at ECWA had recommended telling Karen she was adopted, and we agreed completely. We promised we'd always be honest with her. Often we prayed, "Lord, show us the right time." She was only two-and-a-half years old when it happened.

Karen and I were bathing together because water was scarce in Sudan. Oh, how scratchy that concrete tub was! She patted my breast and said, "When I was a baby, did I drink milk the way the African babies do? You had chocolate milk in one and white in the other, right?"

I smiled, silently thanking God for the perfect opening.

"A mother doesn't have milk in her breasts unless her baby comes out of her tummy," I said. "God gave you to us another way."

"How, Mommy?"

"Well, let me tell you your story." I pointed to a long scar on my abdomen. "See this? It's from an operation that probably saved my life. But it kept me from having a baby. Ever since we got to Africa, I wanted a baby. It seemed as though everybody had one except me. One time I got pregnant—"

"What's 'pregnant,' Mommy?"

"Pregnant is when a baby is growing in your tummy. Something went wrong, and it came out too soon, before it was big enough to live. I was terribly sad. After a while, we heard about a place in America where we might be able to adopt a baby."

"What's 'adopt,' Mommy?"

"Sometimes a mother can't take care of her baby herself," I explained. "Maybe she's sick or too young or all alone. Maybe she has no money and no job. She loves her baby very much and wants it to be happy and have everything it needs. So she gives her precious baby to a family who will love and care for it forever. That's adoption.

"We wrote the adoption place and asked if they had a baby for us. They said there weren't nearly enough babies for everyone who wanted them, but they hoped they'd find one for us. We said we'd like a newborn baby girl. Then we prayed and prayed.

"A few months later when we got to America, a miracle happened. The adoption agency told us they had a baby for us. The mother couldn't keep her, and she wanted only a missionary family to have her baby. Our letter arrived at exactly the right time. God wanted us to have you."

Karen and I got out of the cold tub, dried off, and put on our nightgowns. She was satisfied with the story. It became her favorite one. As she got older and could understand more, we added other details we'd heard at ECWA. Eventually she knew everything we knew.

How often I wished there were some way to thank the young woman who had given us her baby! Sometimes I wrote letters addressed to "Dear Other Mother," but there was no way to deliver them, and I prayed, "Lord, give her joy, a husband, and other babies."

Karen was a gregarious child who preferred playing with her African buddies to eating. She loved real babies as well as dolls. "Let's adopt another baby, Mommy," she said regularly.

When our next furlough time came, we contacted ECWA. Unfortunately, their rules had changed, and now they could give babies only to residents of Illinois. Although we tried other organizations, each time the answer was no. As it turned out, it was for our good. The next couple of years would have been difficult with a new baby.

Sudan closed the door to missionaries, and we had to change direction. We spent the winter in Switzerland learning French, then resettled in Zaire. After only four months, a civil war erupted there, and all missionaries were forced to evacuate. Since the situation in Zaire remained unstable, we transferred permanently to Kenya, where we began serving at a boarding school for missionary children.

One Sunday at the English church service, a visiting preacher reminded us that we have a God who delights to give us our heart's desires. "It's perfectly simple," he said. "Know what you want. Ask God for it. Then wait for God to answer."

I glanced at Karen and saw her laughing. When we got home, I asked, "Were you listening to the sermon?"

She nodded.

"What did he say?" I asked.

"Know what you want and ask God for it," she said.

"Is there something you want, Karen?"

"A baby!"

"What do we do next?" I asked.

"Ask God for it."

We knelt down beside the white chenille-covered bed—Dan was out preaching. "Dear God," Karen said, "I want a baby more than anything else in the world. Please, could you give us one?"

"Amen!" we said together, for I agreed with all my heart. From that day on, Karen asked daily, "When is God going to send the baby?"

"In his perfect time," I answered. Although I had no idea how long we'd have to wait, I hung on to God's promise: "Delight yourself in the LORD and he will give you the desires of your heart" (Ps. 37:4).

Three months later, we received a letter from Esther, a friend in the States. She wrote,

About a month from now, a baby will be born to an unmarried girl, the daughter of a woman in my Bible study. She wants to arrange an adoption now, even before the birth. For months, I've been trying, but I can't find anyone who would commit beforehand. One wants only a boy, another wants only a girl, everyone wants to wait and see if it's healthy. Suddenly today I thought of you, remembering you tried to adopt last furlough and couldn't.

If you'd like this baby, I'll be happy to take him or her from the hospital to care for until you return in August. Please answer immediately. I feel God's hand leading. I will pray and wait to hear from you.

Love, Esther

Totally convinced this was God's answer to our prayer, we immediately sent Esther an express letter.

> We'll be delighted to take that baby, whether boy or girl. We're overwhelmed with God's answer to our prayer and with your offer to care for the baby until we arrive. Thanks for having your lawyer deal with legal matters.
> The names are Mark Daniel for a boy and Erika for a girl.
> Love, Jean, Dan, and Karen

The day after we arrived in the States, Esther delivered three-month-old Erika to us. She put the darling, dark-eyed brunette into Karen's arms. Then a dozen joyous relatives took turns cuddling the newest member of the Olsen clan.

Erika learned about her adoption early, as her big sister Karen had. In our family, we're not afraid or ashamed of the word *adopt*. It's a happy word, one we celebrate.

When, as adults, the girls mentioned wanting to locate their natural mothers, we urged them to do so—for their own sakes as well as ours. Praise God, they were both successful, and we were finally able to personally thank the dear women whose hard times and sacrifice had brought us such joy.

Adoptive Breast-Feeding
Anne Calahan

My husband and I were waiting excitedly in the hospital corridor. We looked up when we heard a nursery cart rolling toward us. "He was born twelve minutes ago," the nurse said. We jumped up and walked alongside him to the nursery. Kati, his birth mother, would be in recovery from the cesarean for several hours.

The nurses let us come into the nursery and give him his first bath. As I bathed him with clean, warm water, my husband and I poured our prayers over him as well. We prayed blessings of love and acceptance, life and joy, and a sense of belonging.

The nurses were wonderful. They could see how thrilled we were to be an integral part of Ezra's first moments outside the womb. We rented a room at the hospital so the nurses could call me to come feed him his bottle in the middle of the night.

Before we took our son home from the hospital, we were thankful to witness Kati cuddling, kissing, and admiring her baby. She had originally intended to relinquish him without ever holding him. We know her loving words and embraces affected him in the deep recesses of his spirit.

I breast-fed my biological daughter and enjoyed the bond we shared during our special time together. So it wasn't too unusual for me to try nursing my first adopted son with the aid of a supplemental feeding system. With Ezra it was even easier, because of the things I had learned while nursing his older brother and with the help of La Leche League.

This time I did not try to induce my own milk supply with an electric breast pump. I had two other children to care for and I didn't want to take the time. I nursed my first son in the hospital, but I was confident even if Ezra first took a bottle, he would be able to transfer to the breast when we brought him home at two days old.

Once home, I had no trouble moving right into the routine of breast-feeding. The supplemental feeding system allowed me to connect with my adopted infant in one of the closest, most intimate forms of bonding.

While nourishing his body I wanted to nurture his heart as well. The close cuddling and warmth of my skin against his little cheek, the smell of my body, the beat of my heart, the sound of my voice, and looking into each other's eyes all became the essence of comfort to him.

When my son was ready to eat, I needed to find a private place to tape the tubes in the proper position on my nipples and hang the warmed bottle around my neck. Once everything was in place I had to make sure the formula was flowing properly. Knowing beforehand this system took lots of planning and preparedness, I decided to commit to three months. This experience granted me a satisfaction that far outweighed the hassles of dealing with the supplemental feeding system. And I established a cherished bond with my son during our special time of breast-feeding.

Part 3

A Father's Focus

Stories from Men

Papa's Perspective

Greg Patchell

I was ready to adopt about a year before Donna was and was given some great advice: "Don't start adopting until you have dealt with infertility, and don't plan on adopting until you are both ready."

If God wanted us to adopt, he would have to change Donna's heart. She struggled with her God-created desire to give birth versus the apparent reality that the Lord was not giving us natural-born children. It helped her to read *When Empty Arms Become a Heavy Burden* by Sandra Glahn and William Cutrer, M.D. The authors expressed the same feelings Donna was grappling with.

Once Donna was ready we began the paperwork to adopt a baby from Tuzla, Bosnia. A few months later, my army reservist unit was called to go to Bosnia for nine months. My unit spent a lot of time at the orphanage in Tuzla. While playing with the kids I wondered which one might become Donna's and my adopted child. It was in Bosnia that I first thought about adopting siblings. I really grew to love the Bosnian people, not just because of their tragic history but because they loved their children.

A month after I returned home we found out that our adoption agency, Bethany Christian Services, was closing their Bosnian office.

That night I cried in the shower over the death of our dream. I felt such sorrow for the children living in the Bosnian orphanage. But as I cried, I realized God loved those children more than I did.

Since then I have learned that adoption is a calling from the Lord. It is something very close to God's heart. He even prepared the way in his sovereign timing.

From the time we started the process until we walked through the front door with our children, it took over three years. We adopted three siblings from Russia: Artyom, age five;

Vladislav, age four; and Kristina, age two. If we had tried to force things according to our own timing, we would have had one child from Bosnia, or just two kids from Russia, since Kristina hadn't even been born when we started the adoption process.

The first day at the orphanage we spent some time getting to know the kids. By the second day, as soon as they saw us their faces lit up, and they ran down the hall into our arms.

Returning home to the States, we arrived at the airport at 4:00 A.M. exhausted and with jet lag. After all the excitement of seeing the house, we put the kids to bed, then crashed into bed ourselves.

One hour later they woke up. Within the next several hours, they discovered all the ways in which we hadn't childproofed our home. That's when it really sank in that we had three kids, because I had to deal with three Tasmanian devils of energy and enthusiasm. I thought, *What have we gotten ourselves into?!* Fortunately it was only a fleeting thought. When that thought does reoccur, it helps to recall how God brought us to the point of adopting them.

Since we brought them home, the kids have been adjusting extremely well. It isn't a honeymoon, but it isn't a nightmare either. The kids are, well, kids. I had read books about adopting older children and had been to classes. Yet, I still harbored an expectation that the three kids would be perfectly behaved, as if God owed me that.

I am learning to give those expectations over to the Lord.

In the last two months it has been my joy to experience:

- Seeing the kids wave out the window as I drive off to work, watching for me as I come home, and then running to greet me at the door, yelling, "Papa! Papa!"
- Watching their eyes light up as they learn a new word in English.
- Telling stories about them at work.
- Holding all three at once, or being held onto by all three when they are being shy with other people.

- Carrying them on my shoulders.
- Running with them, throwing balls, sledding, and tossing them in the air.
- Playing pretend and making things for them out of cardboard boxes.
- Hearing them say *Moya Papa* ("my daddy" in Russian) and hugging me when they go off to sleep.
- Listening to them tell my parents on the telephone that their family name is Patchell.
- Teaching them about God—who he is and who his son Jesus is.
- Watching them play together with their blankets and a couple of laundry baskets as *maschinas* (cars).
- Working on behavioral issues such as hitting each other, pouting, lying, and falsely accusing each other.

Kristina is now three and has been going through her "terrible twos." This is expressed in a very strong *Nyet!* with fiery eyes and as strong a frown as she can muster. Though the twinkle in her eyes says, "See if you can make me," it's hard to keep from laughing.

There are challenges with parenting any child, adopted or not. I'm learning it is a mix of love and justice, not laughing (much) while disciplining, and maintaining consistency between parents.

Protecting my relationship with Donna has been very hard work in these initial months of adoption. It is hard to find uninterrupted time to talk about the kids, let alone about ourselves.

I try to take into account how Donna's day is going, keeping tabs on her physical stamina. I write little notes of appreciation and try to call from work to encourage her. Once I get home, I make sure the kids see that she is my priority as they clamor for my attention as I walk in the door.

We have received much financial and practical help from family and from friends in our church. I don't know how we could have made it these last few months without the catered meals, guys coming over to childproof our house, teens helping Donna, and one friend who helps Donna take the kids to medical appointments. People from all over the world are praying for us and encouraging us.

God even blessed us with Russian-speaking friends. The first time they came over, the kids told them Donna and I fold our hands, close our eyes, and take a little nap before we eat. We can't imagine not having them as our children or not having the three of them together. In just a few short months the children have come to know without a doubt that we are Mama and Papa and love them unconditionally.

No Greater Joy

Jeff Adams

Rosemary and I searched from coast to coast for a child. When we inquired about adopting a special-needs child, we were informed we weren't qualified. When a newspaper article pleaded for parents to adopt older children of mixed ethnic origins, we said, "We'll take one!" But because we weren't multiracial or a minority, we were not considered. And then we were told we were too old to adopt.

But in August 1997, it appeared our long wait for parenthood was over. A single mother of three was pregnant again. After several phone calls, we agreed to meet with her and flew back East once more.

Jennifer was everything we had hoped for in a birth mother. To this day we love her dearly. She insisted we stay at her home instead of a hotel. We bought pizza, read stories, and played with her children. We shared our dreams with Jennifer and gratefully accepted when she said she wanted us to adopt her baby.

For six months we prayed and waited. As the day approached, we were on red alert, carrying a cell phone and pager. We religiously adhered to our daily routine, so we could be notified day or night when Jennifer went into labor.

Rosemary picked up the plane tickets, telling Brandy, our travel agent, she planned to fly back immediately to be there for the birth. As soon as I got the call I would follow.

The lawyers had prepared the documents for the relinquishment proceedings. The hospital, doctors, and nurses were informed of the protocol they were to follow. Nothing had been overlooked.

Then the call came. Jennifer could not even speak to us on the phone. She left an anguished message on our answering machine: "Don't come. The father won't relinquish." Rosemary almost collapsed when she heard those words.

That night we cried. Our pastor and his wife cried with us. So did our family and friends. Each failed adoption was like a miscarriage. Emotionally exhausted, Rosemary wanted no part of another failure. We would learn to be content with one another. Perhaps God's promise had been nothing more than wishful thinking.

The next day I phoned Brandy to cancel the tickets. She asked if Rosemary had told me about her friend Sarah who was due in two months and feeling desperate to find someone to adopt her child.

Apparently when Rosemary had picked up our plane tickets, Brandy had asked her if she knew anyone who might want to adopt. Thinking all was well with our adoption thousands of miles away, Rosemary had not mentioned the conversation.

The weekend passed and I decided to give Sarah a call. To shield Rosemary, I secretly arranged a meeting with Sarah at her grandparents' home just a few miles away.

I didn't know what to expect when I pulled up to the singlewide trailer. Shielding my heart against another broken promise, I knocked on the door.

After so many failed adoption attempts, and with my own emotions still raw from the latest rejection, my questions were blunt. Sarah never flinched. Her candor assured me of her intentions and motives.

She told me the reality of raising a three-year-old son alone was almost more than she could manage. She seemed determined to place her baby for adoption. So I agreed to tell Rosemary.

A few days later they met. Still numb, Rosemary limped through the familiar question-and-answer routine with Sarah.

We ached so much for a child that we were willing to try again. But this time I immediately contacted our county attorney's office, and they placed the required legal notices in newspapers in an attempt to locate the birth father. When no one responded, his parental rights were irrevocably terminated by the court. Overnight my mourning turned into joy as I considered what God might be doing for us.

One month later, a visiting evangelist spoke in our church. At one point, he called everyone to the front of the sanctuary. Pacing back and forth, he suddenly stopped, wheeled around, pointed at Rosemary and me and said, "God says you've waited long enough! It is being done in heaven even now." We almost fainted, because we knew what he was referring to.

We felt God's smile on us that night and we could hardly contain our joy. Over the next month we leaked the news to our immediate families. Still, we said nothing to even our closest friends.

Two months after meeting Sarah, our fourteen-year heartache ended with the birth of Meaghan Elizabeth. Holding a tiny new life, my fingertips softly brushed her downy hair. God covered us with his blanket of peace as I sang softly to my daughter: "Jesus loves me, this I know." Overcome with unspeakable joy, tears rolled down my cheeks as Meaghan fell asleep.

I wasn't aware Sarah was watching us, but later she told me that when she saw me singing to Meaghan, she knew she had made the right decision.

When Meaghan was three days old Sarah signed the relinquishment papers. Her shaky signature revealed how difficult the decision had been for her.

Only a few people in our congregation, including our pastors, knew about our new adoption prospect, and they were all admonished not to breathe a word to anyone. They faithfully cloaked their joy until the night we introduced Meaghan to the entire church.

That Sunday morning the senior pastor encouraged everyone not to miss the evening service. He added, "Tonight we will have a very special guest here with us for the first time." Everyone assumed he meant a guest speaker.

That evening Rosemary and Meaghan entered the building through a locked unused side entrance. They stood in the wings just before the service was to begin.

Our pastor strode to the platform: "I told you this morning we would have a special guest this evening. I would like to introduce to you Meaghan Elizabeth."

The entire congregation simultaneously inhaled as Rosemary carried Meaghan onto the stage. Jumping to their feet, they roared their approval. Their joy for us erupted into deafening shouts.

The night before she was born I wrote Meaghan a letter. I told her tomorrow would be like any other day. I would wake up, shower, shave, dress, eat breakfast, and go about my business until she was born. Then nothing would ever be the same.

Meaghan is three now. I smile when she runs to me with arms upraised, gleefully shouting, "Daddy! Daddy!"

Every time I gaze into Meaghan's brown eyes I catch a glimpse of what I always wanted to be, her father. With four little words she takes my heart captive. The world stands still as two tiny hands embrace my cheeks and she softly says, "I love you, Daddy." Tilting her head back, eyes wide open with wonder, she stands on her tiptoes to kiss me. There is no greater joy than this.

My Little Guys

as told to Kelly Fordyce Martindale

Having Tyler and Matthew join our family was the greatest gift I've ever received. We've been a family for over seven years and it's been wonderful. Our lives are so complete, I don't want anything to change. I have one concern, however, and it's been gnawing at me for the last few months: When should we tell the boys they are adopted?

I suppose if my wife and I had talked about this right from the start, I wouldn't be facing this dilemma. But we didn't. For me, it didn't matter. I'm their dad, they are my sons, and our family has grown close naturally. The boys were just a few days old when we met them and I feel like their natural father. Right now they see me that way too. I love them completely and they love me. I don't want that to change in any way.

Life is difficult enough without adding yet another hurdle. I want to give the little guys a good solid start, and learning they're adopted would undermine their sense of security. We've bonded like any other father and his sons, and I'm afraid telling them they're adopted would change our bond, our natural connection. I've seen sons lose respect for their adoptive fathers once they learned the truth. Hearing the words "You're not my real dad anyway!" would devastate me.

My relationship with the little guys is great. We camp and fish and play together. There's so much I want to teach them. Right now we're restoring a little motorcycle that I had when I was a boy. It's a 1969 Honda Trail 50. My dad bought it for me when I was about six. When I moved out of the house it got passed between my siblings a few times, and I finally tracked it down.

It was exciting to bring it home. I hollered at the boys and they came running into the garage. Tyler raised his fist and, with the exultation of a true winner, jerked his elbow back to his hip and gave a resounding "Yes!"

I couldn't have asked for a better reaction. The boys were thrilled when I explained the history of the bike. "Hey, look guys. This was my bike when I was your age. We're gonna work together to fix it up so you can ride it." The boys took turns sitting on it, tinkering with it, pulling the levers, and pushing the buttons. They wanted to ride it right away but, of course, they couldn't.

We've torn it completely apart so the boys are learning about tools and motorcycle parts. They tinker with it for a while and then they run off. But they always come back.

Once when I started the chain saw to cut down an old tree, Tyler heard it and thought it was the motorcycle. He ran to his mom and yelled, "Dad got our bike running. I got the best dad in the whole world!"

I'm also trying to teach the boys a good work ethic. They have their own chores and they know how to do them well. While I teach them the "tough stuff," their mother teaches them the "soft stuff." They're well-rounded little fellas. They treat their mom with respect. They protect her, worry about her, and pray for her. They are both sensitive and tenderhearted.

It sickens me to even think about what the boys might go through if we tell them about their adoption. We should have told them when they were able to grow into it. Sometimes I even worry about extended family members letting it slip.

I've often asked myself how I would feel if I found out I was adopted. I believe I would still love and respect my dad as much as ever, but I just don't trust it would be the same with my boys. I'm not sure why.

I would like to tell them when they're about eighteen or so. By then they would have a solid foundation and I would have taught them everything I could. They would be adults and perhaps better able to deal with the news. Of course that's if we ever tell them at all.

The bottom line is I don't want to lose the opportunity to take these little people and mold them and teach them to be good people in society. It's so rewarding to be able to love them and teach them and watch them grow. Right now I'm their hero. Telling them they're adopted could jeopardize that. And I want to be Matthew and Tyler's hero as long as I can.

Part 4

The Choice for Adoption

Making the Adoption Decision

A Mother's Sacrificial Love

Jennifer Ciminski

I had just celebrated my twenty-first birthday and was about to take the biggest test of my life: a pregnancy test. I was a typical college student with a major, a minor, and a boyfriend, though was long gone shortly after the four-minute timer sounded. Those four minutes were the longest four minutes of my life. Ding. I had passed the test and it changed my life forever.

Earlier, I'd walked into the counseling room at the local pregnancy center with an air of strength and determination. I wanted the world to know, *I don't care what you think. This is my body and I will do as I please.* But when I learned I was pregnant, my defenses crumbled and my fear and disgrace were obvious.

For the first several minutes I studied the pastel wallpaper, felt the softness of the cushion beneath me, and listened to the indecipherable whispers through the wall into the next room.

I couldn't stop the tears from falling or the shock from taking over. I wanted to bolt out the door, but the counselor wasn't about to let me off the hook that easily. Kindness showed on her face but her words were like slaps of reality. She started asking questions—hard, deep questions.

"What are you going to do?" *I don't know.*

"Will the baby's father be there for you?" *I think he'll marry me. . . . I really do.*

"Do you know what your baby looks like right now?" *I just found out I was pregnant.*

"How will you support a baby?" *I don't know. I can barely support myself.*

"Do you plan on keeping your baby?" *I don't know.*

My answers were short and quick. In truth, I didn't have a clue what I was going to do. So, I sat and listened as the counselor shared with me her own experience with an unplanned pregnancy and how she'd made the choice to abort. She explained that she wished someone had told her the whole truth about abortion. Given the choice, she wouldn't do it again.

The counselor also wanted to make sure I knew exactly what was happening with my own body and how much the baby was already formed. She showed me pamphlets and a tiny, accurately detailed model of a baby that fit into the palm of my hand. It was her task to explain the severity and long-term consequences of abortion.

By the time I left the pregnancy center, I was so overwhelmed I actually thought it would be better and just plain easier to get the abortion. Nobody would have to know. Thankfully, that was a fleeting thought, and in my heart, I knew I could never abort my baby.

I wanted to run and hide, but instead I drove to my friend's house. A year before, she had been in this exact situation. Now, she was loving her little girl. I supported her while she faced her crisis pregnancy and I knew she would support me. When I got to her house, I just held her daughter and cried.

I decided to call my boyfriend. I wanted us to get together so we could talk. Instead, I was so upset I just blurted out, "I'm pregnant."

"Okay, well, I'm going to come home next weekend and we'll tell our parents together," he responded.

But he didn't show up the next weekend. I had gone all week waiting for him to be here with me and he deserted me. I was an emotional wreck and I was afraid.

I needed to tell my family. Here I was, a legal adult, yet I felt like a little child caught stealing or something even more horrendous. I loved my parents and my brother completely. We were a close family and I was about to disrupt their whole world. As embarrassed as I was at the pregnancy center, it was nothing compared to the humiliation I felt as I planned to tell them.

Realizing I couldn't wait for my boyfriend's support, I decided to tell my family immediately. We needed to talk about my pregnancy so we had time to prepare, though for what I wasn't yet sure. I caught myself hugging my abdomen. I loved my baby already. I was surprised I felt that way so quickly. At the same time it was sad having to face the fact that my boyfriend would probably never know this feeling. It was his loss, but it still hurt.

I heard my dad's car pull into the gravel driveway. Mom had just put the last dish on the table for dinner. They had a system. Their lives were smooth and functional. The atmosphere of the whole house felt peaceful, and I felt more ashamed than ever. I felt sick to my stomach. I didn't know if it was nerves or nausea.

Mom called us to the table and we started dinner with thanksgiving and ate heartily—at least everyone else did. I could hardly swallow and I seriously doubted I could keep down what little I did eat. The dinner conversation was so *normal* and reflected the harmony that was common in our home. I wanted to bask in the warmth of the love flowing around the table but I feared it would be short-lived.

"I'd like to talk to everybody after we clean up from dinner," I stated timidly.

"What's up?" Dad asked, as I escaped to the kitchen acting like I didn't hear him. I kept my eyes averted from everyone as I loaded the dishwasher and washed the counters.

As each person made their way to the family room for an evening of popcorn and movies, I interrupted them with the reminder that I needed to talk. Dad reached out his arm, aiming the remote at the TV, and shut it off. All eyes were on me. I was terrified. *Where do I begin? Should I just blurt it out? Help me, Lord.*

My eyes filled with tears as I choked on my own breath. My mom came to me suddenly, her hand on my shoulder as she sat down next to me. "What's wrong?" Fear was in her voice. Her eyes searched mine, but I couldn't yet speak.

Dad sat his recliner forward. I had my brother's complete attention too.

"I . . . I'm . . . preg . . . I'm pregnant." I buried my face in my hands and sobbed.

Neither Mom nor my brother made a move. My dad was silent, but I felt his hurt and anger. I could barely look at him. I shrank into the back of the couch. I saw the disappointment in his eyes. I looked from my mom to my brother and back again. They were shocked. I knew the feeling.

My mom's silence drew my attention as I gained control of my own emotions. Normally very demonstrative of her feelings, it seemed very strange that Mom wasn't crying or talking or something. After a long time, she finally asked, "Do you know what you want to do?" I shook my head no.

My brother gave me an understanding smile and a hug and left the room so Mom, Dad, and I could talk. I loved my brother so much. I desperately wanted to talk to him but I knew my parents had to come first.

No one said anything until Dad was ready. He was composed but shaking. My mom repeated her question.

"I don't know. I mean, you know, I didn't mean for this to happen. I can't believe it happened to me."

Mom shushed me, "We need to know what you *think* you want to do."

"I went to the pregnancy center for the test and they explained my options. We didn't really discuss anything at length, but I know about adoption and parenting."

"Did you talk about abortion?" she asked me.

I was stunned. It must have showed because my dad finally spoke. "Is abortion really an option for you?"

"I couldn't do that," I finally responded, my voice quivering.

"Then we all agree abortion is not an option," Mom said matter-of-factly. "What about the father of the baby?"

"He didn't say much," I choked. "Last weekend he said he would come home with me, but he didn't." I started crying again. I was realizing this wouldn't be the last time I would have to do the hard things alone. This was the first of many promises the father of my baby would not keep.

I knew my parents would support me regardless of what I chose, but it was comforting to know they wouldn't try to force me to get an abortion. I didn't really think they would, but I was fearful of the possibility. I'd heard too many stories of "good little Christian girls" whose parents cared more for their own reputation than the life of their grandchild.

Finally, my mom wrapped her arms around me and concluded the night's talk with, "Well then, it seems your choices are going to be parenting or placing your baby for adoption. I'm sure it's been a long week for you. Let's call it a night and talk more tomorrow. Is that all right with you two?"

Dad and I nodded in agreement. "I'm really tired. I'm going to go to bed," I said after returning Mom's embrace. I hugged Dad. He didn't seem to want to let go of me. It occurred to me I was no longer his little girl. Maybe he was hoping he'd wake up from the nightmare. I'd been hoping that for weeks now.

I still hoped to hear from my boyfriend. My heart ached to hear words of encouragement, support, and even marriage, but I was wondering, *Will he be here for me? Where is he? Will he be a father to our child? I don't want to do this alone.*

As I went down the hall to my bedroom, I glanced over my shoulder and saw my dad slump onto the couch next to Mom. I had done the right thing by telling them, even though I had been afraid I wouldn't live through it. My parents had reaffirmed their love for me and I knew they still respected my opinion and me. I poked my head into my brother's room. He was stretched out on his bed with his hands clasped behind his head. "Good night," I told him.

"Good night. I love you, Jen," my brother said. I could tell he was in deep thought.

I had a rough pregnancy. I lacked any kind of "pregnant glow." Not only did I have to contend with all the emotional turmoil associated with an unplanned pregnancy, but my health suffered as well. I was under incredible stress with the decisions I had to make about school, my baby's future, and my absent so-called boyfriend. I was unprepared emotionally, physically, mentally, and spiritually.

What's going to happen to us? I questioned myself. *I have so many plans. This wasn't part of the plan. College, a career, then maybe marriage, and only then a child—that was the plan. Look at me: pregnant, alone, empty. I thought he loved me. I gave him everything and now he's gone.* I would cry to exhaustion and then finally fall asleep.

Just starting my second trimester of pregnancy, I woke up one morning with excruciating pain in the lower part of my torso. Since I'd never been pregnant before, I had no idea what could be wrong, whether the pain was normal or an indicator of something bad. I called out for my mom.

"It hurts to walk and I feel really sick," I tried to explain my symptoms as I curled around myself in pain.

"I'll get you to the doctor," she said without hesitation.

After seeing the doctor, he admitted me to the hospital with a severe kidney infection. The hospital stay turned out to be just what I needed to reflect on all the events of the last few months. Except for the numerous blood pressure and medicine checks, I was left alone. Propped against several pillows, I found myself constantly smoothing the sheet and blanket over and around my legs. They kept giving me glasses of ice, but I was so preoccupied with my thoughts I just sat there watching it slowly melt until I had a glass of water. Every few minutes a new tear would drip down one of my cheeks adding to the growing wet spots on my hospital gown. During this time, I made a decision about my baby.

I have always believed a child needs a mother and a father if at all possible. I knew I was not ready to parent, even though I was already a parent, and the baby's father had made it clear he wasn't ready for parenthood either. I thought of all the love, support, and security my parents had given me through the years, and I knew I couldn't give anything close to that to my child. Not yet anyway.

My heart ached each time I admitted to myself how unfair it would be to try to raise my baby alone. In my heart, I knew how much I loved my baby. I also knew I would be a good, safe, and nurturing mother. But how could I truly be the best mother for my baby if I was going to school full-time or working full-time? And if I put off school or work, then how could I provide for us financially? I was completely torn between love for my baby and the practical necessities of child rearing.

My hands again stroked my abdomen. *What have I done? Why won't somebody just tell me what to do?* I desperately wanted and needed to make the right decision. *It isn't just me anymore is it, little one? I have to make a decision that is right for you. How I love you. Please know I love you,* I begged the tiny being within me.

My parents and my brother visited me every day at the hospital. Many of my friends came between classes or on their way to work. It was my baby's father who never showed his face or called to see how we were.

My head made the decision before my heart would let my mouth speak it, and once again, I found myself having to build up courage to tell my family about my decision to place the baby for adoption. This time I waited a long time. I was trying to stay focused on my classes, or maybe I was only hiding behind them. The painful reality continued to grow just as my body grew to accommodate my baby. When I did tell them, my family wasn't surprised at my decision, but they were nearly as sad as I was.

When things settled down somewhat, I revisited the pregnancy center to get information about adoption. They gave me phone numbers of local agencies and helpful literature about adoption planning. I was relieved to find out I could choose my baby's parents.

I called a few agencies and after choosing one, made an appointment. Once there, I met a counselor who would support me throughout the rest of my pregnancy. The counselor explained all the details necessary to plan my baby's adoption. It was frightening but also exciting to learn how many families desired to adopt. There were numerous portfolios of couples wanting to adopt. Each portfolio contained photos and letters written by the prospective families. Every letter was really a plea to adopt and all the reasons why they thought they would be the best parents.

Everybody I talked to about choosing a family said, "As you read the information, you'll know almost instantly which family you want to raise your baby."

I studied all the portfolios at the agency but didn't find the right family. My counselor told me to be patient. She made appointments for me at other agencies, but I still couldn't find the right parents. I was nearing the end of my pregnancy and starting to panic.

Adding to the stress was the reappearance of my baby's father, even though he had ignored the baby and me thus far. Because of our mutual friends, he was always kept aware of what was going on during my pregnancy. I'm not sure why he chose this particular time to start calling me, but he seemed intent on causing trouble for everybody.

"I want to have custody of the baby," he informed me on the first phone call.

"That's ridiculous," I responded. "How can you say that when you haven't even been around?"

"If you're going to give it up, then I want it," he said as if the baby was just some object to possess.

I was speechless and angry. My heart burned and my blood boiled. *Where were you the last several months when I really needed you? How will you raise a baby? Why can't we raise the baby together? There is no way you'll get this child.* I hung up on him.

That would be the first of many unexpected calls, each one catching me off guard. I had spent so much time trying to cover every angle to ensure the well-being of my baby, and now all my planning was blowing up in my face because of him. It seemed he was determined to ruin my whole life. I knew one thing for sure—he would not be a good father. He had proven that.

I finally confided to my mother that he was threatening to take me to court for custody of our child. Thankfully, she calmed me with her wisdom. I knew she had been praying all along. My mom sensed he was just bluffing and explained to me how I was playing right into his hands. We talked a lot more and I was ready for the next phone call.

As usual, the conversation started out with him telling me what he was going to do. "OK, fine," I said.

"What?" he asked, astounded.

"You can have the baby and raise him or her yourself," I stated. I was scared but I trusted my mom's instinct. We hung up.

The next call he added another glitch. "My mom's going to adopt the baby."

"Whatever," I said, hoping to sound nonchalant. I tried to act like it didn't matter to me.

Funny thing was, he quit calling. I didn't hear from him until he asked if he could be at the birth. Again, I acted like *whatever*.

When I was eight and a half months pregnant, I still had not settled on a family. I had some conditions that were very important to me. I wanted my baby to be raised by a mom and dad committed to marriage and family. Like me, I wanted my baby's parents to take her to church and teach her the values found in the Bible. I wanted the parents to look like the father and me. I didn't want the family to have any biological children because I didn't want my baby to grow up feeling different. I wanted my baby to fit into their family. Where my baby was concerned, I wouldn't settle for less.

Very nervous and at the end of my pregnancy, I called my adoption counselor to see if other portfolios had come in. None had. A little later she called me back and said she was getting some from yet another organization. I went over and picked those up.

Almost without hope, I sat down on my parents' living room floor and spread the latest portfolios out around me. I read through one, then another. Nearly in tears I picked up yet another. I looked pleadingly at my mom. "What if I don't find the right family?" She gave me a look of encouragement to keep trying. I started reading.

About halfway through the letter, a letter written to a birth mom, I knew: This was the family God had chosen to raise my baby. "Mom, this is the one," I said, passing the photo to her.

She looked at the picture and back at me. The woman looked like me and the man looked somewhat like my baby's father. They were involved in church and, more importantly, they had one daughter and she was adopted also. Relief flooded my soul.

A few days before I went into labor, my brother, my precious little brother, gave me an incredible gift. He embraced me and, despite the sorrowful weeping, said, "Jen, I know how hard this is for you. If I could, I would adopt your baby so it would have a dad. I'm sorry I can't. I want you to know that I am so proud of you and the decisions you are making."

It wasn't long before I found myself going into labor. Thankfully, my friends were in the lobby and my family surrounded me in the hospital room. They supported me with love and prayers and their presence. The baby's father was also there off and on. My mother finally asked him to leave since he wasn't doing anything except causing me anxiety. Every time he came into the room my monitors escalated.

I was in labor forty-eight hours before my precious daughter arrived. Everybody loved her instantly. Her father must have felt that way too because he proposed: "Let's get married and raise her together."

"You're nine months too late," I said. Emotionally, I wanted to, but intellectually I knew it wouldn't work. More importantly, it wasn't the best thing for my baby daughter.

One by one, my family members and friends paraded into the room to meet the most precious person I've ever known. They said their congratulations and took turns holding my daughter and giving me hugs before they left. Finally, I had her to myself.

"My precious gift from God," I whispered, nuzzling her soft cheek. I cuddled her to myself and cried. I told her, "I love you so much," over and over. "I know I can give you all the love a mother can give, but you deserve a daddy's love too." Through broken sobs I continued, "You deserve everything that brings joy to life. I am so sorry I cannot give you that right now. I love you so much my sweet, sweet baby.

"Your new mommy and daddy can give you everything you need. They will love you like I love you." I tried to tell her a lifetime's worth of words in just a few hours. But even a lifetime wouldn't be long enough to tell her all the things she deserved to hear.

"I don't want to let you go. I want to keep you close to me. But you deserve so much more." I could not understand how, in just a few short hours, her life became more important to me than my own. My head relaxed against my pillow and I finally understood the true meaning of motherhood. I let my tears soak the pillow as she slept against my breast.

Too soon the day came to surrender this precious gift into the loving arms of her new parents. My adoption counselor had a small ceremony planned for us—my daughter and me, the adoptive parents, my parents and brother, and the birth father.

The counselor started with a prayer of blessing for each of us. She knew we would go our separate ways in just a few minutes—a family with a new baby and me with empty arms. I felt God's presence. It was comforting, though bittersweet. I didn't have the emotional strength to release my baby to her parents. Instead, I handed her to my father.

He held her close and said, "God bless you, little one. Remember we will always love you dearly." He gently kissed her forehead. It seemed he too didn't ever want to let her go. My dad bent to let me kiss her one last time and then gave her to her new parents, who welcomed her gratefully into their combined embrace. They cried and laughed and rejoiced. I cried.

I knew they cared for her and would give her everything a little girl needed to grow up emotionally, physically, and spiritually healthy. For that I had peace. We three parents shared a moment of complete connection, and then it was time to let go, time for them to go home, together.

That was the saddest day of my life. For I, too, had to go home that day, but alone.

It's been six years now. Not a day goes by that I don't think of my daughter. I miss her terribly, but I have no regrets. I continued on in school and received my master's degree. I've had a few relationships but nothing so special as to make a good marriage.

I've mourned greatly over the years. My daughter's birthday is an annual reminder of my loss; on that day I grieve and then thank God for her life and her family. It's comforting to know my daughter is all right. God took care of that the day I sat on my parents' living room rug and chose her family. I have a deep sense of peace about her well-being.

My family and friends are still concerned that I have not fully dealt with placing my child for adoption. Some even push me toward counseling. In the end, I know I did the right thing—for myself and more importantly *for my daughter*.

God's Faithfulness

Anne McNamara

I will sing of the LORD's great love forever; with my mouth I will make your faithfulness known through all generations.

Psalm 89:1

I'm from a large family of seven children with two loving parents who devoted their lives to our family. I grew up knowing Jesus and in high school decided to commit my life to him.

As the second born, I had many responsibilities, but my favorite was helping my mom with my twin baby brother and sister. I was only seven when they were born, but it was then that I started dreaming of holding, loving, and caring for my own babies. I loved baby-sitting and constantly thought about getting married and having a large family of my own.

I met my husband in 1982 and the first time I saw him, I knew he was the man for me. We had a beautiful wedding two years later. Happy and in love, I began to plan out my life. We wanted to start our family immediately and have three, four, or five children. I knew we would live happily ever after.

One year went by, then two, and still our arms were empty. We yearned for a baby to hold, to smell sweet baby scent and to brush our hands against soft baby cheeks. We wanted so much to hear our child call us Mommy and Daddy. Our hearts ached to be a family.

Family members and friends prayed and encouraged us to keep our faith and keep trying. My mother continually sent cards with special words of support. In one card she included the words of Psalm 20:4: "May he give you the desire of your heart and make all your plans succeed."

I silently asked God, "Why, Lord, would you plant a desire so deep in my heart and then deny me that very thing?" I even asked him to take away my desire to have children, but my desire only increased as time went on. I prayed and prayed, but it just didn't seem that God heard my prayers.

Every time we heard the news of another pregnancy or birth, our hearts ached. We were happy for those couples, but with each announcement, our hopes and dreams of having a family grew dimmer. I felt like we were chasing something that kept getting farther and farther from our grasp.

I was getting tired, depressed, and defeated. But a certain Bible verse kept coming to my mind: "All things work together for good to them that love God, to them who are called according to his purpose" (Rom. 8:28 KJV). I, however, could not see *any* good in our situation.

I tried to pour myself into school, sports, and crafts. Each changed my focus, but only momentarily. The activities never took away my desire to have children.

My emotions were continually up and down. I was a wreck. Some days I felt encouraged and sensed God's closeness. Other days I cried all day and didn't feel God at all—rather I felt angry, hurt, empty, and very much alone.

We pursued extensive infertility tests and procedures. We not only put our lives in the hands of the doctors, but we placed all our hopes there as well. We believed their words and the statistics more than anything else. It got to where we felt we were living at the doctor's office. Despite the roller coaster of emotions accompanying the needles, tests, and fertility drugs, each procedure gave us a tiny measure of hope.

In May of 1990, my husband and I underwent the GIFT (Gamete intra-fallopian tube transfer) procedure, where doctors placed my eggs with my husband's sperm into my fallopian tube in the hope that fertilization would take place. We would have to wait two weeks to find out if it worked.

On a Friday afternoon in the first part of June, we received a call from our nurse. "Are you ready to be pregnant?" she asked me.

Could this really be happening . . . to us . . . for us? I could hardly believe it. We called everybody. Our family and friends were overjoyed.

I immediately started journaling. My entry on June 19, 1990, reads, "Yesterday was the big day. I was so nervous. Here we were for an ultrasound and to see our baby or perhaps babies. But I wanted, I needed, to see my baby for myself. I needed to see to believe. As we were in the ultrasound room, my husband and I were both nervous. I couldn't talk. I just held my breath. My husband, on the other hand, babbled away. His babbling abruptly stopped when we saw the baby. We had our baby. This was one very special GIFT baby and God chose to give him to us. This is truly a Gift from God."

Tears streamed from my eyes as I saw our baby, just 3mm big at the time. Even so small the baby was already taking form. The most wonderful thing we saw was the baby's heartbeat—a small, fast flicker of light on the ultrasound. It was then that I realized there was truly a baby living inside of me. I couldn't imagine a more wonderful feeling. When we arrived home, the phone didn't stop ringing. Our family and friends wanted all the details. It was exciting to share our joy.

About three weeks later I went to spend the weekend with my parents about seventy miles away, and on Sunday morning I woke up and found that I was spotting. I wept at the sight of the blood. I knew right away that my pregnancy was over. Our baby was gone.

My mother held me tight. I sobbed. She said over and over, "I wish I could take away your pain." She held me in her arms as our bodies swayed back and forth. She tried to comfort me for a long time as we sat on the bed. I needed my mom and she was there.

I called my husband and we made plans to meet the next morning at the doctor's office. We had another ultrasound and it only confirmed what we did not want to hear. Our baby was truly gone; our baby was now with the Lord.

The memory of that painful day remains vivid. The pain we felt was so deep and so sharp that I was physically sick inside. I remember lying on that ultrasound table, crying, "I don't think I can take any more . . . I can't go through with it . . . What are we going to do?" I cried out to my Father in heaven, "How could you have taken my baby away?"

My husband held me tight. He reminded me that God would help us through this. He told me over and over again that he loved me. He stroked my hair and wiped my tears until they finally quit falling.

After that fateful day, we continued with more expensive procedures for another year. Nothing worked. By 1991, our arms that longed to hold a baby and our hearts that ached to give our love away were empty. All the hope we placed in doctors and all the money we spent on infertility had given us nothing but more pain and loneliness.

I started wondering if God was allowing this to happen as some sort of punishment. Maybe he had not really blessed our marriage. Maybe my husband and I weren't really supposed to be together. One thing I knew for sure. The thought of living my life without children caused me a pain I could never endure.

Then one day, my husband and I were driving along a beautiful mountain ridge in New Mexico, and he asked me, "Do you really want children?"

I answered with tears in my eyes, "Most definitely." That was when we began to look into adoption.

After researching a number of adoption agencies, we chose one. The adoption process, at times, was overwhelming. We each had to write an autobiography, go through counseling, and take a three-day extensive preparation class. It was frustrating at times because we felt we had to prove to everyone that we would be good parents. But we got through it and in the fall of 1991 placed our adoption letter into the agency's profile.

In January of 1992 a birth mother chose us. Our hearts were filled with renewed joy. We couldn't believe we might have a baby soon. On a Friday in February we learned our birth mom had given birth to a baby girl. I will never forget the day we first met our beautiful daughter.

We were in the hospital with the birth mother when the nurse brought our baby in. I walked quickly to the cart. Reaching for my dear daughter, I held her tight against my heart. I didn't even give the nurse the chance to tell us to wash our hands.

We took one look at her, so tiny, so beautiful and perfect, and we fell in love. Two days later we brought our precious little Christine home. At long last, a tiny little baby, one we had waited for for so long, had already filled our lives with joy, happiness, and love.

The next few months were filled with celebrations, showers, and parties as our family and friends shared in our excitement and happiness. Our prayers of having a family were answered much later than we anticipated, but we began to see God's perfect plan for us. At last we were seeing how all things do work together for good to those who love God.

When Christine was three years old, we began procedures to adopt our second child. God closed doors where necessary and opened them as well. It seems we were more patient the second time around, or perhaps it was just smoother and faster.

In the spring of 1995 we met our second birth mother and her family. It was an incredible meeting. We seemed to have much in common and felt a closeness right away.

In late June we received a call that the birth mother was in labor. As we left for the hospital, Christine told us she wanted a baby sister, and a few hours later Laura was born. They were meant to be sisters—God knew exactly what he was doing.

The day was filled with emotion, especially during the adoption ceremony. After the birth family took turns holding Laura, our birth mother's father took this beautiful baby girl and placed her in our arms. I sobbed. I was filled with joy and happiness, yet I felt a sense of pain and guilt. I felt I was stealing their joy and happiness by taking this beautiful baby from them.

We brought our sweet little Laura home from the hospital to meet her new big sister. Christine was excited to meet her. She sat on the sofa and checked out her sibling, examining her from the top of her head to her tiny feet. She fingered Laura's tiny toes and touched her sister's head with her cheek.

Looking at our two beautiful girls, our hearts were filled with a sense of completeness. Later, my husband and I walked onto our deck and there in the sky at a distance was the most beautiful rainbow. We felt at peace. My eyes filled with tears, for I knew God had sent this rainbow to us. It was then that I realized what a faithful God we have.

We endured multiple losses through infertility, including the loss of dreams. But each loss gave us more insight into the pain a birth mother must feel as she makes an adoption plan. The love a birth mother must have for her child is beyond my comprehension. At times I still feel a sense of guilt because it was through the pain of our birth mothers that we have so much love and joy.

I have no idea why God chose to give us our children through our birth mothers and not biologically. But we thank God every day for our birth mothers and that they chose life for their unborn children. We know it is an honor to raise these two precious angels and we thank two wonderful young women for giving us the privilege. We are not perfect parents, but we can say that we love our girls with all our hearts. We believe they are truly miracles of God!

Part 5

Who Will Rock My Baby?

Wanting the Best for My Child

Taxi Driver Rescue

Wanda Lee Robb

I was the oldest of six children. My father, an abusive alcoholic, abandoned us. My mother worked two full-time jobs to keep a roof over our heads, and the responsibility for my five younger siblings fell into my hands: cooking meals, doing laundry, signing report cards, administering cold medicine, changing beds, changing diapers.

My straight-A grades fell until I just quit school completely. Mom seemed relieved; now I could help even more by taking on a part-time job.

And then I met Jeff. At nineteen, he seemed mature and understanding. He made me feel as though there was more to life than work and responsibility. He took me to parties and showed me how to have fun. He made me feel valuable and wanted, instead of just needed, until I got pregnant. Then he made me feel worthless.

I was only sixteen. While teen pregnancies seemed to be rampant in 1972, no one in my family wanted me to be one of them. Everyone wanted me to abort.

I couldn't explain why I felt so protective of a child I had never seen, fathered by a boy who didn't want any part of it. I just was.

Determined to do whatever I could to keep my child, I went to work full-time, hoping to save enough money to be able to raise my baby. My mother was against it every step of the way. I suppose, looking back, it was unreasonable for me to have expected her to take on any more children. But I resented that my child wasn't wanted there.

When I was six months pregnant my mother's new boyfriend decided I was a bad influence on my younger sisters and demanded I leave the house immediately. I was given three hours to pack and go. One hour later, with one suitcase and a stuffed koala bear, I left.

Alone, homeless, and emotionally devastated, I didn't know where to go or what to do. Not far from where I worked was an abandoned building. I slept there two nights, using my suitcase for a pillow. The third night, rescue came in the form of a taxi driver. Tom had occasionally driven me to and from work. He saw me walking down the highway with my suitcase, recognized me, and stopped.

When he found out what had happened, he had pity on me and took me off the streets. He was willing to give me a home until the child was born. After the baby was born and I was back on my feet, I would have to move on.

Tom gave me friendship. He bought me better clothes, took me to better restaurants, taught me how to talk and walk and act as if I had come from a different side of town.

He spoke of growing up as an only child without a father. Tears filled his eyes when he talked of being left alone much of the time while his mother was working—of never having enough, of never feeling good enough. It was Tom who suggested adoption.

At first, the idea devastated me. I couldn't imagine giving my child away, as if it were a puppy I could no longer take care of. But Tom was right. This child deserved better than being dragged along with no guarantee of a meal that day or a place to sleep that night. After weeks of crying and deliberating, I finally accepted the truth. I wanted more for my child than a homeless and uncertain future.

Reluctantly, I went to the nearest adoption agency. The people there assured me that I was doing the right thing. They said my baby would have two parents, a home, security, and a chance for a better life than I had or could provide.

Even so, I continued to argue with myself. I could keep the child. Somehow. I could find a better job than the one I had washing dishes in a restaurant. I could find some sort of housing. I could raise my child. Alone. Without family. Without security. Without any guarantees.

The bottom line was, did I love this child enough to want the best for him—even if I wasn't the one who could provide it?

I knew the answer even though I couldn't admit it to anyone. If anyone asked, I continued to say that I hadn't made up my mind yet. Perhaps I was hoping for a miracle. Maybe talking about it would make it all the more real before it even happened. I just wanted time with my baby, every precious minute of it.

Early on the morning of January 15, 1973, I went into labor and my taxi driver friend took me to the hospital. Because Tom wasn't family or the child's father, he was sent away. Alone once again, I went through over thirty-two hours of labor, waiting for a child to be born who seemed as reluctant to leave me as I was to leave him. The doctors, concerned that both the baby and I were in distress, gave up trying to get my mother to come and sign the papers for a C-section and delivered the baby the best they could without surgery.

Michael James came kicking and screaming into the world just after five-thirty on the evening of January 16. And I fell in love with him.

Even though I was told not to look at him or touch him, I insisted. He was my son. For the next four days, Michael and I bonded. I fed him, held him, and sang to him. I told him how much I loved him and how proud I was of his fighting spirit. I told him to remember that I would always hold him in my heart and nothing would ever take his love and memory from me. Each night, when they took him back to the nursery, I cried, afraid he might grow up thinking I didn't want him, didn't love him, and had abandoned him.

I begged God to somehow assure my son that I would never stop loving him, and to help him understand that my decision to let him go wasn't because I didn't love him—but because I so desperately did.

Four days later, I was instructed to leave the hospital—and my son. It took every ounce of strength and determination to do so. I walked out of the building knowing I'd left the best part of myself inside. All I could do was pray that someday my son would understand what it cost me to give him more. To give him life. To give him a chance.

For the first few weeks, neighbors and friends condemned me for "giving away my son." I would go back to Tom's in tears, wondering if I was as cold, heartless, and failing in motherly instincts as they said. After two months, I couldn't take the accusing looks and horrid whispers anymore. Packing my bags, I left the state, hitching a ride with a friend who took me to New York City. I started a new life, never talking about my son to anyone, keeping it a precious secret in my heart.

Many condemn adoption—making it appear loveless, hopeless, and worthless, as if it were merely a choice between adoption and abandonment on the steps of a church. Some people condemn mothers who give their babies up for adoption as heartless and uncaring women. Well, they are wrong. Adoption is a choice of love. Of sacrifice. Of giving so that someone you love can have more even if it leaves you wanting.

My son is twenty-eight years old now and not a January 16 goes by that I don't stop and wish him a happy birthday. I wonder if he's happy, if he's married, if he's well. He has a twelve-year-old half sister—another child the world wanted aborted, but this time because she is handicapped. She lives with her dad and me and is a blessing to all who know her.

Michael has an adoptive mother and father who love him, and he also has a mother praying every day for the son she never sees, but has never stopped loving.

Sharing Thaddaeus

Ann Brandt with Alice Gregory

When my daughter and son-in-law, Alice and Willie, began the process of becoming adoptive parents, none of us realized the course they would travel. As my husband and I watched from seventeen hundred miles away, we saw a small part of their hopes, joys, and disappointments.

Their lowest point was when a birth father changed his mind and told them, "I need to parent my child."

Seven months later the father and his baby girl appeared on a television program. Alice told me, "I saw the love he had for his child and cried through the entire show. They were tears of sadness, but they were also cleansing tears. I realized this was his irreplaceable child and understood the difficulty he had faced in making his final choice; it was the right choice for him and his daughter. I know our time will come; it just isn't now."

After a year and a half of riding the adoption roller coaster, Alice and Willie decided to move forward with other aspects of their lives. Alice changed from part-time to full-time work, while Willie became more absorbed at the law office. My heart broke for them, but the only thing I could do was pray.

In the same city, at the same time that Alice and Willie were coping with their disappointment, Stephanie was trying to cope with her own pain. She was all alone, except for her unborn baby. Her boyfriend had left and she had no job. She spent a lot of her time alone pondering how she would be able to care for a child.

When it was time, Stephanie took the public bus to the hospital where she labored through powerful contractions, experiencing the trauma and miracle of birth without a friend or family member by her side.

Holding her newborn son, Stephanie felt a strong need to protect and nurture him. As she held him close to her heart, reality sank in: Babies need a lot of stuff—more than she would be able to provide at this time in her life.

While her son was asleep in the nursery, Stephanie walked into the hospital lounge. After pacing for some time she saw a woman—a stranger—walking toward her. They began talking. The woman's adopted daughter was in labor. She wanted to be near in case her daughter needed her, and of course to see her new grandchild. The two talked for hours. She shared with Stephanie that all five of her children were adopted and most of them were open adoptions. The woman went on to describe how wonderful adoption is for children. She was grateful, she said, for her children's courageous and loving birth mothers. The adoptive mother encouraged Stephanie not to be afraid of adoption.

Stephanie left the lounge and asked a nurse who she should talk to if she was considering adoption. By dinnertime an adoption agency representative arrived with adoption forms to sign releasing her parental rights.

It was a scary moment, but it helped to know she would not have to completely walk away. She could receive updates on how her son was doing and see pictures of what he looked like when he was six and didn't have his front teeth.

A new sense of excitement swept over Stephanie; she could have some control over her child's future by choosing his parents. She decided she wanted her baby to be the oldest in the family so "he could be spoiled rotten."

Stephanie flipped through pictures of prospective parents and skimmed their applications and letters. When she saw Alice and Willie's picture she stopped and announced, "These are the people." She just knew in her heart that Alice and Willie were the parents she wanted for her baby boy. Something special about this couple seemed to shine through their picture.

The caseworker insisted that Stephanie view all the applications, but her feeling persisted and she declared that Alice and Willie should be the adoptive parents.

From their classes at the adoption agency, Alice and Willie learned it was important for adopted children to know from the beginning they had a larger family than just the family they lived with. Alice and Willie sympathized with a birth mother's need to have some contact, even if was only pictures and letters.

Alice and Willie did not promise, or even agree, that Stephanie could visit her baby. But they were open to the idea and would wait and see how things worked out between them. Stephanie wanted so much for Alice and Willie to be her son's parents, even though she might never hold her baby again once she placed him in their arms.

Alice and Willie's openness was the level of openness Stephanie could agree to. On that Thursday, after learning Stephanie had chosen them, Alice called me. "Hi, Grandma!" she said.

It took a few seconds for her meaning to sink in. "What! When? Who? How?" I must have sounded crazed.

During the next few days Alice and Willie scrambled to get ready. Their church threw them an impromptu baby shower, a friend from Willie's office gave them a crib, while another friend offered bottles and clothes.

While Alice and Willie were ecstatically preparing for the baby, Stephanie mourned the loss of her son. Somehow, it comforted her to write a poem for him.

A few days later the happy parents arrived to meet Stephanie for the first time. They talked, sharing stories about themselves and answering each other's questions. Then Stephanie tenderly placed her son into Willie's arms. Later she confided, "It ripped my guts out to hand him over, but it was the best way I knew to make it real."

Stephanie signed the relinquishment papers, but it takes more than writing your name on a piece of paper to emotionally release a child. Determined to go forward with her life, she mailed her poem to the adoption agency. They would send it to Alice and Willie.

My Baby Boy
My little "bundle of joy"
When you were born I was so glad
When you left I was so sad
I did what I thought was best
It put my love to the test
It tore at my heart
And ripped it apart
I wanted you with me
But you needed a family
A family to love and care for you
Even though I wanted to
I wanted to give you a family
So I gave you Alice & Willie

Parents to be proud of
Parents to love
Love them as they love you
Care for them as they have cared for you
Alice & Willie are the parents for you
They are a dream come true
Hopefully you'll come to see
What I did wasn't for me
It was for my baby boy
May his life be filled with joy.

S.W.

Alice stayed true to her word and sent Stephanie pictures and short letters through the agency. Several months later Stephanie expressed how hard it was for her to write letters to people she hardly knew. She suggested they get to know each other better. Alice and Willie agreed and met Stephanie several times for lunch or coffee. On the fourth visit all of them, including Thaddaeus, went to the zoo.

Alice and Willie decided to invite Stephanie to join them again on another outing with Thaddaeus. Their relationship was changing from cautious politeness to honest transparency.

Over the years as their trust and respect for one another deepened, Willie and Alice invited Stephanie more and more into their lives. Now, when Stephanie comes to visit, instead of staying in a hotel she spends the night in their home.

At first they felt awkward about what terms to use for each other. Now when they go places together Stephanie smiles and introduces Alice as, "the mother of my son." Thaddaeus used to tell people he had two mothers.

The terms they call each other may be confusing to people outside the family. But because there is no confusion for Thaddaeus, he is very secure.

Although Stephanie and Alice have differences of opinion on what toys are appropriate, at all times Stephanie respects Alice and Willie's values. Stephanie has taken the role of a good-hearted aunt with Thaddaeus and does not interfere when his parents correct him.

Eight-year-old Thaddaeus has all the "stuff" Stephanie wanted him to have. Thankfully he is not being spoiled rotten as she had first requested. Better yet, she knows Thaddaeus is being taught to run with a football and catch a baseball by a loving father who is a role model of what it means to be a man of integrity.

Stephanie has become a part of her son's life and Alice asserts that she always will be.

Snapshots of an Adoption
Anne Calahan

Before a woman places her baby for adoption through an agency, she receives counseling to make sure adoption is really what is best for her and her child. If she decides it is, she then begins looking through family picture albums of people who are eager to adopt. Anne, an adoptive mother, looks back to the time when she was preparing such a picture album for pregnant women to view. This is her story.

Someone Is Missing from Our Family

When I was a little girl, people would ask me, "What do you want to be when you grow up?" My quick response was always, "A mom!" Seven years after marrying my college sweetheart, Tyler, and unsuccessfully trying almost everything the infertility doctors suggested, I was still longing to be a mom. Tyler and I wanted a baby so badly that we decided to begin the adoption process. To our astonishment, my unexplained infertility turned into a surprise pregnancy. We were thrilled when our precious daughter was born.

Then I became pregnant again, but this time it ended in a miscarriage. We still longed for another child. We had a strong sense that there was someone still missing from our family.

Hoping to Be Chosen

After my miscarriage, we decided to continue with the adoption process. I sat in my kitchen, pictures scattered across the table, thinking about and praying for the pregnant mother who might soon be looking through our photo album. *Which pictures will communicate who we are and what kind of life we can offer her baby?*

I picked up a picture of our three-year-old daughter surrounded by wildflowers and majestic mountains. The picture was taken during one of the camping trips we took that summer in the Rocky Mountains. We had hiked through fields of wild flowers in the high mountain meadows, taking turns carrying our little girl on our backs as she contentedly sat in her child pack, soaking in the beauty of nature all around her. I chose another photo of our daughter sitting in her bicycle seat behind her papa, the two of them coasting along the bike path.

I thought, *I want so much to talk to you as you look through our personal profile and assure you we will love your baby just like our own little girl who came from our marriage union. My heart goes out to you as you question if we really are the kind of people we present ourselves to be. I understand none of us, no matter how good our photo profiles make us appear, are exactly what you want for your baby. We have our faults and make mistakes, but we are offering your child a home with a mom and dad who love and are committed to each other and our family. From the cuddly baby days, through the rough waters of adolescence, all the way to the other side of childhood, we promise, as best we can, to protect and encourage your child.*

I looked down at the photo I held in my hand and wondered how difficult it would be for me to raise my daughter alone. *Do you feel like a mama bird without a nest for your little one?* Tears welled up in my eyes as I thought of you saying good-bye to your baby. I imagined how much it would have hurt to say good-bye to my newborn daughter. *How can I communicate all I feel for you, brave mother? You love your baby so much that you're giving him life.* As I sat at the kitchen table surrounded by pictures, my thoughts drifted and I imagined myself rocking your baby and holding him close and someday telling him how good and caring you were to place him here with sissy, papa, and me.

Months Later

The telephone rang. I answered. It was the adoption agency. One of the several women who looked through our photo album was considering placing her baby with us! The social worker told me, "Jennifer grew up without a father and wants her child to have a dad. She also likes your views on child raising and that you're a stay-at-home mom." We were so excited and honored to be chosen! I knew a part of this young woman would be a part of our child, and I was eager to learn all I could about her.

The Baby Is Born

We were told we could come to the hospital and bond with the baby as soon as he was born. When that wonderful event finally happened, we entered the small hospital room, our presence filling it to capacity with the caseworker, the nurse, Jennifer, her mother, Tyler, and me.

The tiny newborn was crying. He was being passed from person to person in hopes that someone could shush his cries. When the social worker placed my son, who was less than an hour old, into my arms, I felt flooded with joy and excitement. His tiny body felt tense, and his unhappy cries continued. I handed the baby to Tyler, who awkwardly held the little bundle, not expecting the unhappy cries to stop. To everyone's surprise, the baby took a breath, sighed as if to say, "I'm home," and relaxed in Tyler's clumsy hands. My husband sat down and looked into his son's wide-awake eyes. As he fell in love with the "little peanut" he held in his hands, the rest of us quietly watched the two of them together.

After a while Tyler stood and carried the baby back to Jennifer. Although my husband didn't say much as he handed her the baby, his face showed how he felt. Then we left the room so Jennifer could have some special time with her baby.

The next day we brought our son home. We knew Jennifer could still change her mind, but we were willing to take the chance of being hurt and disappointed in order to bond with our new little guy. Tyler and I felt nervous until the day arrived when the adoption papers were signed and he was legally our son.

Aching for My Child's Birth Mother

The weeks rolled by. Though I was thrilled with my baby boy, I struggled with feelings of guilt. I grieved along with my child's birth mother for the loss she might be feeling. I called the adoption agency. I couldn't stop crying as I shared my feelings with a counselor. I wondered if sending pictures of the baby would only increase Jennifer's pain. The social worker encouraged me to keep sending the pictures and letters. She assured me that they would help in Jennifer's healing process. We had agreed to send pictures for only the first year. But after talking to the counselor, I decided to send a bundle of pictures and a letter every year for the agency to pass on to Jennifer so she could watch Jacob grow.

Seven Years Later

I sit in my kitchen, with pictures scattered across the kitchen table. I pick up a picture of Jacob and his papa building a snowman, and another of Jacob and his sister swimming together. I choose the cutest picture of Jacob and his newly adopted baby brother. I slip the pictures in the envelope and begin writing my yearly letter to Jennifer. I tell her how Jacob's older sister is some-times a little too bossy with him, and how he teases her and tries her patience until she yells. And how they make up. I describe the two of them traveling to the land of make-believe, and the adven-tures they share together. I write of Jacob's ups and downs at school, his character strengths, the things we are working on, and, of course, how much we love him. I stop and ponder, wondering if it comforts Jennifer when she remembers how Jacob stopped crying when Tyler took him in his arms. I smile when I think of how much Jacob loves his papa, and how his papa loves him.

I cannot imagine raising this energetic, lively, and sometimes challenging boy without my husband's help. I end the letter by saying, "I know it was hard to say good-bye to your baby when you gave him what he needed then and what he still needs today—a dad. I hope you are happy, Jennifer. It would be won-derful to receive a letter from you. And thank you again for mak-ing my life-long dream of being a mother of children come true."

I recently received a letter after nine years. Jennifer thanked me for the pictures and letters. She said she is happy for Jacob and glad I am his mother.

Samantha's Box

as told to Cindy Sweeney

Mom's life was a big mess. Men were in the house constantly, pot-smokers and drunks. Not a safe place for a fourteen-year-old girl. I was scared.

I enrolled as a ninth-grader at the high school, where I met Tommy. I liked him. One day when we were just hanging out, he asked if I wanted to experiment with sex. I agreed. Once. That's all. I thought we were just two friends trying something new. I ached to see what a normal relationship was like. It seemed innocent enough. But it wasn't.

That same week at my house, my brother's friends convinced me to try some pot. I didn't know what it was. I was naïve to trust them. They told me it was nothing bad, so I smoked it. I felt woozy and went to my bedroom. Ron, my brother's creepy friend, followed me into my room and started messing around with me. I told him to stop, but he kept saying everything would be okay. I felt out of control, groggy. He had sex with me. I passed out. That's all I remember.

Mom was there, but she pretended nothing was happening. Eight weeks later, I fainted in the shower. I told my mom that I might be pregnant, so she took me to the local Christian pregnancy center. I met Annie, the director, and took the pregnancy test.

When Annie confirmed I was pregnant, a slow panic gripped me. I crumbled to the floor and just fell apart. I didn't know what to do.

I wasn't sure which guy was the father. I was only a kid. Tommy was just a kid too. And Ron, well, I didn't want anything to do with him. Somehow I made it home, though home was certainly no haven of protection.

I don't remember Mom's reaction, but I knew I couldn't stay at our house. I packed a few things and threw my suitcase out the window. I told Mom I was going out for a walk, but I didn't return. I was scared. I didn't want to go back home for fear of what might happen to me. I stayed with friends for about a week, and then Mom sent my brother and Ron to look for me. Ron's girlfriend was looking for me too. She was furious it might be Ron's baby. I was terrified of her.

I stopped going to school. I finally called my pastor and told him everything. He encouraged me to meet with Annie again. That's when things changed. Annie referred me to a program for unwed pregnant girls.

I lived at a Christian group home for three months, but because of an insurance problem I had to leave. I returned to my hometown and turned myself in as a ward of the State, and they placed me with a family from my church as a foster daughter. The mom home-schooled me. She was very supportive, very loving.

My church encouraged me during those difficult months too. One Sunday I went up front to ask forgiveness. I sobbed my way through "Amazing Grace." It truly was amazing. Everyone stood up and started singing the hymn with me. Afterwards, the whole church prayed for me. I felt so loved. I grew closer to Jesus every day—strong for the first time in my life. I knew I mustn't blame my family for my situation—my pregnancy was the result of my own choices—and I took full responsibility. God's forgiveness and his strength filled me. I was free!

Abortion was never an option for me. More than anything, I wanted my baby to have a chance at life, but I hadn't yet thought about adoption. My grandparents said they wanted to raise the baby for me until I finished high school. But they started dictating when I could or couldn't visit the baby.

I wanted my baby to have a safe, loving home, with a kind and nurturing mom and dad—something I had always longed for. How could I give what I didn't have? I was only fourteen.

Annie gave me books to read about adoption and parenting. She encouraged me to make my own decision. One day, in my seventh month, when Annie and I met for prayer, I experienced something very strange. The word adoption echoed in my head. In my mind I could actually see the letters written in red. I told Annie I was sure God wanted me to place my baby for adoption.

My family was so upset with me. I was convinced I had heard from the Lord, but they didn't understand that at all. God gave me a supernatural strength to stand my ground. Doors started opening at that point. I connected with a Christian adoption agency and arranged for a semi-open adoption. I picked an adoptive couple just before the baby was born. Their file impressed me. They prayed a lot. They were a little older and seemed stable. The woman had been adopted herself, and they had a four-year-old adopted daughter. I wanted my baby to be safe and loved. They'd help my baby understand my decision.

A couple weeks later, I felt a little queasy. The next thing I knew, I was in labor. In just six hours, my beautiful baby girl was born. Much to my relief, a blood test confirmed Tommy was the father. I was very thankful. I told Tommy he was the dad, and he agreed with my decision to place her for adoption. At fifteen, he wasn't ready for parenthood either.

The hospital let me keep my baby in the room and take care of her. I spent hours staring at her and holding her close. I wanted to remember every detail of her sweet face. I named her Samantha. My friends and my pastor visited me on our last day. They brought me a beautiful corsage and we dedicated my precious daughter to the Lord.

Letting Samantha go was incredibly hard. I couldn't have done it without my friends. And the Lord too. My daughter and I rode together in the wheelchair to the lobby where I placed her into the arms of the social worker. My baby, my dear Samantha, would soon join her family. I gave the social worker a box. Inside was a doll blanket my mom knit for me when I was little, my favorite stuffed bunny from my dad, and a picture of me. I had kept a journal throughout my pregnancy and put that in too.

"Give this to Samantha's parents," I begged. "Tell them I love my baby. Tell them to take good care of her. And tell them thank you." I wept.

Someday she'll read it and know how much I love her. And how proud Tommy was of her too. He kept her picture in his school locker and showed everyone.

I went to live with friends from church and got a scholarship for the Christian school. Without my baby, I didn't know if my life would ever be the same. Now and then I'd take Samantha's little hospital hat and booties out of my special "Samantha box." I had even saved a lock of her hair. Everything still smelled like her. I'd hold them close, then tuck them away again for another day.

It hurt so much to be away from Samantha. But deep in my heart I felt at peace about my decision to go through the pregnancy and place my baby for adoption. I know it was the best thing, the most unselfish thing I've ever done in my life. It really helps to know that.

I love it when every Christmas a new picture arrives. I can't believe she's already eight and I'm twenty-three. I'm convinced I made the right choice for my daughter, so I don't feel as sad anymore. I hope she wants to meet me someday. I wonder how she is. I miss her.

I would love to be able to tell Samantha how blessed I am that I brought her into the world. Through my pregnancy and her birth I experienced so much—sadness and joy, God's forgiveness and love. Because of her, my life is changed forever. She will always be in my heart and part of my family. I didn't reject her, but chose adoption because I loved her so much.

For the Good of the Children

Kelly Fordyce Martindale

I know two women who are best friends and two other women who are mothers. They live in the same small community and are connected by a common thread: adoption. The best friends, Brenda and Nellie, for years have shared with each other their desire to be parents, while the moms, Darcy and Rosa, struggle with their roles as mothers. Here is their story.

Nellie worked for social services when she overheard a caseworker tell a young girl, "Look, we've tried to help you but you won't help yourself or your son. We have to take him to a foster home until you can prove you're a fit mother."

"Why don't you let them come to our home?" Nellie asked, as she approached the caseworker's desk. "My husband and I are already foster parents. Maybe we can help her get back into school and find a job." Turning to the young woman, she asked, "What do you think?" When everything was approved, Darcy and her son, Isaiah, moved in with Nellie and her husband.

Meanwhile, Brenda and her husband were marking off days on a calendar. They had heard about a prayer service uniquely designed for those struggling with fertility issues and adoption. Held only once a year, the service staff claimed a high success rate in pregnancies and approved adoptions for those attending the event. Brenda and her husband had been trying to have a baby for eleven years, and they wanted to experience the miracles that others were talking about.

So Brenda and Nellie encouraged each other to hang in there during the next weeks and months. During that time Darcy found out she was pregnant again, thus making her situation even more complicated. Since Darcy couldn't handle one child, everyone wondered how she would handle two.

As Darcy's second pregnancy drew to an end, Brenda became more anxious about the upcoming church service. Nellie was simultaneously spurring Darcy on to finish high school and urging Brenda to be patient. Meanwhile, Darcy was becoming more comfortable in her role as foster daughter and less interested in being a mother. She soaked up the attention and pampering.

After much contemplation, Nellie and her husband approached Darcy about the well-being of her soon-to-be-born baby. Darcy admitted, "I'm not sure what I want to do, but I do know I'm not ready to parent two kids. You two have been so good to me and Isaiah, well, I think you should adopt my baby." She continued, "I've been learning so much from you about being a mom so I know you'd do a good job."

Nellie and her husband had been trying to conceive for over six years. This seemed like the perfect opportunity and their hearts were ready for a baby. But was it really a wise decision? By the time Darcy gave birth, they all agreed it would be a blessing for each person concerned, especially the new baby boy. At first it appeared it was too good to be true, but the adoption was successful. Unfortunately, Darcy and Isaiah would have many problems to overcome.

Meanwhile, as the time drew near for the upcoming church service, Brenda could hardly wait. Nellie's adoption made Brenda desire a baby even more. Both women had been prayerfully patient in waiting for God's timing for parenting, but Brenda knew in her heart it was her time also.

Then the unexpected happened. The day they were to go to the church service, Brenda's husband became very sick. There was no way he could make the drive or sit through the long service. Brenda wept and her husband felt a huge burden for causing her heartache. She spent the day in sorrowful prayer and begged God to take away her pain.

Reluctantly, Brenda went to work the next day. As the admitting supervisor at the local hospital, she found herself involved in a miracle. In eight hours time, she and her husband became the parents of a newborn baby boy, relinquished by a mother of two older children. The mother had had an affair and her husband refused to raise another man's child.

The two best friends were finally moms. God had answered their prayers in unpredictable ways. Attorneys had been available, paperwork approved, and babies were settling in with their new mommies and daddies. But their miracles were accompanied by heavy trials.

Despite the closed adoption, Brenda found herself face-to-face with her baby's birth mom, Rosa. Because Rosa's husband refused to raise her newest child, she had reluctantly chosen adoption. Rosa treasured her little boy and knew adoption was the loving choice, but still she missed her baby. So she searched for Brenda who, in our small community, wasn't hard to find.

Brenda asked Nellie to accompany her to the local park where she would meet Rosa for the first of several encounters. At first, Rosa asked a lot of questions about their baby boy. Brenda shared many details. It was uncomfortable, however, because the adoption was supposed to be a closed adoption. Brenda's heart was torn; she wanted to support the birth mom in her decision to relinquish her child by sharing information that all moms desire to know. On the other hand, Brenda feared that Rosa was changing her mind and would try to take her son back.

It was especially helpful to have Nellie at the park meetings because she played the role of mediator and helped the two women verbalize their feelings. By the end of the first meeting, Brenda agreed to give Rosa a photo of the baby.

The dynamics of the two adoptions continued to grow in complexity. Each time Rosa contacted Brenda, she managed to finagle a little more from the adoption plan. First it was to meet, second it was a photo, third it was a much larger photo, and on came the requests until, finally, Rosa was holding and playing with her birth child.

Brenda's discomfort continued to grow but so did her understanding of the grieving mother. Like Nellie, Brenda discovered there was little counseling available for birth moms in their area. Because of economics, birth moms were often unable to make the long drive to a pregnancy center where more support and information were obtainable.

With Nellie's help, Brenda continued to support the birth mom in person and through prayer. Meanwhile Nellie was starting to feel turmoil as well. Darcy enjoyed the security of a family, something she had never known. But realizing their two families couldn't live together much longer, Nellie encouraged Darcy to develop a plan to get back on her feet. Darcy, however, was so comfortable with the care from her foster parents, she just wasn't motivated to parent on her own. Plus, having missed so much of her childhood, Darcy started partying and acting like an irresponsible teenager. She often left Isaiah in Nellie's care, sometimes not returning home for days. Later that turned to months. Finally, Isaiah's confusion about who his mother was forced Nellie to set some strict guidelines.

Isaiah and his baby brother had grown to love one another. Nellie was Isaiah's foster grandma but had grown to treat him like a son, just like her own baby. The relationships were strong, secure, and emotionally stable for the little kids. But the family dynamics weren't what they were supposed to be.

Whereas the birth mom in Brenda's case wanted more and more of her baby despite the closed adoption, the birth mom in Nellie's case was drifting away from her own child.

Nellie and Brenda continued to talk about their situations. They called counselors and did research at the library. They wanted to help their birth moms as much as possible but they realized action needed to be taken in both cases.

As it turned out, Rosa's greatest help came from Darcy. At one of the park meetings, Darcy tagged along and ended up talking to Rosa. It seems Darcy was able to help Rosa understand the magnitude of her decision to place her baby for adoption. Darcy explained the benefits that the baby would receive by having two parents in the home. She also shared her own grief and confusion. Together, the birth moms realized their feelings weren't so unusual, especially since they felt the same way.

The four women are still developing comfortable relationships, working together for the good of the children. Nobody knows at this point whether Isaiah will stay with his biological brother and foster grandparents. Nor do they know when Rosa will be completely at peace with her decision to relinquish her son. But what every person does know is that they each love those little boys. And each adult is striving to do whatever she can to assure a safe and secure upbringing for the children.

Aaron, Forever a Big Brother

as told to Kelly Fordyce Martindale

I was the girl you'd take home to Mom. I didn't drink or smoke. I was a good student. I went to church. My life was peaceful. At seventeen, however, everything changed and suddenly I was on a wild ride.

I could cast blame in many directions for what happened. Realistically, I have no one to blame but myself. But the rigidity of my parents was a factor. I was sheltered from alcohol, drugs, and sex, and that alone played a role in the first major detour I took.

When I first broke away from being a "good girl," life took on an excitement I had not experienced before. I drank and had sex with my boyfriend. No longer wanting any part of religion, I turned my back on God. And not surprisingly, I got pregnant.

I ended my pregnancy abruptly by abortion, and I knew right away it was the wrong thing to do. I was determined to put it out of my mind. I knew, though, that I would never have another abortion.

The abortion stopped me in my tracks, and I changed my lifestyle somewhat. I started drinking less and decided not to date for a while. I tried to make peace with God, but was unsuccessful. I was consumed with guilt at turning my back on him.

Within a year of my abortion, I had a new boyfriend and was pregnant again. I've since learned that studies show many women get pregnant again soon after an abortion. Statisticians call it a replacement baby. Studies also show that men and women have a difficult time bonding to the first child born after an abortion. Perhaps that's what led me to my second detour from God.

Ted, the father of my second baby, had problems. He drank and smoked and was into witchcraft. I felt unsafe with him and afraid. I didn't know what to do, but I knew I needed to get away from him.

I met a woman who worked for a maternity home. Looking back, I realize she was a gift from God. She introduced me to some people at a private adoption agency, and they helped me get into an apartment and establish a new home.

I settled in as the baby within me grew. My new friend and the adoption agency were very helpful. Their support made me feel like God cared about my baby, even though I didn't believe he cared about me. I was truly thankful for this woman's friendship, especially since my own family was ashamed of me. They tried to ignore my pregnancy, tried to pretend the whole thing didn't exist. They offered no support.

I received counseling and decided to pursue adoption. Something inside me kept nudging me toward God and the church, and that's when I decided to go through a Christian adoption agency. I really wanted my baby to grow up in a happy, healthy home. So, nearly eight months pregnant, I started looking at this agency's adoptive family profiles.

The last month of my pregnancy was difficult. I had many decisions to make, and I was very emotional. It was especially hard being on my own.

I finally chose a family and thankfully, as my pregnancy came to term, everything fell into place. My labor lasted more than three days, but I finally gave birth to a little boy. I named him Aaron.

Aaron was placed in "cradle care" until the adoption was finalized. I visited him several times as did my family. The cradle-care family was wonderful, but it was still a very difficult time because, having spent time with him, I didn't really want to give him up. I was only choosing adoption because I knew it was the right thing for Aaron.

Although my boyfriend was with me throughout the pregnancy, I didn't let him get involved with the adoption process. I persuaded him to sign the adoption papers, though I don't think he really wanted to. I now realize I wasn't fair to him.

The adoption process took just two weeks to complete. I'm confident Aaron is with the right family. The family and I communicate at times and they send me photos and videos when I request them. I still feel like Aaron is mine, even though I know legally he is not.

I'm a different person now and my life has changed greatly, but one thing remains the same: I love Aaron and know he will always be a part of me. At the time I could not provide him with what every child needs and deserves. Through the adoption, though, I've been able to do just that. Someday, when I have more children, I will tell them about their big brother Aaron.

There was a time I never would have supported adoption. I always wondered how people could give birth to a baby and then give it up. Yet, as I reflect on my two pregnancies, I am reminded of the fear and anxiety they both produced. Each decision was difficult and heart-wrenching. But having had an abortion and losing that child forever, I know now adoption is the best choice—especially for Aaron.

Aaron, you will always have a place in my heart. Always.

Part 6

Tapestries of Color

Biracial Adoptions

It's Not Black or White, It's Love

Jesika Sorenson

I was born in a small village in Kisumu, Kenya, in Eastern Africa, where the equator divides the world in half. The village is on a high plain surrounded by mountains. Not far from the village, elephants and giraffes roam freely.

Families live in round mud huts with thatched roofs. If the rains come, the rich soil produces enough maize and beans for food. The villagers also grow tea and coffee to sell for export at Lake Victoria, where hippos lazily bask in the water.

I was my father's fifth child and my mother's last—she died shortly after giving birth to me. In my village many believed if a woman died in childbirth it was because her baby was cursed and should be left to die. I was found in my mother's hut, lying on the dirt floor in a coma. The person who found me was a representative for the newly established Child Welfare Society of Kenya. The year was 1958, and I was their first case.

I was allowed to stay at the hospital for six months. After that an African couple and a white lady went around looking for any family—African, Asian, or European—to take me, but with no success. Then someone suggested Derek and Lydia Prince.

Derek was born in 1915, in Bangor, India, where his father was serving as an officer in Queen Victoria's army. Derek's British upbringing was from the old school—"Keep a stiff upper lip and all that." During World War II, Derek served in the British army as a medical soldier in North Africa. After that he was posted to Jerusalem, where he met Lydia.

Lydia was from the northern tip of Denmark. Born in 1890, she pioneered the teaching of home economics. Eventually she felt called to go to Jerusalem, where she established a children's home. There were food shortages and gunfire in the streets, but Lydia stayed to care for over seventy Jewish, Arab, Armenian, and European girls. Lydia adopted eight girls as her own—six Jewish, one Arab, and one of European descent. Derek became the father of these eight girls when he and Lydia married on February 16, 1946.

Eleven years later Derek, Lydia, and their youngest adopted daughter, Elisabeth, left Jerusalem and moved to Kenya. Derek served as the principal of a teacher training college and Lydia taught home economics. Sixteen-year-old Elisabeth attended a boarding school near the Uganda boarder.

Wrapped in a dirty towel, I was brought to their home at the mission school. The white lady and the black couple said, "We were told you take in children."

Lydia answered, "That was long ago. We are too old and too busy with our educational work. We cannot possibly take in another child."

One of the three strangers said, "We are so tired. May we come in and sit down for a little while?" They were given water to drink. After thirty minutes they got up to leave. As they passed Derek at the door I reached my hand out toward him as if to say, "What are you going to do about me?"

Lydia and Derek looked at each other in silent agreement, and then Lydia said, "Give me a week to get a crib and some baby clothes." Mummy was sixty-eight and Daddy was forty-three years old when I came to live with them. I was a sickly baby, but Mummy patiently nursed me back to health.

By 1961 my father had turned his attention to writing books and was receiving speaking invitations. We left Africa and briefly lived in England, Denmark, and Canada. When my father spoke in a church I would sit with him and Mummy on the platform. When he stood by the pulpit and taught, I would often lie at his feet and color until I fell asleep. Lying there I would hear him tell the story of me, and how families can be formed through love and acceptance, no matter the nationality.

It was as though my family was color-blind. As a child I had a sense of belonging, feeling secure in my parent's love.

When we moved to Chicago it was a complete shock to go to school and experience prejudice. In elementary school I was usually the only black student. When I was picked on and called "blackie" I would boldly stick up for myself and call them "whitie." When called "nigger" I would defiantly answer, "Oh, no, I'm not!"

My junior high and high school years in Florida were the most traumatic. I went to racially mixed schools where there was tension between blacks and whites. The blacks did not tolerate me. I was not like them in any way. My features were distinctly African—thick lips and a high forehead. The way I talked was "white." The black kids stole things from me and taunted me every day, calling me "baldy." My self-esteem was definitely affected by those years in school.

Even though I am still troubled by past events, I have never regretted being raised by white parents. Mummy truly had a mother's heart for me, but she had her rules.

As a teenager I tried to find my own direction by separating from my parents, considering my friends' approval more important than theirs. I was embarrassed when strangers and the kids at school saw me with my white parents. Other times I felt embarrassed by my mother, not because she was white, but because she was very forthright, a lot to do with her Danish heritage. Once we were in a meeting and the pastor was droning on endlessly. The congregation was helpless in their seats. Then out of the silence, in her thick Danish accent, I heard my mother say, "Tell that man to shut up!" I was so embarrassed I wanted to slink down in my seat as the red faced speaker quickly finished.

And yet we had our special moments where she'd ask questions that required answers from the heart, like the time she asked me, "Do you want to marry a white man or a black man?" I thought for a moment and said, "I'll marry the man I fall in love with." Interracial marriage wasn't a problem for me. If my mother had an opinion about it she didn't express it.

Even in her eighties she wanted to teach me how to cook, but at the time my heart wasn't in it. I'm glad she insisted. Now when I want to remember Mummy, I bake her wonderful pound cake or make pancakes.

The most meaningful memory I have was of the week before she died. Mummy and I and another lady were in the living room praying and singing and dancing together. It was such a joyous time. I am so glad I was home that afternoon.

Mummy was eighty-seven when she went home to be with Jesus. I would love to benefit from her sage advice and pearls of wisdom now that I am an adult. She was a woman who had such a deep faith and love for God. She prayed daily for her family. I respect how she lived her life, especially her love and concern for others. I'm proud to call her Mummy.

Her death took a lot out of my father; they had been married almost thirty years. I was only seventeen and it was hard to see my father weep out loud. I wanted so much to help him. I had my own grief and wondered what we were going to do without her. My mother was such a unifying factor in our family life.

My father started traveling more, so I went to live with family friends in Kansas City, Missouri. Not wanting to attend the public school, I graduated early by taking the G.E.D. One day some friends and I went to a public beach on a lake. While we were swimming, four white men came out of their homes and told us we had to leave. Later I discovered it was because of me, or should I say because of the color of my skin.

A year after my mother died I went to Israel with my father and other religious leaders. It was a special time with Daddy. He showed me the house in Jerusalem where he and Mummy had lived. I was pleasantly surprised that I didn't experience barriers but felt accepted by the Israeli people.

When I was twenty-one I returned to Israel. I connected with the people and the land and felt peaceful and free to be my true self. As a person I felt complete. On one of my walking adventures I met a young Israeli woman. We started chatting about something when she said, "I love the color of your skin."

I just about keeled over. Never had I heard such a statement. I said thank you, and thought, *Well, black can be beautiful.* I didn't feel small that day. It is remarkable how one word or statement can make such a difference in someone's life for good or for bad.

After my year in Israel it was an adjustment to be back in the United States. I felt unsettled. So my father made arrangements for me to live with a black Christian family in Kingston, Jamaica, for six months. While there I worked in a Christian radio station, answering letters from listeners and counseling people who'd walk in seeking help.

Jamaica was my first experience of living in a mostly black society. Because I still carried the hurt and the painful memories of how the black kids treated me in junior high and high school, I would walk with my head down, trying not be noticed. I feared at any given moment the situation could change and I would be verbally attacked again. I never really relaxed. Though usually treated well, there were odd moments when I was told I was not pretty because my features were African instead of Jamaican.

It was in Jamaica that I began to actively seek God to heal my emotions. It was painful, because part of the process was facing my hurts and forgiving the people who had caused my pain. I accepted the empty place in my heart from being abandoned at birth and chose to look at what was positive about my life. I came to understand what is really meaningful and discovered it was my adoptive family.

The healing did not happen overnight, but I was more able to overcome doubts and insecurities. I thank God for sustaining me and bringing healing to my wounded spirit.

After my time in Jamaica I went to Africa with my father and new stepmother, Ruth. My father had several speaking engagements in Kenya, so we were able to visit the village and the hut where I was born. Some of the African Christian women remembered me. They were excited to know I was doing well and was a Christian. They introduced me to my birth mother's brother.

It was a joyous reunion. Through a translator I learned my African father had just recently moved away. Due to time constraints we could not go see him.

When I returned to Florida I received a letter from him. While opening his letter I became light-headed and had to catch my breath. Then a giddy feeling came over me. It was a moment to savor. It wasn't written in his own hand, but the words were his. The letter began with, "I am happy to greet you in the name of God." He said he longed to see me. Then he talked about where he worked. He ended it by saying, "It is me, your father."

It would be lovely to see him. Recently I spoke with my African sister on the phone. God has been good to me.

In 1998, at age thirty-nine, I married Rick, who is white and seven years younger than me. Our wedding was a wonderful celebration with family and lots of friends. During the reception Daddy told again how I came into his family and how much he loved me. Tears came to my eyes as he spoke. My father is now eighty-five and a widower again. He suffers health problems, being weaker in body but not in mind. Daddy took nine orphan girls into his heart and home. Now it is our turn to care for him. Though our hearts are sad, we gladly do whatever we can to comfort our loving father, the one who helped make us a family.

Collage of Colors

as told to Kelly Fordyce Martindale

Many years ago in California we started looking into adoption. My husband and I had four children by birth, but we felt we had a lot to offer a child who needed a home. We knew we couldn't change the world, but because we loved the parenting experience so much, we thought we could help at least one child. We called many agencies to inquire about biracial adoption, but the door was always closed. We were a Caucasian family and we weren't infertile.

We didn't expect to get preference over a childless couple, but we had heard there were children who needed homes, so we kept pursuing adoption. I eventually had three more children and knew, physically, I couldn't have any more. Still the yearning to adopt a baby was strong. We had seven children and our whole family wanted another baby. The desire was so strong, I couldn't force myself to store away the baby clothes.

After moving out-of-state, we again called adoption agencies, but the answers remained the same: "You're not a biracial family and you are not infertile."

At our regular family meeting, we made a commitment to pray for a baby. We felt strongly that there was a baby who needed us as much as we needed him or her. We picked out the name Cody, because it would work for a boy or a girl, and we started praying earnestly for our baby, by name.

We continued to call different agencies and networked constantly, but the doors remained closed. And then a new agency came to our area. We met with them and they listened, and we became hopeful. They also informed us there was a growing need for homes for babies exposed to drugs.

Willingly, we worked with this new agency. We felt that God would prepare us for whatever we would be faced with concerning a baby's health. Our journey officially began.

Not long after, our beautiful African American and Caucasian baby girl Cody came to us. Her mother had used drugs during her pregnancy. Thus, we didn't know if her mind had been affected or if she would be hampered physically. However, we did know we loved her immediately.

We also knew we were committed to at least one more adoption. We could be Mom and Dad, and we could provide good experiences for all of our children, but we couldn't be another color. We believed with another biracial child, Cody would have someone she could share her identity with.

Turning to an East Coast agency, we aggressively networked to adopt another biracial child. Within weeks, we were blessed with Anthony. Like Cody, he is part African American and considered a "crack baby." Again, we didn't know how the drugs physically and mentally affected him, but we loved him immediately.

It always amazed me that people would tell us, "Oh, these babies are so fortunate to have you. . . . Oh, what a wonderful thing you have done for these babies. . . ."

They really did not understand. I would respond, "We are the ones who are fortunate because we are the ones whose lives are changed for the better. These babies help us grow in character and they push us to expand our small way of thinking. We are the ones that are truly blessed."

It's not surprising the looks we get; we are quite a sizable crew now. Our extended family has been gracious in helping us with our growing family. Everybody loves our children. My father used to bounce Anthony on his knee, saying, "You are my grandson. You are my grandson." I loved watching the twinkle in their eyes and hearing the giggles my father encouraged.

It's easy to love a baby, especially for little kids. However, I was sometimes concerned about our older children. My mind was put to rest the day I pulled up at the high school to pick up my oldest son. It was a stretch for him to acknowledge me in the car waiting for him, so I was amazed when he yelled, "Hey, guys. Come meet my little sister." He introduced them to Cody and then I knew all was well.

Being a biracial family draws challenging questions at times. One of those arose when Anthony was in first grade. He was reading a book on history when he padded into the kitchen in his stocking feet and crawled up on the stool at the breakfast bar: "What does n-i-g-g-e-r spell?" He asked so innocently it caught me completely off guard. I pulled Anthony off the stool and into my lap as we took another chair. I wrapped my arms around him and began to explain. I realized it was my responsibility to tell him now, surrounded by love and acceptance, rather than let him find out on his own when someone spit the word out at him in a much less loving environment. Sadly, there will always be hateful, closed-minded people to contend with.

One night while my husband was at a meeting, I got a call. A caseworker on the phone said they had a two-and-one-half-year-old boy who needed foster care until they could figure out what to do with the child.

I barely had time to tell my husband of the situation when there was a knock at the door. The caseworker stood there with our new little guy, Darrell. Darrell had come with a lot of emotional baggage. He too was the victim of hateful, irresponsible people.

This was our first experience parenting a little person whom we didn't know from birth. Also biracial, he fit into our family perfectly. But sadly, Darrell suffered from attachment disorder. We soon realized he had no ability to bond with us. It was extremely frustrating until we finally realized we had to treat him like a newborn and teach him to be dependent on us so he could learn to trust us.

Until then, I hadn't appreciated the importance of changing diapers or holding a bottle to a child's mouth. Darrell hadn't experienced anything loving. I spent the first year making up for the time Darrell didn't get to spend with us. I bottle-fed him for a while and then moved to spoon-feeding—actions imperative to bonding. I had underestimated these responsibilities with my other babies. Through Darrell I learned that feeding contributed to the perfect harmony between parent and child. As a mother, I was being stretched more than ever. My unconditional love, patience, and perseverance were all put to the test.

We needed to gain Darrell's trust and love, but it was difficult because of his previous experiences. We had to commit him to the Lord on a daily basis. In his few short years, Darrell had learned he couldn't count on anybody, not for food, shelter, or warmth, and especially not for nurturing. We had to prove him wrong.

Darrell taught us much about being parents including the true meaning of unconditional love. Because of Darrell, we had a renewed commitment to parenting. Even though he was supposed to be in foster care, we loved him as our own and we knew we wanted to adopt him. Though it took some time, it all eventually worked out. Now he's six and officially our son.

Once again, with all the children toddling about, we figured we were ready to stop. Then the phone rang. It was a friend calling about a family in need. They asked us if we could take their six children until they could get their finances and household in order. At the time Darrell was still fragile, so I told them we could only take the fifteen-month-old baby, Carlos. He was supposed to be with us for about three weeks, but it's been over two years now. We are hoping Carlos will be able to permanently join our family. He has added joy and a new hue to our home and we love him dearly.

Our kids range in age from three to twenty-eight and we have two grandchildren. We've had a delightful time with every one of them. We believe we are finished adopting, but only God knows that for sure. We've been given so many miracles. Each of our children is free from any complications that might have been caused during pregnancy. Often I am asked, "What if there *were* major problems?"

And I respond, "You have to ask yourself how bad you want to be a parent. Then it doesn't matter how your child comes to you. You just go from there."

Mommy, I'm Different

as told to Kelly Fordyce Martindale

We are a multiracial family, but our daughter didn't see skin color as relevant until she entered preschool. There, her little friends taught her what they had learned from their parents— that skin color makes a difference.

Our youngest daughter entered our world just over five years ago. They've been wonderful, joyous years. Our family is primarily Caucasian, but I am part Native American as well. When we decided to pursue adoption, we made one simple request— we wanted a baby girl. We were blessed with our adorable little girl, who happens to be part Native American and part African American. I suppose you might consider our family color-blind because we just don't see the difference, not in skin color and not in status—adopted or biological. We love each of our children, and believe me, they each have unique personalities that set them apart from one another.

For the most part, being a multiracial family isn't unusual. Unfortunately, the outside world focuses on the difference. My sister explained it perfectly: "Little children are protected by their parents and the walls of their home. It's only when they go outside to the cold cruel world that they find out they have a *carrot top*, or are *fat*, or have *four eyes,* or in our situation, have a *different skin color.*"

We've had biracial experiences that made us cry, laugh out loud, or even completely change the way we think (and sing).

- Family and friends from all over our own state welcomed us when we brought our little girl home. Sadly, there were two people missing from the crowd. My father-in-law and my brother-in-law simply couldn't put away their prejudice. Most of our family welcomed our daughter unconditionally. Some took a little time but now can't imagine their lives without her. But my father-in-law passed away without ever seeing or knowing his granddaughter. It remains to be seen if my brother-in-law will accept the privilege he's been offered. He has a huge blessing awaiting him should he ever choose to meet his niece.

- It only took two days at preschool before our daughter came home and asked, "Why is my skin dark and yours isn't?" Maybe I was being naïve, but I didn't think it mattered or that people even noticed. In our home, we truly don't see color. Maybe we did at first, but the color blindness happens so quickly. It's like childbirth—the pain is excruciating, but once you hold that beautiful bundle in your arms, it seems to disappear.

- We even changed the words of the song "Jesus Loves the Little Children." We'd been singing that song with each of our children and continued to do so with our youngest. Then one day, probably after preschool, we sang the song again. This time, after singing the line "red and yellow, black and white," my song was interrupted with, "Mommy, doesn't Jesus like brown children?" Now we sing, "Jesus loves the little children, all the children of the world. Red and yellow, *brown* and white, they are precious in his sight, Jesus loves the little children of the world."

- One day my husband, daughter, and I were outside feeding the horses and doing other chores. It was fairly cold and I had put on a jacket. My daughter was running around without a coat and barefoot when her dad yelled to her, "Go get your shoes and socks on and a coat."

  About fifteen minutes later, my daughter had not put on the required attire. Her dad squatted down before her and asked, "Do I need to get the paddle?" She shook her head no and her dad went back to the chores. My daughter approached me with a quivering lip, "Will Daddy really spank me?"

  He never had before but I responded, "I think you should do as you're told instead of finding out."

  She turned toward the house and then abruptly changed her path back to me. Her big brown eyes wide with concern, she said, "Well, you never see an Indian in a movie wear a coat."

I know we still have much to teach our daughter about her heritage, but right now we're focusing on good parenting and building a strong family foundation for her. Her grandpa says, "Yep, she used to be adopted but she's not anymore. She's ours!"

Over the years, I hope the humorous incidents will outweigh the hurtful ones, but regardless, our daughter will know she is loved unconditionally by her parents, her sister and brother, her grandparents, her aunts and uncles, and her cousins.

Part 7

Crossing Continents

International Adoptions

Finding Grace

Nancy Petty

I have long been fascinated with Chinese culture—the mystery of Asian calligraphy, the delicacy of Asian art, their exquisite silken fabrics. I used to linger in the dimly lit quiet of the Asian collection at the Philadelphia Art Museum and then walk the bustling streets of Chinatown. This early affinity reflects the beginning of a love that God was planting in my heart.

My husband and I met in 1979 in the Dominican Republic while volunteering in a clinic. We were married that same year. Steve was in medical school and I was in college, so we decided to delay having children for five years.

As those five years drew to a close, I developed a condition that we nicknamed "baby brain." I obsessed and daydreamed about what it would be like to have a baby. I felt sure my dreams would soon be a reality. But there was one problem—Steve was not yet ready to have children.

Rather than wait until we were in agreement, I stubbornly clung to the idea that our five years of waiting were over. Steve reluctantly gave in to my pressure. When our first son, Jon, was born, Steve felt displaced by our new baby. Many of the normal stresses and insecurities of new parenthood were magnified by Steve's resentment and the unresolved tension between us.

I tried to ensure that our precious new baby would not bring any changes or disruptions into our home. This, of course, was an impossible task.

It was during this time that I vowed never to force Steve into having more children. If we were to have a larger family, then God would need to change Steve's heart.

And he did. It was shortly after this that God softened Steve's heart and turned him into a wonderful and enthusiastic father. When our first son was just over a year old, Steve suggested we try to have another baby. Our second son, Tim, was born nine months later, and our third son, Chris, came along two years after Tim.

116

My first two pregnancies had been difficult and my third was even more dangerous. So after Chris was born we thought it medically prudent to have my tubes tied.

Steve and I reminded each other that we had three wonderful, healthy boys. I suggested maybe someday we could adopt a daughter, and Steve agreed. But neither of us was really serious; we were just trying to console ourselves. When it came to everyday reality, we were up to our eyebrows in toddlers and preschoolers for several years. We were simply too exhausted to seriously consider adoption.

In 1993, an acquaintance mentioned that China was beginning to open up to foreign adoption. She showed me a brochure that briefly described the situation—thousands of girls living in Chinese orphanages. Instantly something leaped within my heart. I wondered if there was a daughter for us in China. Although the idea was new to me, it immediately felt right.

At the same time I was overwhelmed with the gravity of such a decision. Steve and I would need to be in complete agreement. I prayed, asking God to give me a sign. I then had a strong impression that if God wanted us to adopt a daughter from China, he would inspire Steve to bring it up without me ever mentioning it. I knew if this were to happen, it would be a truly miraculous sign.

Time passed, and I continued to pray for the little girls in China. My heart was filled with love and concern for all of them. Each time I prayed, I was more certain that someday we would travel to China to meet our daughter. I daydreamed about this moment and pictured myself as the mother of four children.

My condition was similar to the "baby brain" that I had felt years earlier. This time, however, I was determined to be guided by God's perfect plan for us rather than to force my own desires on Steve. I never mentioned these thoughts and hopes to Steve. I was trusting God to do that. At first, I fully expected Steve to bring it up at any moment.

My resolve in this was tested as the months stretched into years with no mention of adoption. I had to be willing to embrace whichever answer God chose to give, even if his answer was a resounding No, expressed in complete silence.

Gradually my expectation turned into resignation. I began to wonder if I had been mistaken all along. Eventually I put my adoption dream on the shelf and tried to forget about it. I moved on to other things in my thought and prayer life. God, however, did not forget.

October of 1995, Steve was attending a weekend conference on worship music in Colorado Springs. During this conference his eyes were drawn to two Asian men who were standing with their hands raised to God, immersed in the reverence of the music.

As Steve watched them, he felt certain God was speaking to him. It was not in an audible voice, but he felt strongly impressed we should adopt an Asian baby. He left the conference with the assurance that God's plans for us included an Asian child.

The following evening we attended a wedding. The oldest child of a friend of ours was getting married, and we suddenly felt old. While sitting at an elegant reception table, Steve turned to me and said, "I know that this will sound strange, but I have to say it. I believe God wants us to adopt an Asian baby." He told me of his experience at the worship conference and of his conviction that God had spoken to him. I was stunned! Out of the blue came the exact confirmation I had requested. I told Steve about my prayers and hopes and dreams. We were both amazed, and we went home that night confident of the course we needed to take.

Almost immediately this confidence was tested. I mentioned our intention to a friend who works in children's health care. She strongly cautioned me against adopting a child from a foreign orphanage. She recited a list of daunting medical problems that such children could bring with them. That was scary enough, but then she proceeded to tell horror stories of mental and emotional problems and of families which had literally been torn apart by post-institutionalized adopted children.

As I look back, I am surprised at how quickly and easily I was drawn in by her terror. In the course of one conversation, I went from being confident and excited to being paralyzed by fear. Completely shaken, I confessed to Steve that I was too afraid to go through with an adoption. I told him of my conversation with my friend and of the subsequent terror that had enveloped me.

Steve looked at me calmly and said confidently, "If you aren't ready yet, we can wait. However, I believe that God has clearly spoken to each of us individually. At this point, I would be more afraid to deliberately walk away from God's plan for us than of what might happen if we adopt a baby."

Steve's calm and unshakable faith sliced through the cloud of fear that engulfed me. My excitement and confidence returned. Even if we might be embarking on a difficult path, I knew it was our path. And I was ready.

The next morning I began to contact adoption agencies. By the following week, we had submitted an application and started the paperwork process for our adoption. We began to pray earnestly and specifically for our daughter. That very same week her mother in China was taking the heartrending step of letting her go. In God's perfect timing and plan, as soon as she was released from her birth mother's care, she was received into our care, from afar, through our prayers.

I have never prayed so earnestly and consistently for anyone in my life. I knew that I had a daughter somewhere in China, and I felt responsible for her. Yet, I had no physical way to participate in her care, no control over her environment or over the kindness of her caretakers. Prayer became a vital link to my daughter in China. It was only through prayer that I could shower her with love and concern and have an effect on her circumstances.

The next nine months were spent plowing through paperwork, praying, fantasizing, and reading everything we could find relating to adoption and to China.

During our wait, our family spent ten weeks in the Dominican Republic. While Steve taught surgical techniques to Dominican students, the boys and I studied a comprehensive unit on China. We immersed ourselves in the history, geography, art, language, and culture of the country that we would soon visit.

We were excited about the possibility of taking our three sons with us on the journey to meet their new sister. Even though it was expensive to bring our whole family to China, it was important to us that the boys be a part of this pivotal moment in our family's history. This particular trip to China would become a memory we would treasure as a family.

Exactly nine months after we filed our initial application, we were on a plane to China. It was July of 1996, and our sons were seven, nine, and eleven years old. We brought with us a tiny color picture of our daughter and the knowledge that she would be twelve months old when we finally met her.

Our suitcases were stuffed with baby formula and disposable diapers, things to occupy our boys on the long plane flight, and medicines of every description. We traveled with nine other couples who were also adopting daughters. Steve's mother accompanied us and became the designated "grandma" for the group.

We spent several days in Hong Kong, sightseeing and getting to know our new travel companions. Nervous excitement seemed to be the dominant emotion that coursed through the group. As we sailed on a traditional Chinese junk through Hong Kong Harbor, we probably looked like any other group of American tourists. It hardly seemed possible that within hours we would hold our new babies for the first time.

We flew from Hong Kong into the People's Republic of China late on a Sunday afternoon. By the time we had checked into our hotel rooms, it was after nine o'clock. We had given up hope of seeing our babies that day, but then the glass elevator began to ascend bearing three adults and ten babies. They exited the elevator on our floor and hurried into a hotel room, closing the door behind them. We all assembled outside the door shouting with joy, "The babies are here!" Nervous and excited, we waited for our names to be called. One by one, couples entered the room and emerged carrying their babies.

Our name was called near the end of the list. Steve and I, along with Jon, Tim, and Chris, crowded into the tiny room. An orphanage official handed our baby to me. She did not cry or respond in any way. She just stared at us curiously. It was almost like a dream. We walked into that hotel room with three children and walked out with four.

We named our daughter Graceanna. Since both Grace and Anna signify grace, her name literally means "a double portion of grace." We viewed this as God's grace to her in giving her a family, and God's grace to us in giving us a daughter.

We took Graceanna out to see the sights of China. Everywhere we went we were approached by women who were amazed at our good fortune in having not just one, but three blond-haired, blue-eyed sons. Then they would turn their attention to our little dark-haired, brown-eyed daughter. They patted her in hopes that her good luck would rub off on them.

Although she was already one year old, Graceanna was initially unable to sit up, crawl, or even roll over without assistance. But these developmental delays were quickly overcome as she was given opportunities to move and exercise. Over the next days, weeks, and months, Graceanna came alive. She quickly changed from being almost unresponsive to being a lively child with an infectious giggle.

Every day was like a miracle as she raced through developmental milestones and generally made up for lost time. It became clear to us that she was extremely bright. Despite having heard no English during her first year of life, she quickly became very verbal.

It was my joy and pleasure to carry, hold, and snuggle Graceanna throughout most of our first couple of years together. I was acutely aware of having missed an entire year of her life. This awareness made me less concerned about spoiling her and more concerned about establishing a strong and trusting bond with her.

When we first returned home from China, we received a lot of attention. Friends, family, and even strangers were curious and excited to meet our new baby. Since that time, we have become de facto ambassadors for adoption in general, and cross-cultural adoption in particular. We have been approached by friends and strangers alike with questions about my daughter. I know some adoptive families are uncomfortable with this kind of attention and find it intrusive. I can understand how they might feel this way, but I have always welcomed the questions as a chance to influence people's attitudes in a positive way. I also relish the opportunity to let Graceanna observe my excitement and pride in her special story.

Over the years, she has had the opportunity to hear my answers to a wide variety of inquiries about our family. She has absorbed these answers and made them her own. Now that she is in school, she is often in situations where she is asked questions directly by other children. They wonder why she doesn't resemble her parents or her brothers. I am not always there to provide the responses. But because she has heard me answer these types of questions, she is confident and articulate in her replies.

One afternoon I overheard her acting out the Bible story of baby Moses with one of her dolls. She tenderly wrapped the doll in a blanket and placed it in a basket. The whole time, she was explaining to the doll that she really loved him, but that she was not allowed to keep him. There were just too many people, and the government was getting nervous. She assured the doll that she would take him to a place where he was certain to be found by someone who could take care of him. She promised the doll that God would watch over him. As I listened to her play, I found myself tearing up. I asked her if the story reminded her of anything. She immediately responded that it was just like what had happened to her. She said, "My Chinese mother is just like Moses' mother, and I am just like baby Moses. I guess that would make you into an Egyptian princess!"

It has been important to us to try to provide Graceanna with a deeply rooted cultural and ethnic identity. Rather than ignoring or downplaying the fact that she is Chinese, we have chosen to celebrate it. Graceanna and I began attending the Joyous Chinese Cultural School on a weekly basis when she was just two years old. We are now finishing our fourth year. We are grateful for the school's positive influence in our lives.

The school, which was started by our adoption agency, is staffed with talented and dedicated Chinese teachers and attended by swarms of little Chinese girls and their adoptive parents. We are learning the Chinese language, which is not as impossible as many Americans think, and we're immersing ourselves in Chinese culture and music. Graceanna is even learning traditional Chinese dance. Something deep within Graceanna has been affirmed and uplifted, and she is proud of her Chinese heritage. Chinese has become a secret language of love between us, and Chinese School is an important treasure that we share.

We have also been able to take the lessons we learn at Chinese School into her regular classroom. Each year, she and I put on China Day at her school with food, music, crafts, stories, and lots of Chinese show-and-tell. This year as China Day was coming to a close, several of her kindergarten friends told me that they wished they were Chinese.

Looking back, I can't imagine what life would be like without our beautiful daughter. God truly does do all things well in his own unusual way. He brought Steve and me together in complete agreement. Somehow, the experience of stepping out on a limb together in our adoption adventure strengthened our marriage and reinforced our love. At the same time, God gave us all an unforgettable lesson in faith and trust. Both literally and figuratively he has changed the complexion of our family forever.

Hope Fulfilled

Ann Cooper McCauley and Megan McCauley

Our biological sons were five and three when five-month-old Megan arrived from Korea at Christmastime. We felt indescribable joy upon her arrival. She nestled into the family just as any birth child would and we felt complete. She smiled and loved me from day one. When I held Megan and patted her on the back, her tiny hand patted me in return on the back of my shoulder. It was the love pat of a very tiny hand, but the large sense of acceptance it conveyed was overwhelming to me.

From the time Megan was itty-bitty we told her she was adopted. We were just crazy about her—she was wonderful. Some of her antics and rituals used to make me laugh. Now I know they were attempts to resemble her new family. Those memories are bittersweet to me now, and I hold them as precious things in my heart. One of those memories is of a bedtime ritual. When Megan was a toddler, pacifier in mouth, she used to point to the only dark freckle on her upper arm. She did this night after night to hear me say, "Yes, Baby, you have a freckle just like me!" My husband, two biological sons, and I are all fair and freckled. In Megan's mind her one little dark freckle was the only physical characteristic linking her with us.

My heart would ache to look at Megan, so deep was my love and gratitude to God for giving her to me. But she would always cry when we got out the baby pictures and told her about how we had been praying for her before she was born, about how happy we were when she finally came home to our family. From a tender age she tried not to hurt our feelings by crying. Nevertheless the tears came, and she could not express to us why.

By age four Megan was only saying a few disjointed words, but no sentences. I had her hearing tested, and we visited a speech therapist. Her hearing was fine, but she lagged behind peers in her expression of language. Coupled with this growing inability to verbally express herself was an escalating sadness. The two things seemed related, and yet they didn't. I watched as Megan retreated into a large world as a make-believe cat. Day in and day out Megan the cat roamed in the yard. The cat ate her cat food (popcorn) from a bowl on the floor. I patted the cat, and the cat patted me back.

In second grade with great frustration Megan struggled to read. It was then that we discovered that she had an auditory processing difference. Verbal directions, phone messages, and sentences were processed in a different word order from the way they were spoken. This is not atypical for children who are right-brained, but it is different from the way most people perceive and learn language. For years Megan had misunderstood what we were saying when we told her she was adopted. The adoption issues Megan struggled with were intensified because she could not understand what we told her and she could not express how she felt. Her response to all of this was to bottle up her feelings.

But at age twelve those feelings surfaced. One morning she saw a picture of an orphan and she exploded with anger. She was disturbed she had flown on an airplane with strangers and that I was not with her. With tears in her eyes she asked me why I had left her all alone. She had not been able to tell me this before. Her words spelled *rejection*. She cried and cried and cried. Why had her mother left her? Why had it happened to her? Why was she unwanted? Why didn't God fix it? "He could have!" she shouted. "God could have helped my mother!" she cried. "He could have brought her to America too! Then I could have stayed with her and I wouldn't be so different!"

I had known for years this moment would come, and when it arrived, I didn't know what to do. I held her and suffered with her, praying for the Lord to give me the right words. Finally I said, "I wish I could have gotten to know my dad before he died. I wonder what about me is like him? Do I move like him, think like him, laugh like him? It's a hole in my heart that will never quite be filled. I understand, Megan. You can cry. Anytime you feel like it—you can cry. I know you feel sad." God had answered my cries for help and given me the right words for my daughter.

That same year Megan went through what I call her Korean stage. She got out every Korean thing we had ever given her— a small flag, a map, etc.—and displayed them in her room. She ate nearly every meal with chopsticks. About a year later our home-school cooperative decided to study countries from around the world. We did Korea the first month. A whole day was dedicated to everything about Korea. When Megan came home she was very happy and built up. Slowly, the Korean things were moved from their prominent positions in her room and she began using a fork. She had to find what part of her was Korean and balance it in her mind with what part of her was American.

Megan is fourteen now, and her sadness appears to have faded. Still, I am aware there may be more under the surface and wonder when it will bubble up again. Though Megan sometimes still struggles to understand what people are saying, she is learning techniques to help herself, such as note taking, and not being shy about asking people to repeat themselves. She does grade level work using challenging private school materials and is one of the most talented artists I know. We have been encouraging her to explore and try new activities and are excited about what she is discovering within herself.

When Megan was little, I searched for the keys to unlock her loneliness caused by being different and her pain of not understanding. What Megan needed was time to become who she is and to discover that God loved her more than I could, understood her when I didn't, and was with her all the time. Now I see a more self-assured young person standing before me.

The other day Megan heard that a new girl in her youth group needed a friend. She was absolutely shocked this girl was needy when she appeared to have everything. Megan was bothered to the point of tears that a person could feel excluded or left out when it was within her power to make a difference. Shyly, afraid of rejection, Megan made herself available to this girl, and the girl wholeheartedly reciprocated the friendship.

In the process of making a friend, Megan discovered the enormous amount of compassion, love, and acceptance she has stored up inside herself for others. Megan now holds the key to unlock herself from loneliness. For she understands that a person who shows friendliness will always have a friend. Beautiful, sensitive Megan, how valuable you are!

Megan's Side of the Story

By Megan McCauley, age 14

When I think back on the day that I really opened up and talked to my mom about being adopted, I feel stuck. I can't change my life or what happened to me when I was a baby. I can't make my story different. I know my birth mom was probably in a situation where she was forced to give me up. She was probably scared and sad too. And I know if I wasn't adopted, I wouldn't have my family and friends here. They are important to me. They love me. Being adopted is sad, but being adopted is glad. I lost something but I gained something.

Each day I deal with the fact that I am adopted—that I am both Korean and American. I have things about me that were from my birth parents and I have things about me I have learned from the people around me—the people that mean most to me in life.

When I see pictures of children living in poverty, I feel lucky to have a home and a family. I realize that God took care of me when he placed me in the home I have. But I still like learning about my heritage, the culture and all, because I'm still Korean. I want to know about where I came from and who I am. But I will always be an American. This is where I grew up. This is the culture that I know best. This is how it is, and I love my way of life.

I'm glad that I live in a country where I have freedom to be who I am. I'm finding out more and more what my talents and abilities are, and this makes me feel good about myself. I know that I am a good artist and want to work someday with that gift. Right now I'm writing and illustrating a book with my cousin. It is for her master's in education. I designed this lobster named Crusty. He escapes from Jean Claude, a French chef, who wants to cook him.

I'm also discovering new gifts and talents in myself. This makes me see that I am unique. One of these talents has drawn me out of my room and out in front of people. I'm the drummer in our church's praise and worship band. Being a drummer has helped me to become more outgoing. I'm not so shy anymore.

I used to be shy because I felt different. I don't look like my family; my mom has red hair and light skin. Also, we live in the South. There aren't many Asian people living here, so I've always felt like I was different. Also, we have a large family with a few handicapped kids, so I've always felt like we were stared at. This made me feel weird. But now that I have developed my talents and feel more secure with friends, I feel better about myself. I love my family and friends and I have learned to be more confident. Learning to do something well helps self-esteem a lot.

Adopting Joshua
Ann Cooper McCauley

When Megan was seventeen months old we saw a picture of a young boy. His image followed us wherever we tried to run. We could not escape the power that he held over our thoughts, and we could not hide from his longing to be loved. That's when we knew that once again a child had been conceived in us. His name was Chan Hee. Abandoned at birth on the streets of Taegue, South Korea, Chan Hee was born premature with serious intestinal problems. He was sent to an orphanage for the mentally and physically handicapped and once there, forgotten. That is, forgotten until our adoption agency took a picture of seven-year-old Chan Hee.

We were flat broke. We didn't even own a car at the time we said yes to adopting Chan Hee.

We were led to believe that Chan Hee's mental and physical development lagged behind but that it was nothing serious. Then only weeks before his arrival we were told that he was profoundly retarded. My husband wasn't moved, but I was angry at God.

We had three healthy, beautiful children whom we loved with all our hearts. Adding Chan Hee meant complicating everything. We had our hands full with a toddler and two active boys. Could we handle a child with mental retardation? Was it fair to the other children to bring Chan Hee into our family? All the years I was growing up my uncle and my mother had worked with handicapped children. I purposefully steered clear of their occupation.

In my battle with God over Chan Hee, God led me to a Scripture passage about the blind and the deaf. I shouted at God that Chan Hee was not blind or deaf! God gently spoke to my heart. He spoke to me about the infirm. He spoke about his love for all children—especially the fatherless. He told me how he loved Chan Hee. I shouted. He whispered. I broke, and he won.

I discovered a truth about myself. If I had given birth to a child who was retarded, I would have devotedly loved that child, not rejected him. God had destined Chan Hee to be our child, and all he was asking me to do was love him. How could I reject Chan Hee?

Seven-year-old Chan Hee arrived to our open arms at Christmastime. We named him Joshua. We were shocked when we saw him. He appeared to have cerebral palsy, taking one step and falling the next, his head lagging.

We discovered hours later the reason for his weakness—severe malnutrition. We fed him nutritious food and tried to stimulate him mentally. Within days of his arrival, we saw him graduate from simple form puzzles to one-hundred-piece puzzles. We couldn't explain how Joshua appeared so bright and intelligent, yet at the same time was unable to learn simple language. He was unable to express himself verbally in his native Korean or in the simple English we tried to teach him. Three months later, he was evaluated at Children's Hospital. There he was found to be severely hearing impaired. Joshua was deaf.

Later that summer he was fitted with hearing aids and at age eight he heard human speech clearly for the first time.

Adopting an older child was very different from adopting a baby. Joshua was happy and he zealously loved every new life experience, but he came with issues. The biggest challenge was his lack of language. Joshua had a crude form of communicating—simple gestures, which he made up. He had never learned to give or receive affection. When I tried to bond with him by holding him in my lap or cuddling with him, he stiffened like a board.

Our home was changed as a result of adopting this child, just as I had feared. But the change was met with fortitude because we knew beyond a doubt that Joshua was our child, given by God. We didn't force him to bond. His ability to show affection would be slow coming and would take time and patience on our part. We had huge hopes for Joshua's potential, and yet each day we made ourselves accept his slow emotional progress. Our loving and generous seven- and five-year-old sons had to work as hard as we did at making Joshua fit into our lives. Each new success Joshua made was a victory for us all.

Two-year-old Megan and eight-year-old Joshua played well together because they were on the same developmental level. Like twins, they had a language that only the two of them understood.

Joshua wiggled his way into our hearts. Whenever I felt low, Joshua could make me smile. However, Joshua was also the child that could make me see red. He managed to push every button I had thought myself too righteous to own. I struggled with guilt feelings. Did I love Joshua in the same way I loved Kirk, Jarred, and Megan? Could I birth and deliver an almost eight-year-old child through the process of adoption and feel the same way I had over a baby?

The breakthrough moment came on a Sunday morning when my patience with Joshua was at an all-time low. I went to church and during the song service I began to fight tears. My best friend leaned over and asked me what was wrong. I replied brokenly, "I just don't think I like Joshua." I felt tremendous guilt on one hand and immense relief on the other—relief that only confession brings.

My friend smiled at me and said simply, "I don't like my son today either."

Her son was a birth child, and a revelation hit me square in the face. There were days that I did not like any of my children—because I was human and their behaviors were trying. My feelings were not an adoption issue at all. I had categorized all of my feelings for Joshua into adoption related issues, but my feelings were life issues. I realized that Joshua was just as much my son as Kirk or Jarred. There were days I disliked them and days that I thought they hung the moon, but every day I loved them. I stopped feeling guilty and I stopped measuring my ability to love. I learned to be kinder to myself.

Each new year with Joshua was a guessing game. Would Joshua ever be able to accept and receive affection or interact socially with people? Within one year of his arrival at our home he began to initiate hugging. Now he is a warm and loving individual who in recent years was awarded honor camper at our church's regional campground.

Would Joshua's legs ever walk steadily? He went on to win ribbons in the Louisiana Gumbo Olympics for kids with motor disabilities.

Would Joshua learn to speak? He learned to communicate, as best he could, both verbally and using sign language.

Would he learn to read? Joshua learned to read at a very basic level.

Would he always live at home? Joshua is at home at age nineteen, and he is an essential member of the family team. He currently holds a part-time job with a bait and tackle company, packaging products. The boy who did not seem to fit any mold found an ideal place to fit—within the safe and loving walls of his family.

When Joshua came into our lives the doors on adoption appeared to close. We felt certain our family was complete. But, were we ever wrong!

A Merry Heart Is like a Medicine
Ann Cooper McCauley

Randy and I felt certain our family was complete with our two biological sons and our two adopted children, two-year-old

Megan and eight-year-old Joshua. We deliberately discontinued our subscription to the adoption agency's magazine and their photographs of waiting children. We did not want to be tempted by another child's longing eyes.

But God does not limit himself to magazines. Four years after we adopted Joshua, another child came to our attention. She had been abandoned at age three in the streets of Manila in the Philippines. She was found battered, her leg broken. One eyeball protruded from her left eye socket having grown huge and tumorous. The other eye was covered in a milky film, the result of a weakened and useless cornea. From the street, she was taken to a hospital, where she was named Joana Doe, and from the hospital to an orphanage. It would be Joana's fate to remain within the walls of an orphanage—blind, sullen, and unloved.

God stirred our hearts for her. Yes, we had the heart to love her. Yes, we had room in our home. But how could love or compassion put food on the table or squeeze a fifth growing child into a 1980 Oldsmobile sedan? The only answer was to know that her need was greater than our own.

In the meantime our agency received our updated home study and pictures of Joshua who was now twelve years old. Because they were amazed at how far our son had come in less than five years, they decided to eliminate all of Joana's adoption fees. God made a way for us to have Joana when there was none.

In 1993, a small five-year-old girl courageously boarded a plane for America, wearing her new red tennis shoes. Upon Joana's arrival we added another letter to her name and began a remarkable adventure.

Tiny Joanna couldn't see a thing. But when she got mad, look out. She'd pull off her little red tennis shoes and nail us with them from anywhere in the room. I would carry her kicking and screaming to her bed. There she would claw at the walls, trying to climb them. Then she would rip all her bedding off and throw it. She was a violent twenty-three-pound tornado.

Randy and I prayed about how to handle her. After she had been home about two weeks I realized how smart she was— she knew that we weren't treating her like the other children.

While the other kids were getting their share of correction, we were afraid we would wound her spirit if we corrected her so soon after her homecoming. But on the day we decided to treat her like the rest of the children, everything changed. At first she almost seemed worse—but then she turned into the calmest, sweetest child.

Then we had to tackle her shunning problem. She had a habit of twisting her body and facing away from people if she was angry with them. After she had been with us long enough that I knew she understood "I love you" (and could say it), I would stand her in front of me after a tantrum. She knew she would be allowed to go on with her day after she made up with me. When she would twist her body to shun me, I turned her back toward me.

One day in the middle of my daily routine—cooking, taking care of the other kids, home schooling—Joanna had a tantrum and I stopped everything. I told the kids to turn the pots off and to entertain themselves in another room. When the phone rang I didn't take the call. After standing in front of each other for two-and-one-half hours Joanna began to sniffle, then sob. She threw her arms around me and hugged me hard. Then she said, "Mamma, I—l—love you!" She knew that I loved her enough to stop life for her—she knew I loved her enough to outlast her stubbornness. We both cried. That day I got a glimpse of how God will outlast me and my stubbornness. She never shunned me like that again.

While Joanna's temper tantrums were challenging, they could not keep us from falling in love with the delightful little girl that she was. I wouldn't have missed parenting Joanna for anything. The word clever has new meaning to me after knowing her. It is astounding how afraid I was to adopt a sightless child and how quickly Joanna erased all those fears.

In a short time she memorized the layout of our home. She had a sixth sense about where objects were located and she was not intimidated to run or skip through the house. We did purchase a small baby buggy for her to push. We thought it would help her to anticipate furniture before she actually had collisions, but the baby buggy was merely a plaything to Joanna.

She loved dolls. She would stroll them all over the house and yard, and she would sit for hours pretending to bottle- and spoon-feed her babies. She would sit and talk to them in her native tongue and make clucking sounds like she was trying to settle the fussy ones.

Her brothers taught her to leap from the front porch and roll in the grass. She never hesitated to follow them. She was a willing participant in any game they played, but she usually got the best of them. They didn't always have time to see her and move out of her way before she jumped.

At dinner Joanna's little hands would glide inconspicuously across her food taking account of what she had to eat, and then she would sneak her fingers over to see what was on the plate of the one sitting next to her. This usually led to an outburst from one of the children whose plate was being fingered: "What are you looking at, Joanna?"

It was several months before Joanna understood that looking was with eyes and not with fingers. I would take her to visit the ophthalmologist and the woman would say, "Joanna, look at me." Joanna's little fingers would race rapidly to find her. The doctor would say, "Look up, Joanna." And Joanna's fingers would race around in her lap. Which way was up?

The first year Joanna was with us, she had four surgeries. She was turning six when an X-ray discovered an enlarged gland within her heart cavity. The gland was removed and proved to be benign—yet the surgery required that her breastbone be severed and wired back. She was hardly out of the anesthesia when she requested her rabbit slippers and walkman. The doctors and nurses fell in love with her as she lay in pediatric ICU, hooked to monitors and lifelines, tapping her bunny-toed slippers to the beat of praise music.

A month later doctors removed her left eye. An implant was placed behind her empty socket to give movement to a prosthetic eye. Three months after that, she was fitted with her prosthesis, giving her a lovely new look. Then Joanna had a cornea transplant in the right eye. This gave her greater light perception. The doctors built Joanna a pupil and the eye was physically restored, but the brain had never developed the messages of sight during infancy. She only gained light and color vision. She also had surgery on all of her teeth, which were decayed and loose from malnutrition. I remember the day she discovered life without mouth pain and enjoyed chewing a piece of meat.

Her grasp of the English language was fast and astonishing. I taught her Braille with a six-cup muffin tin and ping-pong balls. When she was six, she had learned the entire Braille alphabet and had the fine motor skills to begin reading Braille with the touch of her fingers. Normal blind students do not read fluently until age ten or twelve. And only 10 percent of blind individuals have the brain function and finger sensitivity to read Braille at all. But Joanna was reading first level Braille by age eight.

Joanna was a gregarious and remarkable little girl. Our neighbor across the street had watched our children play in the yard over a three-year period and never realized Joanna was blind. I laugh to myself when I see the strain on his face and remember him saying, "Blind! That little one? The one that jumps off the porch, waves at the cars when they pass by, and rides a bicycle all over the yard?"

"Yes, she's the one," I answered, "and she likes to roller-skate too."

Joanna made friends with other children easily and was never afraid to try something new. As time went by, she taught the church toddlers to tie their shoes. As they grew, she taught them to ride their bikes without training wheels, and she gave them lessons in Braille.

By age eleven Joanna had read full-length novels in Braille, including *Little House on the Prairie* and *Little Women.* She was the ringleader of pretend play, organizing an entire wagon train of little women using the picnic table, sawhorses, and a rope. She and her friends in their prairie dresses and bonnets fended off Indians, wolves, and bank robbers. And believe me, Joanna could swoon with delirium and fever out in the middle of the yard like the best of actresses.

Joanna and her older sister, Megan, earned the title "giggle sisters." Every night at bedtime the kitchen ceiling would shake from their giggling upstairs.

Megan now plays the drums and Joanna the piano. They are two very different people, but they've found a place of harmony with each other. When Joanna had a *Beauty and the Beast* birthday party, she chose to be beautiful Belle, whereas Megan found it fun to dress in a cardboard box and painted mustache as Cogsworth the clock.

Recently, when some neighborhood children asked Joanna about God she ran into the house and then came back outside with her Braille Bible. Her fingers glided over the raised dots as she read aloud the story of creation and the fall. The children laughed when she told them, "Jesus died for all mankind." Joanna calmly said, "That means he died for all men, all women, and all children."

I don't think Joanna had much of a childhood before coming home to her family. But she rapidly made up for lost years. Joanna is gifted at spreading joy. And if it is true that a merry heart does good like a medicine, I will live a very long time.

Siberian Adoption

Ann Cooper McCauley

In the summer of 1997 my life had settled into a comfortable lull. Our five children were growing up and doing well. I started dreaming of life after forty and the extra time I would have to work on my novel.

Then God told us we would adopt again and his name would be Caleb. I was thirty-nine years old and panic-stricken. My husband, Randy, assured me if this was from God then we would know when the time came. While looking at pictures on a reputable international adoption web site, we saw a baby boy, born without a right eye. Our hearts went out to this little baby living in a remote orphanage far away in Siberia, Russia. We felt a strong desire to protect and love him. We knew we had found our Caleb.

We were shocked to discover the cost of the adoption. The amount seemed impossible to acquire, so we did nothing for an entire year. The agency stayed in contact with us and even reduced the fees by half. We had never traveled to adopt our other children. The cost of plane tickets and travel expenses, plus the adoption fee, was staggering. But after Randy decided that we needed to do everything we could to adopt Caleb, God met him with an unexpected raise at work.

We were now qualified for another adoption but still needed to raise money for the adoption itself and the travel expenses. We let our friends know we were adopting again and sent out an Internet newsletter explaining the Caleb Fund. Donations would go directly to our pastor, who would see that the money was used only for Caleb.

Money began pouring in from sources all over the country. People who had never even heard of us gave money to the Caleb Fund. Six months later, we were able to go to Russia and bring our Caleb home.

Upon our arrival in Siberia we were thrust into a strange snowbound world. The orphanage director said three families had come to adopt our son and left without him. Randy and I looked knowingly at each other. Her words were another confirmation that God had chosen Caleb to be our son.

This was the moment we had long anticipated. I was numb, weary from travel, and reeling with culture shock when the orphanage director introduced us to our son.

During the adoption process we were sent a three-minute video taken when Caleb was two weeks old. My husband and I fell in love with a tiny baby boy—helpless and still flinching and jerking as newborn babies do. In the video he hungrily sucked on his fist and cried. Our compassion for him was great—our love that of complete adoration.

When we met our two-year-old son he seemed shy. His head was large and out of proportion with his body, and he was tall for his age. He drooled incessantly and carried a small handkerchief to wipe it away. His empty eye socket was very small, giving his face the appearance of a permanent wink. His cheeks were quite red.

Could we transfer our love for the baby in the picture to this living, breathing two-year-old? It wasn't love at first sight. While we felt compassion for the child, it wasn't a parental love. We were strangers to one another.

After two days of visiting Caleb in the orphanage, it was clear that he preferred being with his play group rather than forced into the music room with two adults he didn't know and who didn't speak his language. He retreated to a corner where he could see himself mirrored in the finish of a piano.

He found Randy's pocket tools more interesting than the couple of toys I was able to pack into a carry-on bag. Caleb turned the pocket flashlight on and off a thousand times. When I presented Caleb with a snack-sized bag of Goldfish crackers, he relished eating them, holding back three in his little fist for later. He held them until they mixed with drool into mush.

Caleb was cute, but the drool was disgusting. Moments later he went to the bathroom in my lap. A birth child's drool or urine at age two would not have bothered me. I wondered if I was shallow.

The next day Randy flew two hours away to process Caleb's visa. My husband and I would be separated for four days. Our host family, who spoke no English, took me back to the orphanage to get Caleb. It was a highly charged and emotional few minutes when I took a screaming two-year-old away from the only world he had ever known.

I will never forget the little faces that watched us leave. I could nearly read their minds: "Oh, this is what it's like for a mommy to come and take you away." Since I couldn't communicate, I blew kisses to the caretakers and children while uttering thank you in Russian.

So great was my sympathy for Caleb that I cried harder than he did. When we got into the car with the host family, both Caleb and I were gulping for air, brushing tears away, and blowing our noses. But strangely, Caleb's tears changed to smiles rather quickly.

Caleb immediately began testing his limits and the host family gave in to his every whim. Before Randy and I were reunited, I had been bitten several times and pinched black-and-blue, and had had my teeth knocked loose by our new little son. He climbed repeatedly into the six-story windows of the host family's apartment, disconnected their electronic equipment, ripped the wallpaper from their bedroom walls, and had thrown enough food to make him eligible for tryouts at Yankee Stadium.

When we returned to Moscow I was exhausted, dirty, disillusioned, and ready to break and run from the whole thing.

But that evening in the hotel, after a bath and a nap, I fell completely in love with Caleb. I filled his juice cup, took toys out of the suitcase we had left behind in the hotel, turned on a tape of Russian children's music, and watched him play. He acted out less and started to interact with us more. I fell in love with his pudgy thighs and his winning Jack Nicholson smile.

Randy's presence was calming to Caleb. He seemed to know from the beginning that his new dad was the boss and didn't challenge Randy as much as he did me.

That night we pushed the twin-sized hotel beds together and made him a bed between us. The clincher of adorable to me was when we saw him nestle down between us, smiling at us behind a thumb he had every intention of sucking. As I watched our sleeping son suck his thumb intermittently, I had a glimpse of the two-week-old baby we had bonded with on the video, and I was warmed by maternal feelings.

The next day I felt I had the fortitude to face his behaviors. Caleb tried to run away from us in the hotel lobby, on the street, in restaurants, and in airport terminals. He pushed every boundary while laughing at us, constantly testing us to see who was in control. I was forced to handle him while Randy took care of business, carried bags, and made phone calls.

But by the time we reached the New York terminal and I noticed people staring at us, I just couldn't take it anymore. I made a public service announcement: "He's adopted and he speaks no English!" After that, the looks were kinder, but I was deluged by questions.

Caleb had two disturbing behaviors that especially worried us. Whenever we corrected him, either he crossed his one eye and stubbornly refused to look at us, or he spit at us. We knew that both behaviors had to be dealt with once we returned home to our other children.

Caleb, however, had something going for him that most kids don't. He now had a mother and father who had parented for nearly eighteen years of their lives. I had parented a total of five children before Caleb. I had parented strong-willed, pliable, learning disabled, deaf, attachment disordered, and blind. I had been through the terrible twos before and wasn't easily daunted. In fact, I was determined that Caleb's behaviors would be brought under control and that we would make it together as a family.

After the initial baby shower/reception and introductions into church and extended family, I isolated myself at home with Caleb. I was convinced some of his issues were orphanage-related, but some of his behavior was typical of a two-year-old.

I took no phone calls and I went nowhere for three weeks. Every time Caleb was difficult, I dealt with him in the same firm manner. I loved him hard. The issue was consistency. He tested me and tested me to see if I would always do things exactly the same way.

There were days I just held him and we both cried. As we snuggled together on the couch we ate cereal, looked at picture books, and worked on saying words in English. At the end of those three weeks Caleb had made me his mom, and I knew that the hardest part of transition was behind us. Perhaps I wasn't so shallow after all.

Of all my children, Caleb gave the biggest, juiciest kisses, and I loved getting them. The teenagers got them too, which was quite entertaining. I could always hear one of them saying, "Ooh, Caleb, gross!"

Caleb has been home for a year and a half and is almost four years old. He still reverts to crossing his eye if he thinks he can get away with it and recently he even tried spitting again, but Caleb knows one thing for sure. His family is forever—for better or for worse. He is secure, social, entertaining, handsome, and intelligent. He learns normally and has a winning future despite his missing eye.

The expense of bringing our son home had left the Caleb Fund exhausted. But before we had time to worry about Caleb's empty eye socket, the Louisiana Lion's Club stepped in and offered unlimited funds. When Caleb is older cosmetic surgery may help. But for now and throughout his childhood he will wear a series of conformers—small pieces of plastic that stretch the eye cavity, much like dental spacers make room in the mouth for more teeth.

Periodically, I take the conformer out to let his socket rest. Children ask him about his empty socket: "Where is your eye?" He replies with a shrug, "Oh, my mom took it out." Most kids stare at me after that and wonder what kind of a mommy I am.

Parenting after forty was nothing to fear. The addition of a small child in the family made us feel young again. With teenagers in the house we always have a baby-sitter, and we often have a volunteer to go down the slide with a toddler at the playground.

Of course parenting a young child among teens has side effects. Caleb calls his ABCs his AB—CDs. And he'd rather jam with a toy guitar while his older brothers play theirs than sit in a sandbox. Adding Caleb enhanced our family.

How could I have known that there was so much room inside myself to love so many children? With all six of my kids I have nagging doubts if I am doing things right. I beg God to help me, to tell me what to do with them. Each child has different needs. I have to depend on God to give me wisdom for each particular child. I've made mistakes, but I've always prayed for God to make the rough places smooth and for his love to cover the multitude of my mistakes.

We cannot take anything with us when we pass from this world to the next, but a child can be eternally influenced—children are a spiritual legacy.

Adoption. Is it worth it? Absolutely! What an incredible, faith-stimulating pilgrimage of blessing we are on.

Part 8

Handle with Care

The Special-Needs Child

Transformed by Love

Beth Louis

Adopt a little girl? It didn't seem logical. I was already very busy with our two boys. Our youngest son was nine months old when my husband, Vern, and I flew to Peru to bring him home from an orphanage. A year and a half later, Vern went back to Peru and brought home our second son, a twelve-year-old from the same orphanage. We hadn't had the benefit of gradually growing into a parent/teen relationship with our oldest son, and his moment-by-moment challenges had left me exhausted. But the feeling would not go away. It really seemed as if God was saying he had one more child for us, and this time it was going to be a girl. I even had a vague visual picture of her as I would pray.

I understood how the adoption process worked and had been very assertive when adopting our two sons. But this time I didn't feel I should do anything about the tuggings on my heart— except pray. So I waited, which is not my favorite thing to do, and talked to God about a little blond-haired girl with freckles I had never met.

I invited over the social worker who had helped us adopt our youngest son. As we drank coffee and ate muffins, we chatted about Nathan. We talked about her busy household and adopted children. Casually, I mentioned I felt God had one more child for us, and this time it would be a girl. Then we went on to talk about other things.

The weeks and seasons passed as I quietly waited on God. Nevertheless, a day did not go by that I did not pray for the little girl who needed us. I was so excited when Vern said he also felt a little girl was waiting for us.

A few weeks after Vern told me he was ready to adopt, I received a phone call from the social worker. She told me that eighteen months earlier social services had removed a two-year-old girl from an abusive father and a neglectful mother. Everyone who met the little girl immediately fell in love with her sky blue eyes, straw blond hair, and sun-kissed, freckled nose. But after taking the sweet, winsome-faced child home, her foster parents discovered her temper tantrums and destructive behavior were far more than they could handle. In fact, within the last eighteen months, the little girl had lived in at least six different foster homes. She had even been returned to her birth mother, only to be rescued again.

Because social services could not find a foster parent who would keep her for more than a month or two, they were now talking about institutionalizing the child. The social worker told me that every time she looked at this little girl, our family came to her mind. "I know you are Christians. Is this God?" she asked.

Was this a coincidence? I was eager to know more, so I set up an appointment for Vern and me to meet the little girl. After I hung up the telephone, I began worrying. Fear gripped my heart, and my thoughts became confused. I wondered, *Are my motherly longings and impatience causing me to run ahead of God? This child is in such need and so desperate for a loving home, but is she the one God laid on my heart? What if, out of compassion, we bring this little girl home and find we can't cope with her any better than her previous foster parents could?* I anxiously turned to God, "How will I know, Lord, if this child is the one?"

In the quiet of my heart, he clearly answered my prayer. I would need to hold the child in my arms, walk with her, and silently pray. If the "peace that passes all understanding" was there, then we would know she was the one. It gave me great comfort knowing Vern was also praying and seeking God's direction for our family.

Finally, the day arrived for us to meet the little girl. As I anxiously reached down to pick her up, her long legs grabbed tightly around my waist. She latched onto me as if I were her only hope from drowning in the turbulent waters of fear and insecurity. Compared to most four-year-old children, she was light and delicate, very easy to carry. I sensed she was yearning and dreaming to be held in arms that felt secure, arms that would not quickly put her down to pick up another.

I didn't want to take another child in my arms. I just wanted to hold her for as long as she needed me to. Then Vern held her. Looking at the two of them together, her skinny legs around his strong body, I thought of two puzzle pieces fitting securely in place. Vern immediately felt she was the child we had been praying for. He also knew from our heartaches and struggles with our adopted teen that if we were going to be able to stick it out with her, we needed more confirmation than just the emotions we were feeling. Vern is very pragmatic and wisely insisted that we walk through the process slowly.

Taking her back into my arms, I walked up and down the hallway, silently crying out to God, listening for his voice. "God," I pleaded, "if this is the child for us, please draw us to her and make our feelings stronger. If she is not the one, Lord, please release us and place her in a loving home."

We started with short little visits. Soon she was spending weekends with us. The peace came, and our feelings for the child grew stronger and stronger. All was going well, until one day I suddenly became plagued with doubts and fears. I felt guilty for taking a child away from a mother who loved her and wanted her back. Would it be best for this little girl to be with her birth mom, even though the mother had proved repeatedly that she couldn't take care of any of her children and was even abusive? At the same time I was harassed by fears. I worried her mother would find our home, steal her away, or hurt my little boy out of revenge.

I went to a prayer meeting at my church and found myself sharing my concerns with my pastor's wife. Like me, she had two adopted children. She listened and then excitedly took my hands and said, "Let's pray!"

When we finished praying, she was smiling and said, "I think you will literally be rescuing this child from the hands of darkness into the hands of light." Her words of faith helped us stop wavering and calmly move forward with bringing the little girl to our home—permanently.

At first, we took the little girl into our home under the title "temporary foster child," not knowing if the courts would relinquish her for adoption or return her to her birth mother.

Regardless of our status as temporary foster parents, I knew she was the little girl God had birthed in my heart; the one I had ached for and labored over in prayer.

We wanted to give our little girl a new beginning. Because my name and hers sounded so much alike, we started calling her Stacie, which means transformed heart.

Although Stacie was showing signs of improvement in our home, a young psychologist who had been working with Stacie did not want her in our care. We had expressed our intent to stop Stacie's sessions where she was told a clay man was her father, and she could pound him all she wanted to for abusing her. The psychologist had also decided Stacie needed the expertise of a special school for severely abused children. She wanted to send Stacie to a school that was on the far side of town. The plan was for a bus to arrive every morning at 7:00 and return Stacie home by 6:00 in the evening. Little Stacie had just turned four years old. We didn't think it would be best for her to be with troubled children like herself all day long.

We yearned for Stacie to be "normal" and believed what she needed more than anything was a loving, stable family environment. We wanted to take her for bike rides, eat ice cream cones with her, and play at the park, not give her more therapy!

I felt it with my whole being that Stacie needed to spend her daytime hours in a secure, quiet home—something she hadn't experienced in her four years of life. And in that home she needed a patient, loving mom who served her nutritious meals and had her take naps on a regular schedule, a mom who would rock her and sing to her, a mom who would sit on the couch with her little girl tucked under her arm and read stories to her. Stacie needed a mom who would take her little girl out into the sunshine and push her back and forth on a swing as she laughed and sailed up into the blue sky. She needed both a mom and a dad to soothe her hurting heart.

God answered our prayers for help through a special foster mother named Karen. Karen had had Stacie in her home and truly cared about her, but could not cope with Stacie's screaming tantrums and destructive outbursts. This dear lady was Stacie's only friend. Karen followed Stacie from foster home to foster home. She would stop by for little visits or take Stacie out for ice cream. Karen hoped her friendship and love would give Stacie a sense of security and order in the midst of her chaos. Karen saw how Stacie was beginning to show signs of emotional healing while under our care. She called the social worker, insisting and pleading with her to let Stacie experience what it's like to be a little girl with a stay-at-home mom whose purpose is to nurture her child. So Stacie was allowed to join our family and to stay home with me.

Stacie effortlessly found her way into our fifteen-year-old son's heart. Richard's acceptance and playful attention meant so much to her. Stacie was more like a baby than a little girl going on four. Although Nathan was six months older than Stacie, he was very much a big brother to her. Nathan became Stacie's constant playmate and interpreter.

After being in six foster homes in eighteen months, Stacie needed constant assurance she was wanted. Throughout the day she would come to me for a quick hug and then run off again to play. In the evenings Stacie would snuggle into the arms of her new father.

Vern's gentleness had a calming effect on Stacie. He would spontaneously play with her and tickle her. Here was a man with a healing touch, not a hurting one—a father she could finally trust. Stacie's perception of men was changing right before our eyes. Vern and I would pray with Stacie asking God to help her birth parents and to help Stacie forgive them.

Two other psychologists had been working with Stacie for months, trying to teach her basic academic skills, one being her colors. Stacie was in our home for about three weeks when they informed me of their assessments. They pronounced her learning disabled, a condition caused by her early years of trauma and abuse. They also said she might never learn to talk or be able to identify colors.

A few days after the psychologists' visit, I sat down with a handful of M&M's. I called Nathan and Stacie over to me and told them, "If you want an M&M, you must say the color first."

Four-and-a-half-year-old Nathan boldly declared, "Green."

Stacie watched her new brother pop a green M&M in his mouth.

"Now your turn, Stacie," I said.

"Geeeen!" she blurted. Next she chose "lellow," then "boo," and "red."

She had known her colors all along. From that day on, Stacie could tell you the color of any piece of candy. The social workers and psychologists were amazed. Even Stacie's birth mother, who had supervised weekly visits at the social services' office, noticed a new sense of security in Stacie and seemed at ease with her daughter living with us.

But day-to-day life with little Stacie was not a candy-coated adventure. She was a screamer, up to four hours a day. In fact, her vocal cords are permanently altered due to screaming so long and so hard the first four years of her life. Shopping at a department store where candy and bright colored toys are strategically placed to catch a child's eye could quickly escalate into a whirlwind of screams complete with flailing arms and legs.

We wanted to bless our little Stacie with pretty dresses, toys, dolls, and sometimes candy, but we especially wanted to give her the gift of learning to control herself. It was hard not to give in to her piercing screams just to shut her up. Vern and I yearned for her to grow into a well-adjusted child, so for her sake we sometimes told Stacie "No" or "Not today."

On one of those days, all eyes were upon me as I embarrassingly carried out of the store a kicking, hitting, screaming four-year-old girl, with little Nathan trailing quietly behind us. As we made our dramatic exit I heard a woman loudly tell another, "Some people just don't know how to parent their child!"

Lord, I silently cried out, *I am trying so hard and feeling all alone and judged by people who don't understand*. I wondered if I was up for these daily challenges. How could I be different from all the others who sent Stacie back to social services?

Six months after Stacie joined our family, the car felt small with five of us crammed inside and two car seats squished together. Vern wanted us to shop alone for a bigger car. So we left our fifteen-year-old son in charge of the two four-year-olds. When we returned home, we found that Stacie had taken a pen and dug into the wood and fabric of our living room and dining room furniture.

With the expense of buying a new car, it would be a long time before I would be able to replace the furniture she ruined. I felt totally defeated and very angry, but deep down I knew she was the one God handpicked to be our daughter. Without his strength and grace, we would have been just another stop at another foster home along Stacie's way to an institution.

A year whirled by and I thought Stacie was ready to attend a neighborhood vacation Bible school. I stood in the hall peeking into the classroom, watching my little Stacie sit quietly at the table, interacting nicely with "normal" five-year-old children. Other mothers were passing me in the hall, so I tried to stop my tears. I was so full of gratefulness and hope, the tears ran down my cheeks. In my heart I knew God was giving Stacie a brand-new childhood. He was restoring her socially, mentally, spiritually, and even physically.

I look at my seventeen-year-old daughter today, and she is a thriving, well-adjusted, busy, energetic teenager. Stacie loves God and is the youngest Sunday school teacher at our church. Her greatest passion in life right now is small children.

She loves her older brothers, and they love her. Stacie and Vern have a great father/daughter relationship. One of their favorite things to do together is to follow daily sports events. Stacie and I have grown from having a mother/child relationship to one of friendship and mutual respect. She enjoys her schoolwork and spending time with friends. She is content and enjoys quiet hours working on her hobbies.

At times I reminisce about those early years with troubled little Stacie. Looking back, I realize it took great courage to adopt and accept responsibility for her. I know the courage came from God. The only thing Vern and I did that was special was we were obedient to our heavenly Father, doing what we thought he wanted us to do. We heard his quiet, yet sure voice directing us to let a little girl interrupt our lifestyle and consume more emotional and physical energy than we had to give.

Looking back I realize how much Vern daily supported me emotionally by listening to me. We are now reaping a harvest of blessings from seeds of love and security God helped us plant in a little child's life.

For the rest of our lives, we will enjoy the beautiful person God intended Stacie to be. I sometimes wonder how many other little Stacies are out there, just waiting for the right family to answer the call and welcome them into a loving, stable, and, of course, imperfect home.

Last Hope, Final Chance
Marisa and Lauren Gray

Marisa, age 13: One of my earliest memories was when my sister, Deb, and I made the kitchen drawers into a ladder and raided the cupboard. We snatched the baby formula off the shelf and stuffed the dry powder in our mouths, half of it falling on the floor. When our mom came home I was still hungry and went to find her, hoping she would give me a bottle. But when I found Mom she was passed out on the floor with her bottles scattered around her.

Lauren, age 32: My attitude about adoption was, "Adoption is great, but not for me." Maybe I would give birth to a child some day, but adoption simply didn't pique my interest. As a teacher, I had great satisfaction in loving my fourth grade students. I didn't have "baby fever" like my peers.

Marisa: Deb and I were alone in our house when a lady wearing high heels came and put us in her car. She took us to my grandma and grandpa's house. I remember eating peanuts and saltwater taffy. But that probably isn't what they remember. Deb and I were used to running around without supervision. We didn't cooperate when they asked us to eat at the table, to not run in the street, and to go to bed. They loved us, I know they did, but one day we weren't with them anymore.

I don't remember it happening exactly, but I found myself at Chris and Marvin's house as their foster child. But Deb wasn't there. Everyone assured me she was okay, that someone was taking good care of her. But that didn't help me. I wanted Deb to take care of me. I wanted my sister back. I was three. I didn't understand Deb was just a little girl herself and couldn't really take care of me.

I was lonely for my sister and looked for her wherever I went. I felt hollow and empty inside and kept wondering why, why, why can't I see Deb, what did I do wrong? It would hurt so much I would get angry, scream, and throw tantrums, trying to have some control over something.

I came to believe that Chris and Marvin were my "real" parents. They let me pick out a puppy named Simon, and I always liked it when Marvin played his guitar. Two years after I went to live with them, Chris and Marvin got me a baby sister from overseas. Soon after the baby came, so did the lady in high-heeled shoes.

Lauren: One afternoon, I browsed through a magazine. The article read, "Three hundred thousand children waiting for homes." I had no idea. Tears wet my eyes. The next day as I taught my fourth graders I pictured each one as a waiting child without a forever family. I would gladly be "Mom" to any one of them.

"Look at this," I said to my husband as I held out the article that night. "We need to do something!" We hadn't tried to start a family until that day. But now it seemed clear. It was time.

Marisa: The sun was shining when Chris and Marvin kissed me good-bye. Then the lady in high-heeled shoes put me in her car. We drove for a long time. Buckled in my seat belt, looking up at the sky, darkness fell both outside and inside of me. Rejected again.

Finally the car stopped. There in the dark of night stood a three-story farmhouse. When I walked through the door, six women greeted me. Each took turns holding me on her lap and welcoming me to their home. These six nuns would be my next

set of foster parents. I liked all of them, especially Sister Patty
and Sister Mary Ann, but I was confused. Why was I taken from
Chris and Marvin? Where was my first mom? More than anything in the world, I wished I had a place I could stay forever
and could stop worrying—about Chris and Marvin's love, about
Deb, but mostly about me. The lady in high heels could come
anytime and whisk me off again.

Sometimes, I asked the sisters to be my parents. "We love
you very much," they would say, "but we can't adopt you." What
hope was there? I would erupt like a volcano, take off my shoes,
and throw them at seventy-year-old Sister Mary Ann. A few
times she ducked just in time, but other times I hit my target.
My target—this woman I loved and called Mama, who treated
me with such amazing care. She would calmly put me in time-
out on the basement stairs. And while my anger still boiled,
regret and sadness washed over me too.

After I cooled down, I felt limp like a rag doll, empty and sad.
Sister Mary Ann was never short on forgiveness and hugs. Her
kind words told me that maybe I was worth something.

I would hear the nuns pray every day, "Please find Marisa a
good mom and dad."

Lauren: My husband, Anthony, and I began our mandatory
adoption classes and home study. We didn't tell anyone at first,
but I was bursting with excitement. I dreamed of our child . . .
boy or girl? Athletic, artistic, smart? Brown hair or (a far shot)
red like mine?

Marisa: I had been living with the nuns for three years when
Sister Mary Ann came to me with good news: "They found a
mom and dad for you, Marisa! Hallelujah!"

"Great!" Or was it? I had grown to love the sisters. And yet,
I felt a spark of hope dance inside of me. "Are they here yet,
Sister Mary Ann?"

"Not yet. Tomorrow."

The mom and dad, Maria and George, finally came, both
wearing big smiles. Maria brought her spinning wheel and
showed me how to spin. When I moved in, they hired an artist
to paint angels on my wall—just like I asked. Finally, at seven
years old, I had found my forever family.

But I knew things weren't working out when I spent almost every minute at home locked in my room with those angels. George looked at me with disgust and fixed me the same lunch every day—bologna sandwiches. The deepest loneliness I had ever felt colored my world. "Please let me call Sister Mary Ann and Sister Patty," I would beg with a lump in my throat.

"No, *we* are your family now," George would say. "You have to get over the past."

I felt like I had lost everyone I once knew or loved. It felt like my new parents were cutting part of my heart out. "We will always be your family. You are never going back to them," they said. "We love you, Marisa. Please cooperate."

But I didn't.

One afternoon, after the school told George I had misbehaved again, he yanked me to the car and raced home. He stuffed only half of my belongings in a bag and threw me and the bag in the backseat. Before long, we were at the nuns' home and he was pushing me toward them.

"Daddy!" I said, holding out my arms.

"I am NOT your daddy, and I don't want your hugs!" His eyes shot darts. "I will make sure that every stunt you ever pulled is in your records, and no one will ever want you!"

No one will ever want me? That was my greatest fear. The nuns could not keep me forever. So where would I end up? What would happen to me?

The nuns talked to George, but I was glad he didn't listen. Their open arms brought life back into my dulled heart. At least I would be okay for a little while.

Lauren: Most of the children's profiles showed teens or large sibling groups. We were not in the position for either. I was only twenty-seven, and we had a small home and a full calendar.

We were told about a girl named Marisa, but we declined. She had deep-rooted behavioral problems. But as time went on, we decided to look into her file.

"Read this," I said to my husband. "Red hair." I had always dreamed of a redheaded daughter.

"And she's sharp," said Anthony. "Maybe she'll like reading and playing games like we do." But the deciding factor was a tug on our hearts that we couldn't describe.

"We heard about a girl named Marisa," I wrote to a friend. "We told the agency 'no,' but for some reason, I think she just may end up as our daughter."

The day the nuns described Marisa, we knew we had found a match. Anthony and I listened to stories of her creativity, compassion, and love for learning. When we looked at each other, both of us had tears streaming down our faces. And when we saw her photo, we had tingles. She was my twin. The nuns let us borrow the photos, and we drove all over the city showing our friends and families our new daughter-to-be.

Marisa: I didn't know what was going on when Anthony and Lauren came to the sisters' house. The nuns didn't tell me; they didn't want me to be upset. Lauren wore a jumper with white polka dots. I thought she and Anthony were nice. We played on the swing set—I still have a picture of it. Later, they visited again, and we fed ducks at the park. When Anthony and Lauren said they were going to adopt me, I still had hope. I don't know why, maybe because I wanted to be adopted so badly. I packed a suitcase and spent an anxious night in my new bedroom.

Anthony's parents adopted his sister at the age of six. Her name is Ellen, and the first time I met her, she said, "We don't give children back in our family." I imagined how Ellen would object if they took me back.

Lauren: We knew what we were getting into when eight-year-old Marisa moved in. Her grim files filled a copy box; her multiple diagnoses were strings of letters all ending "D"—disorder. She was one tough cookie. Daily tantrums, wailing, lying, and constant arguing made our once-peaceful home a battle zone.

But Marisa also had a sweetness that was evident from the minute we met her. She had sat between us on the couch, reading a fairy tale. "Isn't that beautiful?" she said over and over as she pointed to the drawings. To this day, I have never met a child who appreciates beauty—whether music or art or flowers—as much as Marisa does.

Marisa: I was scared when I moved in. Life was so unsure, I was afraid of aliens outside the window and monsters in the pipes. I even wore a whistle when I showered so Lauren would come if I needed her. But I eventually stopped being scared— I don't know when—and I don't know where that whistle went.

Lauren: The first three years were bordering on impossible. Every word in the files proved itself. But we refused to be another bead on a string of rejecting parents. We believed that if we kept loving Marisa, she would respond. Little by little, she began to trust us and let down her guard.

Now, through therapy and prayer, we continually get direction. Marisa loves being held, possibly because she missed it as a baby. Holding her each night at bedtime has brought a big change. It's as if a tightness inside of her is softening.

Firmness is necessary. We are consistent and do everything we say we will do. But Marisa would rather win her fight and get a consequence than cooperate and be consequence-free. We finally figured out that the one consequence that matters to her is isolation. When she acts in an unkind way, we separate her from us. Usually, she reacts with crying and yelling, but comes back with apologies and hugs. And sometimes a bit of humor will pull her out of a mood much better than anything else.

Certainly, it is time-consuming to parent Marisa. Checking to see that she gets her homework done is frustrating for all of us, and unless the teachers sign her planner, she doesn't write down her assignments. We have pared down her responsibilities to the "two Hs"—homework and hygiene. She is less overwhelmed and does not grasp so hard for control.

Because consequences are enforced so frequently and unpleasant moments abound, we try to find fun times to be together with no agenda. Each Wednesday, Marisa and I go out for breakfast before school. I don't discuss any of her responsibilities or shortcomings. It is a safe time for both of us. Our words are vulnerable and our bond consequently grows deeper.

Marisa: Being adopted for keeps has helped me be a better kid. I am just like other kids now. My parents come to my special events, like my flute concerts. Dad and I play games on the living room floor, just the two of us. Mom and I get pancakes before school and talk about boys and stuff as we watch the sunrise. I even baby-sit my cousin, who has never known our family without me in it.

My mom and dad really love each other. Sometimes they go on weekend trips while I go to my grandparents' house. While my parents bike on trails, Grandma takes me clothes shopping and paints my fingernails, and Grandpa spoils me and gives me lots of hugs.

I was very angry before because everyone I knew had a real family, but me. Now, I don't argue as often or throw tantrums like I used to. And I don't have to worry about my sister, Deb, because my parents let us talk on the phone, even though she lives in another state.

My parents forgive me and start over again and again. I'm glad they stuck with me. It has been hard for them sometimes. But I can tell being with me also makes them really happy too. I certainly am.

Lauren: We still go through periods of great struggle. Marisa's misbehaviors are less mature and more frequent than other thirteen-year-old girls. But I have faith that every seed of love and firmness that has been planted in her will eventually grow up to choke out the weeds that first took root. I saw it in Anthony's sister, Ellen. For Ellen, the transformation didn't happen until she was thirty.

I do know this: We are her last hope and her best chance.

In many ways, Marisa has blossomed into a beautiful girl, both on the inside and the outside. Her creativity and artistic talents abound, and her craft box is always sprawled out in the middle of her bedroom. She has a great love for the poor, the handicapped, and the elderly.

This year at school conferences, Marisa's seventh grade teachers bragged about her thoughtful contributions to class and her budding leadership qualities. Tears streamed down my cheeks as I drove back to work and told her on the phone, "I am so proud of you, Marisa. You are becoming the young lady God had in mind when he created you."

She replied, "Every day as I walk to school I pray that God will help me be my best. I think that's made the difference."

And I know it has.

Every day I pray too—that God will heal the brokenness inside of Marisa and help me be the best mom she could ever have. Without God's peace, power, and provision, I might have just become another mother who failed Marisa. But with Christ, love never fails and hope never dies, unless I let it.

Our love for each other is deeper than many mothers' and daughters'. This redhead brings joy into the lives of so many with her infectious smile. My biggest regret is that I have not been her mom from her very first breath.

Given Life, Given Love

as told to Diane York

> Many are the plans in a man's heart, but it is the Lord's purpose that prevails.
>
> Proverbs 19:21

Our day starts at six o'clock in the morning. I wake up my daughter and my two sons and get them ready to leave the house. I help JJ and Bradley get dressed while my daughter, Marya, dresses herself. Sometimes we have bedding to change after nighttime accidents. Everybody gets their medicine and we head into the kitchen for breakfast. Bradley puts bread in the toaster and picks up a cup to indicate he wants some hot chocolate. This may seem normal to a mother with preschool children, but my children are sixteen, eighteen, and twenty-three. My daughter has learning disabilities and my sons are severely retarded. These are the children I have chosen, and I have never regretted adopting them.

I suppose I dreamed the typical dream of a young girl. I envisioned a romantic courtship, falling in love, marrying a handsome young man, having babies, and living the fairy-tale life of a happy wife and mom. The best-laid plans, however, get changed.

Over the years I've had time to ponder those best-laid plans. Not only has my life turned out completely different than I anticipated, but my children's lives, also, are not what I predicted.

I did get married, but that would be the only part of my dream that came true.

Sadly, I was unable to get pregnant. My husband and I both loved and wanted children, so we became foster parents. The void seemed filled by my foster children, but when they left, the emptiness was overpowering. After several such losses, I realized I wanted my own children. I couldn't handle them being taken from me any longer.

We pursued a private adoption when I was thirty-two. We found a birth mother who was six months along and wanting to relinquish her baby. It seemed another of my dreams would come true after all. I felt such joy as we started planning a new future that included our own baby.

It hadn't occurred to me to prepare for complications. I naïvely believed we would have a happy, healthy, sweet-smelling baby. When Bradley was born, it was immediately obvious that something was wrong. We didn't know what at the time, but I realized my baby boy was in for some struggles. But Bradley was my baby boy and I loved him.

We were still in the process for the adoption and had the option to change our minds, but I wanted him. If I had birthed him myself, I felt I would have been faced with the same struggles. In my mind and heart, there were no options. God gave me this precious boy as a gift, perfect or not.

Bradley was diagnosed as having problems with his spine, bordering on spina bifida. The normal connection from his ear to his brain was missing. Later, we also found out that Bradley had fetal alcohol syndrome.

We had been having marital problems but my husband loved our new baby and I hoped that we could pull together as a family. However, having a baby could not solve the other problems, and eventually our marriage ended. I knew I had to move on with my life, so I adopted Bradley by myself and joined the ranks of millions of other single moms.

The connections in Bradley's brain that enable the ability to speak never properly developed. Thankfully, Bradley learned to hear and comprehend what others say to him. But his only form of communication to others is hand gestures.

Our life, although very different from "normal" families, was good. As in any single parent household there were difficulties that could have been handled more easily with two parents, but it was manageable and we were happy. Bradley was five years old when I decided I wanted a little girl. Once again I pursued adoption.

It was a great blessing the day I was introduced to tiny Marya, just seven weeks old. She has Minus 9P Syndrome (also known as Alfi's Syndrome), which means she is missing part of a chromosome. Her doctors and parents had no hope for her future. Although Marya's parents were highly educated, they didn't feel they could deal with raising a disabled child.

They made the decision to place Marya for adoption. Her parents were so afraid of getting attached to her that they only did what was absolutely necessary for her. They changed her diapers and fed her. They didn't hold her for feedings or touch her in any other way.

Thus it took, seemingly, a lifetime for Marya to respond to me. She had not been introduced to touching and holding and fought it each time I fed her. But I held her tight to my breast and let her hear my heart beating—a song of love to her. I prayed, *God, please help her to bond with me. I love her and I want her to love me too. Help her to feel and accept my love.*

My two children were perfect for me. And I was called to be their mommy. We filled each other's lives with what was needed and nothing more—just lots of unconditional love. Bradley quietly loved his baby sister. Over the years, Marya would become his best friend and helper.

Marya had had five major surgeries to correct problems with a clubfoot, a double herniated navel, a cleft palate, and her hearing. Then at age eleven, she lost one of her kidneys. Marya is now eighteen. Though her birth parents and the doctors didn't expect much at all from her, she has far exceeded everybody's expectations. She helps me with laundry and does small chores around the house. Sometimes she doesn't follow through with what she is supposed to do, like the time I sent her to put some ice cream in the freezer in the garage. Instead, she put it on the floor in front of the freezer. I discovered it too late.

I find it interesting how relative things are. For instance, Marya has severe learning disabilities. To most people that would be so far beyond their scope of experience that they couldn't handle it. In our home, however, they're simply learning disabilities. Compared to the boys, her problems, for the most part, can be overcome.

Marya will probably never live by herself, which makes her different from other eighteen-year-olds, but she does have interests just like other teens. She likes boys, her cockatiel, boys, her computer, and boys. She still likes Barbie dolls also. She takes good care of her cockatiel, Babe. She taught the bird to talk, but only Marya can understand Babe. Marya is taking speech lessons and we're hopeful the speech lessons will help the bird as well.

I didn't really plan on adopting any more children, but when Marya was two years old, the adoption agency told me about a little boy born to a drug addict. He was two-and-one-half months old, had Down syndrome and heart problems, and he was exceptionally hard to place. My heart, as always, took over and I accepted him as my own. His name is JJ and he was the tiniest baby I'd ever seen. A friend of mine made Cabbage Patch Kid doll clothes for him. Within two days of placing him with our family, he had heart surgery.

I fed JJ with a pink preemie nipple. Because he had difficulty sucking, I had to squeeze the nipple so the milk would come through. Every other feeding was a tube feeding. I'd have to stick a tube through his nose and into his stomach. It was difficult and somewhat frightening. I had to listen through a stethoscope to make sure the tube was not in his lung.

At one year old JJ went in for more surgery and got spinal meningitis. He almost died. It was hard seeing all the IV needles poked into my tiny baby's head. He survived, thankfully, but the disease affected areas of his brain associated with speech. He can verbally say "Ma" and "apple," and he learned some sign language, such as "more," "please," and "fight." I'm not sure where he got it, but he likes to sign that people are "dirty pigs."

The visible evidence shouts *my family is different!* But it isn't really. I love my kids unconditionally, even when they're being rotten. I feed them and provide a roof over their heads and clothes for their bodies. I teach them the Golden Rule. As much as they are able, they learn manners and right from wrong.

I've learned what each child needs and wants, both physically and emotionally. Instead of toys, I get the boys things like pajamas, blankets, and their favorite foods. Bradley and JJ love lights. In fact, they are so in awe and attentive to lights, I put up lights for Christmas, Valentine's Day, Easter, and Halloween.

One of our pleasures is going out to eat. I take my children to restaurants but am often discouraged by the reactions I get from other patrons. Too often I hear the muffled whispers of "They should be institutionalized" or "They shouldn't allow them in restaurants." Too many people focus on their first impressions.

I do have one fear—sometimes I worry what will happen when I am unable to care for my children. For a long time I felt that I was the only one able to understand their needs. But I'm encouraged to see them relating to others and communicating in ways others understand.

Many parents are anxious for their children to get out on their own, but I want to take care of my children as long as I can. In some ways I'm lucky my children will never be as rebellious as some teenagers and young adults. But they will never outgrow the need for someone to take care of them. The options for disabled adults are limited. Though there are places that could take care of their physical needs, few will provide a home environment and the unconditional love I give them. I realize that eventually I will die or will not have the strength to care for them.

This is a point where I have to let go. I have to believe that if God used me to raise these kids, then he'll provide someone else to finish what he started through me.

Some people wonder how I can care for these children, but I have to say, my rewards are great. JJ loves to give me bear hugs and at sixteen, it's sometimes difficult to get him to release his strong hold. Bradley at twenty-three still gives me kisses on the forehead. Marya at eighteen still tells me, "I love you, Mama," at least a dozen times a day. Most of my friends with kids these ages hardly talk with, let alone receive affection from, their kids. I am blessed.

So much has been said about a mother's right to choose abortion. Many don't want a baby that isn't perfect. However, if they will only give birth to these children, they will find others, like me, who do want them. I am grateful to the natural mothers of my children. They gave them life and now I give them love.

The Year of Jubilee
as told to Kelly Fordyce Martindale

After multiple adoptions, our last baby was now a toddler, so we packed the baby clothes away in the cedar chest. I breathed a sigh of contentment. This was the first time I truly felt ready to quit changing diapers. I suppose it was time, since my husband and I were just about ready to celebrate our twenty-fifth wedding anniversary. Then the mail came.

I sorted the junk from the bills, flipping quickly through the unimportant pieces. The last piece was the quarterly newsletter from our favorite adoption agency. I threw the junk mail in the trash and took the newsletter to the couch. Pulling apart the taped edge, I read the first page.

As I opened to the middle pages my eyes were quickly drawn to sweet innocent little faces that touched my heart as only babies can. I felt the familiar twinge of desire . . . no, the baby clothes are packed. Getting control of my mothering instincts, I continued to gaze at the little ones and then read the head-lines below. HARD TO PLACE BABIES—WE NEED HOMES. As I continued reading I understood why. Some of these babies were biracial, some had been exposed to the HIV virus, drugs and/or alcohol, and some had serious medical conditions. My heart was beating terribly hard.

Who do I know who would take a baby? I asked myself. I went through a mental list of friends and acquaintances who were looking to adopt. I decided to call the agency and get more infor-mation before I phoned potential parents. After all, I wanted to give them as many details as possible so they could make an informed decision.

I found that most of the babies had already been placed and the others were in process. Phew! I could sleep tonight know-ing the children were cared for. If there is one thing I can barely handle, it's a homeless child. No need to worry now.

A week passed and the phone rang. I answered only to hear, "You're it."

"I'm sorry . . . who is this?" I asked.

"You're it," they repeated. "The family backed out and your family is the only one qualified to care for this baby."

It was sinking in. The adoption agency thought I had been interested in another adoption. "You don't understand," I said, "I was just calling for information for some other people who are interested in adopting."

"Oh, well, then . . ." they said.

"Tell me what you called about," I encouraged. They did and we hung up. I felt suddenly tired. When my husband returned from work that evening, we called a family meeting, as we always do under these circumstances.

"There's a baby due in December and it's been exposed to the HIV virus," I started to explain. "The agency might need us to take the baby until they can find a permanent home. They think we would be a good foster family for the baby because we have experience with medical conditions and we are already a biracial family. What do you all think?"

After discussion and prayer, we voted unanimously to take in the baby when it was born if another family did not adopt the baby first. The next day I applied to renew our foster license. We didn't have any time to waste because licensing can take months and the baby was due in five weeks.

It must have been God's will for us to have this child because within one week we received our license. It arrived on Friday and the baby girl was born Saturday! It couldn't have been more obvious that God was in control.

So this little one joined our family for her temporary foster care. We named her Grace. Because of the possibility of the HIV virus, we had to give her a special medicine every six hours for the first six weeks of her life. We couldn't give it fifteen minutes early or ten minutes late—it had to be exactly every six hours. Needless to say, our lives revolved around little Grace.

Until then, we hadn't had such serious events touch our lives. Some of our babies had been exposed to drugs in the womb, but they were perfectly fine and required no special treatments. However, along with Grace's medications, she also required weekly blood tests. The agency had hoped to find a foster family located much closer to the medical facility that offered specific care for children with HIV. Unfortunately, we lived on the other side of the mountains. So, once a week for six weeks, we made the three-hour drive to the hospital and the three-hour drive home. After that, we made the trip once a month for blood tests.

It was to be a time of stretching and rejoicing. Doctors explained that if Grace's blood tests were negative for eighteen months, then her body's immune system would be strong enough to naturally rid itself of the HIV virus.

At Grace's six-month blood test she tested positive. It was a long drive home with such sad news in our minds and on our hearts. I couldn't get the words out, but I wondered how long my precious Gracie would live. I was heartbroken to have to call another family meeting.

We explained to our children that Grace's medical condition was probably worse than we had anticipated. We couldn't give the kids a lot of information because at that time not much was known about AIDS. What we were familiar with, however, was the stigma connected to those with AIDS. We talked about Grace and what she might go through and how each family member might be affected.

There were tough questions. What if it turned into full-blown AIDS? What if parents won't let Gracie in the church nursery because they refuse to touch her? There were moral dilemmas. Should we even tell people? We had considered HIV babies in the past and even our Christian friends made comments like, "You wouldn't bring them here, would you?" This was a big pill to swallow and our family took it very seriously. We knew one of our own was in for a long journey.

Our older kids most definitely understood the repercussions. None of us had ever had to face our own mortality before this. We all knew this was a big step and we had to make some serious decisions since Grace was still in the foster care system.

My husband and I assured each of the kids that their vote was important and we respected them no matter what their vote was. The votes were cast. It was unanimous. The response from our kids was clear: This is our baby. This is our sister. We're not sending her back. She's not going anywhere. Whatever lies ahead, we'll do it and we'll do it as a family. If she's full-blown or whatever, we'll take this journey with her.

I immediately changed doctors and demanded he create two files, one marked CONFIDENTIAL with her important records and the other to hold her shot records and regular checkups that the office staff would see. I felt this was Grace's story and she should be the one to tell it when she was ready. I didn't want gossip started in our small community.

The same week Grace tested positive, she had to go in again for a retest. Once again, we loaded up the car and headed over the pass. This time, however, the test was negative. We praised God all the way home. Apparently, the earlier test was exactly that, a test for our family and our love for Gracie. We passed.

Every month we made the same trek to the same hospital. Our first visit to the medical facility was somewhat shocking. I approached the desk to check in Grace, and there by the clipboard was a huge basket filled with condoms. Posters and warnings about same-sex issues papered the walls. As I turned to find a chair, I realized I was looking into the faces of mothers, grandmothers, foster mothers, and other women, all here for the same reason—to get care for their babies. They were just like me. We were all tied to this thing called HIV.

But one thing never ceased to amaze me. The nurses, knowing full well that some of these children and adults had full-blown AIDS, greeted us with love and enthusiasm. Every single visit, we were hugged. They would ask, "How are you today? How have things been going? Do you have any questions? How can we best help you this month?" And they completely enveloped the babies. They would hug them and hold them and touch them. They would shower the babies with kisses as they examined their tiny bodies. The nurses had not one bit of fear or attitude of judgment.

Plus, for every new baby patient, the caretaker was given a handmade quilt. A local group of women made these quilts specifically for the babies affected by HIV. And in each quilt there was a tiny pocket with a note about Jesus. What a ministry these nurses had. I am still touched by their love and kindness.

Month in and month out, over winter mountain passes, we took Gracie in for her blood tests. It was such a comforting feeling knowing how much we all loved her, no matter what. The agency knew we wanted to adopt her but we had to wait until her final blood test results. Finally, at her eighteen-month blood test, Grace was declared negative for HIV. Our family was jubilant.

She was immediately placed on the preadopt list and then on the ready-to-adopt list. It wasn't long before Gracie joined our family officially. What a year of jubilee indeed! Grace is now five years old and has been declared completely healthy.

Part 9

Ready-Made Families

Multiple Adoptions

What's in a Name?

as told to Kelly Fordyce Martindale

The post office has a heyday with our household mail. Being remarried, there's mail addressed with my husband's last name and my children's last name. We've had several exchange students at our address. And thankfully, our address also has the names of our "adopted daughter" and the grandkids we are raising as our own. The ongoing instruction at the post office is: "Anything addressed to that box number, don't send it back—it belongs to someone."

When we combined our households, I brought with me four birth children and an "adopted" daughter, and my husband, Jack, brought two birth children with him. We had seven children between us. Society has many titles for us: stepdad, stepmom, adoptive mom and dad, stepbrothers and stepsisters. But in our home, we are Mom and Dad, period. Having different last names is the only obvious indicator of our previous lives.

I don't think I ever planned on raising other people's children—it just sort of happened. In my first marriage I had four children and during that time, I was befriending a single mother. Her name was Carla and she had a seven-year-old daughter named Megan. Their life was filled with trauma and insecurity.

One night, fairly late, the telephone rang. It was Megan: "They're hurting my mother." Megan was calling from her grandparents' home where she and her mother were currently living. I didn't understand at first and then I heard screaming in the background. "Megan, are you all right?" She told me she was and again stated, "They're hurting my mother. Can you help her?" I told her I'd be there shortly. And I was. On the way there my mind envisioned an array of horrific scenes waiting to greet me.

I knocked on the door and it opened, allowing me to see Megan's grandfather pacing like a caged animal. The grandmother's head poked tentatively from behind the door. Her obvious attempt to act like everything was fine was at odds with her words that assaulted me: "I hope you don't think we're barbaric."

The atmosphere that greeted me was surreal. I took in the sight and smell and remembered the little girl calling me to help her mother. Yet before me, Megan danced. As if in a glass bubble, this little girl twirled with her hands above her head like a ballerina, her nightgown flowing out around her. Megan was quietly singing a song from *The King and I*. She was in her own world as the grandmother led me around the corner to what I presumed was Carla's bedroom. The room was eerily dark except for the streetlight coming through the window where the curtains had been torn down. Cowering in the corner, Carla was shaking and moaning. I moved towards her and drew her to me to console her; Carla was a mess. I took in the surroundings and noticed clumps of hair matted to Carla's shirt. It was her own and her scalp was bleeding.

"I think you need to leave here," I said to Carla. She was disoriented and ashen. It took a long time to talk her into coming back to my home. I asked, "What about Megan, will they hurt her?" Carla didn't have the ability to answer or make a decision about her own daughter. Megan did, though. Standing in front of me was a seven-year-old's body with an adult's mind. *Poor child*, I thought and then I held them both.

Later on at our home, after Carla was settled into bed, I asked Megan how she had come to call me. After all, Megan barely knew me. I had talked with her mom many times, but never Megan.

As she fiddled with the tie on her bathrobe, Megan said, "That time I came here with my mom." Her legs, too short to touch the floor, swung back and forth from the chair. "I saw your telephone number on the phone and I remembered it."

I was amazed at the levelheadedness of this child.

Carla suffered from mental disorders, and for the rest of her life would be in and out of institutions. Megan's father walked in and out of Carla and Megan's life at his convenience. He came around when he needed something. When he got it, he left.

Megan became a part of our family and lived with us until she was an adult. There were two occasions when her parents petitioned the courts to get her back. They did get her back the first time, temporarily. Megan returned to their home and immediately regressed to a fearful insecure child. My kids went to the same school as Megan so we saw her regularly while she lived with her parents. But during that time, it was obvious her parents did not care for her properly. She came to school with her hair uncombed and her clothes dirty. The hardest part was that she would not talk to any of us. She avoided us even though we loved her as our own and felt she returned that love.

Later, we found out her dad had threatened to hurt us. He went so far as to tell Megan he was going to put a bomb in our church. Megan, bless her heart, was trying to protect us when she couldn't even protect herself.

We wanted to officially adopt Megan, but neither her parents nor the courts would approve adoption or permanent custody. They would only allow temporary custody. In reality, we already had permanent temporary custody. She was raised as our own and lived with us until she moved out on her own. Megan grew to become a beautiful, intelligent woman and today her life is one that glorifies the Lord.

Shortly after my second marriage started, it became necessary for two of Jack's grandkids to come live with us. Kyle was about four and his sister Amanda was a toddler. Jack and I now had the responsibility of raising nine kids.

We didn't know how long Kyle and Amanda would be with us. As time passed, however, we realized it too was a permanent situation. Over the first year or so, we learned that Amanda had been sexually abused. My heart ached at the thought of what happened to this tiny girl before she could even speak.

After much prayer and discussion, Jack and I again pursued adoption, this time for Kyle and Amanda. Like Megan's situation, official adoption wasn't possible. This time, though, the courts did award us with permanent custody.

Even though we are their grandparents, Amanda and Kyle call us Mom and Dad. Kyle is grown and on his own now. Amanda is our youngest and is preparing to be on her own.

Sadly, because of the sexual abuse, Amanda has continued to struggle with major issues such as drugs and an unplanned pregnancy. She has a long way to go for complete healing but does see God working in her life.

Each of our nine children has specific individual needs and personalities. They all have hearts that ache from abuse, neglect, abandonment, or broken homes. Each of their personal trials and tragedies have affected our whole family. But through all the heartache and pain, we've stuck together. By the grace of God, we've supported one another in all the different healing processes.

People always ask me to explain how we were able to parent nine children. The simple fact is, our hearts were open. When these children were in need, we were available. I am so thankful for Jack because our hearts were united. We agreed and supported one another in caring for the kids. And our own kids took in each newcomer as a family member as well.

The things that have happened to my children have left ugly and inflamed scars. Some scars have faded, but others threaten to fester and infect the whole person. We continue to apply the Balm of Gilead, available only through the healing power of God, and we watch and wait and love and hold.

It's a Boy, It's a Boy!

as told to Kelly Fordyce Martindale

I fumbled with the keys trying to find the one that would unlock my door. My purse slipped from my shoulder as I precariously balanced a small sack of groceries atop a box from the post office. I was so anxious to get into my home and to the VCR, I was forgetting an all-important proverb: Haste makes waste. I took a deep breath, dropped the keys to the ground, and care-

fully set the packages on the concrete step. The last thing I
wanted to do was clean up broken glass, spilled pickles, and
sticky jelly. Unlocking the door, I took part of my load in and
set it on the kitchen counter next to the video I was nearly dying
to see. Finally, I brought in the last of my parcels and hurried
to the TV.

In place, I punched the remote buttons to start the video. I
knew I should be waiting for my husband, but I just couldn't. I
had already waited five years to review the events that took place
the first two years of my twin boys' lives. I'd finally had our 8mm
film transferred to VHS—all I needed now was popcorn.

It didn't take but just a few minutes for me to realize what I
really needed was a box of tissues. Tears streamed down my
face as the view before me took me back seven years. Gratitude
flooded my heart for the precious memories my mother-in-law
had captured on tape.

I cried as I watched myself walk toward the bassinet holding our babies. *Oh, my gosh. That's when our lives changed forever,* I reminded myself. Mesmerized, I watched myself wipe
tears from my face as I bent toward the tiny bundles lying in
their makeshift bed. My husband looked petrified as the caseworker picked up one baby and placed him in my husband's
arms. I reached for my other child. Grandma watched us
through the viewfinder on the camera, the new daddy, mama,
and two babies. We were a family.

I wept with joy as I watched those events of seven years
ago—events that brought to an end our thirteen-year journey
to parenthood.

When you first marry, it doesn't enter your mind whether
you can get pregnant or not. But after the seventh year of marriage we'd grown to accept the fact that pregnancy wouldn't
happen naturally for us. So for the next five years we would go
through lots of different testing, use various fertility pills, and
get sperm counts. We were working hard to get pregnant. So
hard, it came to a point where we said enough was enough. We
were losing the intimacy in our marriage. Our relationship had
become mechanical and mundane as our objective changed
from growing a solid relationship to simply getting pregnant.

I missed the intimacy we used to have. After contemplating our love, our relationship, and our family status, I realized it wasn't that important for me to carry a child to term. I had been living month to month. After a while, those months had rolled into years. I was so consumed with getting pregnant I had forgotten how to live my life. I finally concluded we should consider adoption. I felt strongly that we should focus our energies on adoption rather than on trying to get pregnant.

Our decision to adopt was finalized after doctors made the suggestion that undergoing surgery might allow me to conceive. We seriously considered the procedure and weighed the end result versus adoption. We felt surgery gave only the possibility of conceiving and having a child but adoption would guarantee us a child. My husband and I knew at the end of the adoption process we would have our baby.

Through it all, the hardest part about waiting for a baby was the constant questioning from others. When are you going to have kids? What are you waiting for? Wouldn't it be great to have little ones? People can be very insensitive to a couple's inability to conceive. Many don't consider there may be infertility issues. After several years, everybody just quit asking, including our family. The silence and the waiting took its toll. Our sadness lingered like a heavy fog. It wasn't until we made the decision to adopt that the sun finally burst forth again.

Looking back, surgery may have been faster. First we met with the bishop to get our church's support for the adoption. We received his and others' recommendations, but one fear stalled us. We kept hearing heart-wrenching stories of birth parents taking their children back from adoptive families. I wouldn't be able to live through that. My heart ached for a child, but my heart also wanted to protect its vulnerability.

Finally, we submitted all the paperwork, did the home studies, and completed other requirements. Then we waited. It would be two-and-one-half years before we heard anything.

One day, we received a call from our caseworker telling us there was a birth mom who would be relinquishing her baby for adoption. He informed me we were one of three couples she was choosing from. It was finally happening . . . all we needed to do was write her a letter. Of course, we did it immediately.

I laugh at what happened next. That is, I laugh now. It was a Sunday night and I was sick to my stomach and in and out of the bathroom constantly. I decided to stay home from work the next day because of how sick I was. My husband would also miss work the next day because of a funeral he was attending several hours away for a family member. I woke up feeling that if I wasn't going to go to work, I should at least support my husband at the funeral.

And while part of me wanted to stay home and recuperate, I decided to go with my husband to the funeral. We arrived home about eight in the evening to find our answering machine filled with messages from the caseworker. One message after another said to call him immediately. We later found out he had come by our home, my workplace, my husband's parents (who were with us at the funeral), and called everyone he could think of to contact us. I, even today, could kick myself for not paying attention to that little nudge inside me that told me to stay home. We called the caseworker immediately.

We were flabbergasted when he said, "Your babies were born Friday."

"Babies. You mean there are more than one?" I asked.

"Yes, you have twin boys," came the response.

"But the birth mom wants to talk to you," he said. That was a little disturbing because this was supposed to be a completely closed adoption—no contact or anything. Of course we said we would talk to her. On a Tuesday, the caseworker set up a phone call to protect each one's identity. We talked only a few minutes. I'm still not sure exactly what she was looking for, but we wanted her to feel comfortable with us and with the possibility that we would raise her babies. Looking back, I think she needed to hear our voices. She needed a sense of security that her babies were actually going to a real family. She needed to know that the relinquishment wasn't as final as it felt, that she could reach us through the caseworkers if necessary. We assured her we would keep in touch occasionally.

I was dumbfounded. We had heard there had never been twins adopted through this agency. I wracked my brain trying to remember if we had checked the box marked "multiple." We asked our caseworker, "Why didn't you tell us there were twins?"

"What would you do if I had?" he asked.

"We would have bought two of everything," we quickly answered.

"What if she had changed her mind about the adoption?" he asked.

We could only shrug; we didn't know what we would have done. It didn't matter anyway because *our* babies were waiting for us. Just one more detail remained before we could officially become parents—the birth mom. She was unsure about the finality of giving up *her* babies.

Our caseworker knew how much this adoption meant to us and offered to pray and fast with us the next day. So for all of Wednesday, we joined together asking God to help the mom make the decision, the decision that would be best for the boys.

On Thursday of what was becoming quite a long week, our caseworker called and said the birth mom was scheduled to sign paperwork in the morning. "Please call us immediately after she signs and we'll be there," we told him. We were several hours away from the babies' birthplace, but we couldn't leave until all the paperwork was signed.

Instead of pacing we used the time to prepare for the trip. We buckled in the two car seats and marveled at the vision of them. It was happening. We were on pins and needles waiting for the 9:00 A.M. court time when the birth mom would sign the last of the papers. We tried not to allow ourselves to think about the possibility that she would change her mind at the last minute. We stayed focused on what we had to do for the moment.

I'm not sure we slept that night. There was so much excitement and anxiety, we were beside ourselves. Sometimes my husband and I talked circles around each other and other times we were silent as we pondered our future as parents.

The call finally came—the birth mom had signed the papers. Grandma was waiting with us, so the three of us piled into the car amongst the car seats, baby clothes, and diaper bags.

It was our understanding that we had to fill out more paperwork before we could legally take the boys. We thought the paperwork would require their names, so much of the drive was devoted to discussion of names, meanings, nicknames, and how names sounded both young and old. Grandma, Daddy, and I finally settled on Matthew and Tyler.

Rewinding the video, I watch again the moment Grandma asks me, "Which one is which?"

"I don't know. Let me have another look," I respond as I look at the two boys. "This is Matthew," I say to the camera. "And this is Tyler."

The last seven beautiful years have flown by. I can honestly say, knowing what I know now, I don't regret our infertility. In fact, my family is more perfect than I ever could have imagined. We were given double the joy because of each boy.

As I blow my nose and rewind the tape for the second time, I wonder if I'll be able to act like I had waited for my husband before viewing the video. I'm sure with the third viewing I'll cry the same tears of joy I cried the first and second time I watched, but I'll tell him anyway. I'm sure he'll forgive me the second he sees himself cradling his tiny bundle.

Part 10

Sharing My Parents

Siblings Share Their Stories

No Fake Sisters

Emily Trisdale

I had prayed for my baby sister. Her picture came on my twelfth birthday. We had waited so long for it. She was older than I had hoped, but she was cute. The form said she was four years old and her name was ChunShui. Dad suggested we call her Samantha ChunShui, and we all agreed.

Soon Mom and my older sister went to China to bring her home. Mom called from China and told us her name was really Ah-soy.

When Ah-soy got on the phone she sounded darling. Hello was the only word she said, but she said it over and over again.

Ah-soy was smiling and holding Mom's hand when they walked off the plane. I could tell she was nervous, but I couldn't imagine just how much.

Once we were home, Ah-soy became absolutely terrified. She screamed in Chinese, begging to go back to China. I couldn't comfort her. She wouldn't even let me near her.

My younger sister, Laura, and I had worked hard to make our room appeal to Ah-soy. However, she wouldn't sleep in our room. The only place she would sleep was with Mom. I got so mad at her. I guess I didn't think about how she was feeling. At four years old she had been taken away from everything she had ever known and was put with people she couldn't even understand.

The next morning was a little better; she smiled some and even let me give her a hug. Ah-soy grew restless, so we went to the museum. Then we went to a Chinese restaurant. The waiter spoke to Ah-soy in Chinese. It was clear she understood him, but she wouldn't respond. She had decided she was part of our family, and since we didn't speak Chinese she wouldn't either.

After about two weeks Ah-soy moved in with Laura and me. She moved in slowly. First she moved from Mom and Dad's room into the hall, then from the hall to our room.

Immediately she began to learn English. Her favorite word was definitely M&M's. She asked for them constantly (and usually got them). Ah-soy started mimicking everything she heard. I had a lot of fun with her. The first phrase I taught her to say was "I'm a pain." She would walk right up to people, smile, and say, "I'm a pain." Some people laughed, while others gave her strange looks. Mom got kind of upset with me, but I thought it was cute.

Ah-soy liked to listen to music and sing. Laura and I taught her nursery rhymes and sang with her for hours at a time. We even made music videos in the backyard.

The day Ah-soy asked to be called by her American name, Samantha, I realized she was growing up. In just one year she had grown seven inches. It became obvious she was really eight, not four, when she stepped off the plane with my mom.

We told Samantha how we had prayed for her. Soon she started praying for a little sister from China. The laws had changed in China so it wasn't possible for us to get another little girl, but that didn't stop Samantha from praying.

My family frequently gets together with other families who have adopted children from China. One of these families was having bonding problems. The parents said things weren't working out, so Mom and Dad offered to help. They talked about the things our family did with Samantha.

The little girl and her family went to therapy to help with bonding, yet things were still not getting better. Soon Chiara was spending more time at our house.

Chiara was put on medication for bipolar disorder. Her family asked if she could visit for the week, and that week turned into two weeks. During that time I decided Chiara was mine.

When Chiara went back to her house, I cried. I knew she was my little sister. The very next day Mom got a phone call. She was shaking as she talked. Then she handed me a note, "Please pray for me. They are talking about giving Chiara to us. Pray I say the right things."

That day Chiara came to live with us. I don't think she was completely aware of what was going on. It was Super Bowl Sunday and Chiara thought the party was for her. I guess it kind of was.

Chiara was only five and had a hard time understanding that she was here to stay. With Samantha it had been easy. Mom and Dad just told her she was adopted, and that was all it took.

Adoption to Samantha meant forever. Chiara had been adopted before and it hadn't lasted. The word "adopted" did not have the same meaning to Chiara as it did to Samantha. Mom finally told Chiara she was glued to our family with the strongest glue there was and she was stuck, whether she liked it or not. When Mom said that, Chiara smiled and giggled.

My parents decided to take her off the bipolar medication, and it turned out she wasn't bipolar at all. She's just very active.

My sisters and I have a very special bond. We all get along, for the most part. We don't fight; we just bicker. We all have very strong opinions. If I see one of my sisters wearing an outfit that doesn't go together, I tell her. My sisters call me the fashion police. Sometimes we have special nights together where we watch old movies, paint fingernails, do each other's hair, eat junk food, and talk. It's great; we stay up late and really get to learn more about each other. We're usually very busy, and these nights give us time to slow down and hang out.

The thing that probably upsets me most about adoption has nothing to do with my two adopted sisters. It has to do with other people—good people, who in my mind are mixed up.

Several people have told me what a good person I am for sharing my stuff with poor little children and letting them live with me. Nobody has ever told me how nice I am to share my stuff with my two biological sisters. The second remark that makes me mad is when people ask me, "How many real sisters do you have?" None of my sisters are fake. There is no doubt in my mind that we are a family, a mixed-up family, but definitely a family.

Maybe Mismatched, but True Family

Janna Graber

How much love can two people have? How does love multiply? How do parents keep everybody connected? These questions plague my mind. It is difficult to comprehend the fullness of my parents' love. Their hearts have expanded to love all of us—three birth children and five adopted children.

The first two of the eight children were my sister and me (I'm the oldest). I'll always remember when we expanded to three girls. I was four when we adopted Sharon. She came to us with rubber shoes and silver teeth. And her hair was the blackest, fuzziest hair I'd ever seen in my short life.

I found some things strange about Sharon. For an unknown reason, she was very afraid of our dolls. We still don't know why. Also, Sharon would pack her cheeks full of food like a squirrel does. She was afraid that was all she would get. She was about a year old when she joined our family, but she had already experienced hunger and neglect. She was adorable and my sister and I loved her dearly.

I was about six when our perfect family of girls changed—Mom gave birth to our brother. And then four years later, a Seattle adoption agency called us to tell us there were two little boys who needed homes. Like Sharon, they were both from Korea. Both boys had physical problems, so my parents needed to consider which child they could truly help. They determined that they could handle Andrew's heart murmur and the medical attention he would require. Mom then had to fly to San Francisco to get Andrew. The rest of us all went to the local airport to meet them both when they arrived back home. Before we could say our hellos, Andrew was immediately thrust into Dad's arms. His look of puzzlement changed as Mom raked her hands over the front of her clothes. A nine-month-old sure can make a mess of a mom on a plane flight.

We moved from one farm to another as kids. On each farm we had animals and plenty of activities to keep us busy. We had a lamb to pet, chickens to feed, and lots of room to run. My parents worked hard to provide a wholesome environment to raise us children.

Looking back, I appreciate that we were raised the way children should be raised. We were allowed to be kids, but as we got bigger our responsibilities grew too. I was the typical oldest child though; I bossed everybody around. For the most part, we were obedient children and were given our own chores to do. Our parents gladly took on the extra burdens that come with many children. I love having so many brothers and sisters.

Sharon and Andrew always knew they were adopted, but none of us dwelt on it. We had a book that we read occasionally, a book about a little Asian girl. Sharon related to the character in the book because kids would make fun of her eyes for being different. When we were all older, Sharon revealed to us she'd always wanted blond hair. Our family is very connected to each other, so the question of "child by birth or adoption" only came into play when outsiders made it an issue.

Thankfully it was only on occasion when others did make a big deal about our unique family. The only fight I ever got into was at the local swimming pool when another boy called my brother a Chink. Instinctively, I attacked him. I wanted to protect my little brother.

Another thing that upset me was when the high school yearbook staff included a section in the yearbook entitled, "Welcome to America." It included photos of all the kids of color, any color. This offended my brother and me very much. The yearbook staff didn't see any problem with it, but we thought it was racist. Too often, other kids are insensitive to families that are different.

Over the next few years, our family took in foster children. They would stay in our home until it was appropriate to return to their own families. I remember a lot of babies that came and went during my early teen years. Most of them stayed short-term, but one of those babies, Mandy, ended up living with us for four years. She was cute as a button and terrified of men. It took a lot of love and patience on our part, but eventually Mandy outgrew her fear. When she became available to be adopted, Mandy had been with our family so long we couldn't imagine life without her. Still, we had to go to court and fight so that Mandy could officially be the sixth child in our family.

The hardest times came as our youngest two siblings reached the teen years. Siblings Brad and Crystal joined our family when Brad was three and Crystal was eight months. Brad had been severely abused. As a result, he was diagnosed with attachment disorder, something common in children without a secure home early in life. Crystal's sufferings were not quite as extreme—she seemed to have escaped most of the harsh treatment.

As Brad grew up, evidence of his abuse reared its ugly head. Although we loved him completely, as with each child his responses were drastically different. It was obvious that he found it difficult to truly bond with us. He could relate well enough to us siblings but he was especially disrespectful to my parents and he rebelled regularly against them. I had a difficult time forgiving him for how he treated Mom and Dad. I was angry with him for a long time. He seemed so cruel considering all that our parents had done for him. His behavior made our lives difficult for many years.

It only got better when Brad graduated from high school and joined the Marines. I can't believe the difference in him now. The Marines were able to break him down, but they also built him back up. Brad is pretty much a different person now. I am very proud of the changes he's made, and he continues to work on overcoming the huge obstacles in his life.

Crystal is still at home. She deals with the normal issues that affect teenagers, but she's doing great. I'm sure life is different for her now that the other seven siblings are out of the house.

Many years have passed and we still visit each other often. All eight siblings, our spouses, parents, and the grandkids, make it a point to spend New Year's Eve together every year. We get a cabin in the mountains and have a wonderful time. Each year I marvel at how our family grows—not just larger but closer too. As a child, I loved my brothers and sisters. Now as adults, we are best of friends and I consider each person a gift—a gift from my parents.

My parents are wonderful role models. They taught us to stick together; they taught us family loyalty. Despite the struggles that Brad had with bonding, our family is completely united. Once, a friend of mine looked at our family photo and said, "That's your family? You don't match."

My response? "Maybe we don't match on the outside, but we do on the inside." That is what true family is.

Part 11

The Grandchild in My Heart

Grandparents Tell Their Stories

LifeSaver

Shirley A. Reynolds

I retreat to the quiet of our deck and open the recently sent photos of Mandy. In each picture I see happiness through camping trips, school photographs, family holidays, and a sister's hug. Seeing Mandy astride a horse, I'm shocked. *I do believe she has those same brown eyes. Yes, she's the spitting image of Sarah at eleven years old.*

Seeing Mandy dripping wet as she climbs out of a swimming pool, her older sister's arms wrapped around her, I feel no regret.

Watching from afar as another grandparent hugs Mandy, I feel a sadness, and yet a sense of peace and contentment knowing she is growing up in a Christian home. Wiping my tears away, my thoughts return to Mandy's birth and baby dedication.

I stood in the doorway of Sarah's private hospital room, watching as she cradled her tiny infant. My daughter, a mother at seventeen years old—it's still hard to grasp.

The adoptive parents, their three-year-old daughter, our pastor, my husband, and Sarah all gathered together to dedicate little Mandy. My husband silently prayed over Mandy as he tenderly held her to his heart. Then he cradled his tiny granddaughter in his arms and stared down at her as if trying to etch her memory into his mind.

He handed her to me. Tears fell, wetting the blanket wrapped around her. My lips trembled. I couldn't form the words to say, *"Oh, little Mandy, we love you more than you know!"*

Sarah reached for her baby. As I placed the tiny infant in her mother's arms I wanted to take them both and run. Instead, I watched my daughter cuddle her newborn to her chest and kiss her baby's cheek. Sarah tilted her head and softly sang to Mandy. When no more words could break through her tears, she handed her precious child to our pastor.

Quietly, gently, he spoke. Touching Mandy's face with oil, he prayed: "Little Mandy, I dedicate you in the name of the Father, the Son, and the Holy Spirit. May God bless you and keep you in his care." Weeping broke the silence as Pastor placed Mandy into the arms of her adoptive mother.

Her tears wet the cheeks of her new daughter. Quietly, she lifted her eyes toward Sarah, expressing sorrow for my daughter. Tears veiled her joy over the special gift Sarah had given.

Mandy's adoptive father wrapped his arm around his wife and took the hand of his young daughter standing by his side. With tears in his eyes, he smiled at Sarah, as if to say thank you.

Looking down into Sarah's empty arms, I took her hand in mine. She cried openly, and her shoulders shook with each sob.

The three-year-old standing beside her parents pulled away and walked over to Sarah. With childlike sweetness, she looked into Sarah's eyes. "Why are you crying?" she asked. "Do you want a LifeSaver? LifeSavers help you stop crying. My mommy said so." She reached for Sarah's hand, and for a moment their hands enclosed upon one another. The adults smiled and chuckled over the sweetness of the little girl. The strain in the room lightened.

Then the nurse came and took Mandy to the nursery. Pastor and the adoptive family said their good-byes and left.

Silent tears, empty arms, stillness—*what do we say to each other?* The child who found her way so deeply into our hearts in a short time was now gone. Sarah had given a special gift to this family. She would hold her child for only a brief moment and then entrust her to them. It was an act of love.

Sarah lifted her face up to her father and me: "She has a special family, doesn't she?"

"Oh, yes, Sarah."

Looking down at my daughter's hand, I saw the white peppermint lying on her open palm. "Do you want me to throw that away?"

Sarah cupped her hands together and looked down at the candy LifeSaver.

"No, Mom, this LifeSaver is like a promise to me. I'm going to keep it. Someday I will see her again. I know I will. But for now, I have to say good-bye!"

How like God to use a three-year-old moved with sympathy and a desire to help. From her chubby little hand came hope and a tangible reminder of the Lifesaver, Jesus.

In the months and years that followed there would be times when Sarah felt like she was drowning in sadness and regret. But each time she reached for her Lifesaver, he kept her from sinking deeper and deeper into grief.

Sometimes when Sarah smiles, it's hard to hold back my tears of thankfulness. I'm so proud of her. Although she could have given Mandy love, the timing just wasn't right. Though it hurt, and sometimes still hurts, she made a wise and brave choice.

Sarah is now a counselor for abused and wayward teens and shares her own story with hurting young mothers, using a white peppermint LifeSaver to show there is hope for the future.

When It's Your Daughter and Your Grandchild

Sheri and Paul Smith

Our seventeen-year-old daughter, Kathy, had been dating Steve for over two years. We were confident she was maintaining her commitment to "wait" until marriage. When she told us she was pregnant we couldn't believe this had happened to our daughter.

After a few weeks we realized we had a grandchild on the way. While sitting around the kitchen table, Kathy informed us she planned to place her baby for adoption. She said, "Why should I trash my baby's life while I'm trying to get mine together? I don't want my baby to suffer for my mistake."

Kathy had observed friends from junior high and high school who were trying to parent their babies on their own. From what

Kathy saw, she felt the babies weren't getting what was best for them. She had been asking God to reveal his desire for her baby, and she believed adoption was the answer.

That day at the kitchen table was the beginning of our family's journey down a road we had never taken. We had always understood adoption to be a wonderful way for people to become parents and for children to find homes. But now we weren't considering "other" people. From our perspective it was an overwhelming and frightening dilemma.

We had many questions. How does one "give up" a member of their own family to be raised by strangers? Relinquishment— what a cold word that can be to those on the giving end of it. What about life after relinquishment?

How would Kathy be able to walk away from her own child? After experiencing the beautiful intimacy a mother shares with her unborn baby, would Kathy change her mind after he was born? How does a family go on after making the decision to relinquish a child? Do you try to pretend like it never happened, or do you live out the rest of life with a huge empty space in your soul? Do you resolve to go through life never asking what became of the child?

When Steve's parents heard Kathy had decided to place the baby for adoption, they wanted to take the baby. This caused a lot of friction. Kathy didn't want her baby to be in a tug of war between families. She didn't think she could release him emotionally if they took him. Steve sided with Kathy even though his parents were angry about their decision.

It was a difficult time for Steve's parents. We wanted to reach out and try to comfort them but came to the conclusion there was simply no way we could deal with everyone's issues. This was much bigger than us and beyond our ability to fix and make right. We put our complete trust in God to work everything out.

After a while, we seemed to settle into our crisis. We began to take small steps forward. We had met with a wonderful Christian woman who owned an adoption agency. She counseled both birth moms and their families, as well as birth fathers and their families if they chose to be counseled.

She removed much of the mystery and misunderstandings we had about adoption. We learned that the laws had changed and adoptions could be open, allowing birth moms to pick parents from available profiles. Kathy loved having me be a stay-home mom and wanted the same for her baby. We all felt relieved she could choose parents who shared her values.

We discovered that we could receive pictures and letters from the adoptive parents. They would send them to us through the agency. Kathy wouldn't have to wonder how her child was being raised. We began to see some light at the end of our tunnel. The situation was becoming manageable.

Then eighteen weeks into Kathy's pregnancy we were bombarded with new and frightening information. Once again circumstances were beyond our control. An ultrasound revealed the baby had a severe abdominal wall defect. Doctors told us if the child did make it to term, he would not live long and would certainly not be adoptable. Abortion was offered as the best solution to the problem facing us.

While we had very little medical understanding of the problem, we did know that abortion was not the solution. After earnest prayer with our daughter we decided it would be God who ordained the number of this baby's days, not us or a doctor.

We turned to our church fellowship for prayer and comfort. A woman in our church was a nurse for a pediatrician who had experience with high risk newborns. She asked the doctor if he would call us.

Brian called to help us understand the baby's medical condition. He assured us that the condition was treatable with surgery, and the fatality rate was less than 2 percent.

As it turned out, he and his wife had two adopted children through the very agency we were working with.

After a few days he and his wife contacted the agency and said they felt led to adopt our daughter's baby, if she wanted them to. They had been thinking about adopting another child, but had not yet decided, so their profile was not available when Kathy looked through the profiles at the agency.

Kathy met Brian and Pam at the agency. After talking and praying with them, she had complete confidence they were the couple God had chosen to raise her child.

God had used the medical complication to bring this couple and our daughter together. Further, we now had medical expertise to guide us through the medical maze of Kathy's pregnancy.

Pam had worked with premature babies as a nurse, so she began accompanying Kathy to her doctor exams. When we had another unexpected complication, Brian and Pam stood by our side in the middle of the night as we laid hands upon our daughter asking for God's grace and mercy.

Kathy began labor six weeks early. The baby had to be taken by C-section because of the immediate surgery he needed. Our grandson weighed four pounds ten ounces, and Brian and Pam were the first to hold him.

After three months and six surgeries, Brian and Pam were finally able to take their son home. Those three months were difficult for Pam. She wanted to be close to her son in ICU, but she also had two little daughters to care for. As we worked together with our grandson's new parents to sort out things like last name used for medical permission, guardianship, and insurance coverage, a strong bond formed between us.

Kathy had made the decision that if anyone needed to hurt it would be herself, not the baby. She did not think visiting him throughout his life would help her with her sense of loss. But she did need to know (through letters and pictures) that he was loved and safe.

She went back to school and tried to focus on getting the credits she needed for college. When some of the girls found out about the adoption they said, "If you didn't want him, why didn't you just have an abortion?"

But Kathy had thought it all the way through. She thought about everything her son would need from the day he was born until he was a grown man. Kathy was mature enough to understand that you have to be ready. You can't just do the best with what you have.

The testimony of what God had done touched surgeons, nurses, and church fellowships. Most of all it touched us. Over the years, our daughter has shared her story in schools, in the church, and in the community.

It has been ten years since our first grandson was born. Kathy and Steve have each married different people and have other children. Kathy doesn't have contact with the adoptive family except through the pictures and letters Pam sends her.

But my husband and I are like old family friends with our grandson's parents. Last time they asked us over, our grandson reintroduced me to his dog and then showed me his pets: a rat, a snake, an iguana, and a big hairy tarantula named Rose. I laughed and told him that only in this family would he be allowed to have such creepy pets.

I thank God for this special family who loves my grandson so much.

Grandmom's Love

as told to Kelly Fordyce Martindale

When I was a young girl, I dreamed of being a mom with many children. Thankfully, I was blessed with two, a girl and then a boy. However, shortly after giving birth to my second child I was informed that I needed a hysterectomy. My chance of having more children was gone, so naturally my thoughts turned toward future grandchildren. Little did I know that day would come sooner than I expected. I wasn't prepared, emotionally or spiritually, when my unmarried daughter told my husband and me she was pregnant.

She said she had something important to tell us, so the three of us sat together at the kitchen table. I traced the grain of our old oak kitchen table with my index finger. *Is she dropping out of college? Does she want to move in with somebody?* I imagined several scenarios in the growing silence. I was nervous waiting for her to speak, hoping she wouldn't say anything that would upset us. Her dad was drumming his fingers, not so much from impatience but out of anxiety. We are a very close family and what affects one, affects us all.

My daughter's beautiful hazel eyes looked heavenward as tears fell down her cheeks. I prayed silently that God would give her strength for whatever was upsetting her. Then I asked him to give us strength too.

For the moment, all I could do was take her hand. I held it until she pulled away and covered her eyes with both hands. Struggling to regain her composure, she took a deep breath, looked at her father and me, and told us she was pregnant.

Initially, I was dumbfounded. Speechless, I looked to my husband for his wisdom. He seemed so calm, but the disappointment showed in his eyes. I sat there calm and quiet, my mind filled with images of shattered dreams.

It was a long time before I found my voice and had the courage to use it. "What are you going to do?" I asked.

For all of her twenty years, she had been my little girl. Suddenly, everything had changed and I saw her as an individual.

Her unplanned, unwed pregnancy took our balanced, church-going world and turned it upside down. Yet I was moved to see that she cared how we each felt. She understood her pregnancy impacted her own life, yet she realized it would be a major part of our lives too, even her brother's.

Sadly, the father of her baby would not be involved. Knowing this, we discussed the options available to her. We talked about single parenting and we talked about adoption. We also discussed abortion. Thankfully, we all agreed abortion was not going to be the choice for this baby. Even so, parenting and adoption were overwhelming choices.

I found myself angry and sad and confused. After everything we had taught our daughter about premarital sex, I couldn't understand how this had happened to her, to us. I didn't know what the right choice was.

On top of that, my husband was traveling from Sunday to Friday every week for work. Though he and I would talk, I felt like I was dealing with this alone. My daughter and I talked all the time and we cried ourselves to sleep nearly every night. After a while I realized that a very scared part of me was hoping she would miscarry. I prayed that God would take this little one before there was more heartache.

Then my daughter's health seemed to spiral downward. Her sickness increased beyond that of a normal pregnancy. When I took her to the doctor they admitted her into the hospital. She couldn't keep anything down, she was so nauseated. The doctors were worried about both her and the baby so they gave her something for the nausea, but she had an allergic reaction to it. I've never seen a person's body twist to such contorted positions as hers did from the medication. She went into convulsions until the medication finally wore off.

She stayed in the hospital for several days and was released only when she was completely well. The very next day, however, she was in a rollover car accident. After seeing the crumpled wreck of the car, I knew it was a miracle she and her baby had survived. That's what turned me around.

It couldn't have been more obvious that God didn't want my daughter or her baby with him just yet. I stopped praying for a miscarriage and started praying for strength, love, forgiveness, and understanding. I realized God had a plan and I would have to accept it and, with his help, do the best I could under the circumstances.

From that point on, we started walking every evening after work. We had long talks and began planning for the arrival of this baby, my grandchild. My daughter sought counsel and considered the pros and cons of both single parenting and adoption.

I learned the true meaning of bittersweet when my daughter told us she had made the decision to put her baby up for adoption. Still, I supported her completely; we all did. We knew this was the hardest decision she would ever make. Though she had dreamed of family and children, she knew a family should have both mother and father. She wanted the very best for her baby and knew she could not provide that alone. Even with our help, she understood a child needed more than she could provide.

As much as I supported her decision, I was heartbroken. I longed to hold my grandbaby yet to be born. I wanted to play pat-a-cake, buy little surprises, and hear the word "Grandmom." I wanted to be there at every birthday and Christmas. I was already grieving the loss of the grandchild I would only know for a short time.

Inwardly, I cried. Outwardly, I went to support meetings with my daughter. She had an excellent adoption counselor and was walked through the process of planning the adoption and choosing parents. Very close to full term and after dozens and dozens of portfolios, my daughter finally found just the right family.

During her pregnancy I realized my little girl had grown into an extraordinary young woman. I admired her as much as I grieved for her. She was the most courageous person I had ever known.

The joyous and equally sad day came when my grand-daughter entered and left our lives. It was hard to place her into another's arms, but there was comfort in knowing beyond any doubt that my daughter chose the perfect family for my grand-baby. We know she will be loved unconditionally and provided for, ensuring the best possible upbringing.

I miss my granddaughter and think of her daily. In just a short time, she captured my lifelong love, a love only a "grand-mom" can give. That love continues to grow, and someday I'll be able to share it with another grandchild.

Letter from a Thankful Grandma

as told to Kelly Fordyce Martindale

Dear Birth Mom:

I wanted to write you and say thank you, even though I don't know who you are or where to send this letter. I may not know you personally, but I feel I know something about the best part of you—your heart.

I imagine you must be a very loving woman, one with respect for life and for yourself. You might be asking why I would think that. Please, let me share with you.

You made some choices many years ago. I suppose some would say you made poor choices, but I choose to dwell on the positive choice to give life to the baby who would be born before you were ready to be a parent. Sometimes I wonder what your situation was, but it doesn't really matter, considering the outcome.

Your baby boy grew up to be a fine young man. In fact, I am proud to say he is now my son-in-law. He is a loving husband and a generous man. And now, he is also a patient and responsible father to my grandson. Oh, I treasure my grandson. He can do no wrong and he is so cute and has an adorable personality. If not for your choice for life, I would never have known such complete joy. I love your son as my own and he has blessed us with his encouragement, charm, humor, and zest for life and helping others.

In fact, your son is now helping others in East Africa. He and my daughter and grandson are there as missionaries. They plan to be there for several years in hopes of sharing the truth of Jesus with those in their area. He is a gifted communicator and he shares his God-given talents with those around him. He has a strong faith and he wants others to know that there is a loving and forgiving God waiting to embrace them.

Thank you, birth mother, for choosing life for that precious baby boy. I pray that God richly blesses you for the decision you made many years ago. God's work is being done through this young man. Though your decision many years ago must have been a hard one, it is one that will impact many people for eternity!

Sincerely,

A Mother-in-Law & Grandma

Part 12

Fatherless No More

Delayed Adoption Decisions

Ward of the Court

Kelly Fordyce Martindale

If I had to pick one child from the system whom I thought would be tormented by his past experiences as a ward of the court, it would have been Ricky.

Earlier in the day, I was given an assignment to remove five children from their mother's home. They ranged in age from six months to seven years. Reports had been made that there was sufficient evidence of neglect. The removal went smoothly enough. Another worker and I presented the paperwork to the mother and she willingly relinquished the children to us. The children timidly crawled into the van and we pulled away from their home.

The children were silent as we drove to the youngest child's foster home. We escorted Tammy to her new residence and the foster mother greeted us with arms wide. We toured the house and then went outside to play on the swing set.

The four remaining children watched as the foster mother placed Tammy in the specially designed child's swing and gently pushed her. "Is this fun?" she asked Tammy as she carefully pushed off from Tammy's tiny knees. Tammy sucked on the knuckle of one hand as the other grasped the safety belt in front of her. Her eyes began to twinkle as the foster mother continued the soft talk and gentle swinging.

"This should be temporary," I struggled to explain to the older children. "Why don't you go give her a hug now." My voice cracked with emotion as I touched the other children one by one nudging them forward. I'd done this many times before. It's especially difficult to split up siblings.

We had three more stops to make, since we didn't have a home that could take all five children. Reality was setting in as we walked away from the oldest boy. Ricky and his sister walked nearly backwards not wanting to take their eyes off their brother. They understood we were leaving him, just as we had their two little sisters. *The next stop should be easier,* I thought.

200

After all, the two would be staying together. Ricky held my hand to the van.

Finally at the interim home, I helped the children down from the van and took a hand from each. Together, we walked up to the front door of the large brick building. This was actually an orphanage, but these two kids would be going to a foster home as soon as one became available.

The director tried to talk Ricky into playing with the younger children. But even the sandbox with brightly colored toy trucks didn't appeal to the frightened youngster. He turned inward, hiding his face against my leg.

Looking down, I used the palm of my free hand to stroke the boy's towhead blond hair. I wanted to give him some comfort, bring some security before I left him. As I knelt to eye-level, his tiny hands reached for my shoulders. Giving in to the embrace, I allowed his arms to reach around my neck and I wrapped mine around him. Ordinarily, I wouldn't allow physical touch other than handholding, but this four-year-old boy had been through so much today. Ricky gave in to the emotions and wept. I just held him.

Ricky's sister came to the rescue. Taking his hand she led him to a bench where they sat together by the back door. I spoke a few more words with the director and headed for the door. Ricky jumped up and grabbed my hand again; he didn't want to let go. "I'll be back, Ricky. You stay here with your sister while I try to find you two a family to stay with. I promise I'll be back in a few days."

I visited two more times before we finally found a foster home. Sadly, it was for Ricky only. I took Ricky to visit the couple who would probably take him in. A little yippy dog welcomed us, barking and jumping all over. Ricky, petrified, hid behind me. The woman called her dog and put him in another room and closed the door.

Ricky was to spend the weekend at first to see how things would go. Then, if all went well, he would be permanently placed there until things were better at his own home.

By Sunday evening, it seemed clear the couple was anxious to have Ricky stay with them. After spending a couple hours with Ricky it appeared he, likewise, was comfortable in their home.

Ricky took my hand and led me outside. There he showed me the sandbox his foster parents had built for him over the weekend. A smile spread across his face as we proceeded to his bedroom. Pointing with his stubby little fingers, he said with difficulty, "That my dwesser." Then he awkwardly pulled open drawers exposing his clothes, all neatly folded.

"Well, it looks like everything is in order for Ricky to stay here. Do you have any questions?" I looked from one parent to the other.

"We've done this before, so I don't think there's anything we need right now," the foster mother answered.

"Ricky, how about you? Are you happy here? Do you want to stay here for a while?" I asked. We three adults waited for his response.

Ricky nodded his little head up and down. Although he didn't speak anymore, he sat politely on the couch. "OK, Ricky. I'm going to go now, but I'll come back and visit you."

I turned to the foster parents: "His mother will know where he is staying and she will likely visit him regularly. Are you prepared for that?"

"Yes," the foster mother answered.

Satisfied, I shook their hands and, squatting down, I shook Ricky's also. Ricky's eyes sparkled at my attention but he didn't smile or speak. "Good-bye for now."

Over the next few months, it became evident that Ricky had a speech problem. That explained why he was so quiet all the time. Social services worked with the foster family to find him a speech therapist. Ricky was now calling his foster parents Aunt Awice (Alice) and Uncle Dan.

Although Alice would take Ricky to the therapy appointments, she didn't work with Ricky during the week as the therapist instructed. The therapist called me sharing his concerns.

Unannounced, I knocked on Alice and Dan's door. Somewhat taken aback, Alice invited me in. Ricky jumped up and down clapping his little hands together when he saw me. He started to run into my arms until Alice cleared her throat with alarming authority. I straightened and Ricky stopped immediately. He dropped his chin to his chest and stared at the floor, seemingly fearful of looking up.

"How's the therapy going?" I asked as I helped myself to a kitchen chair and drew Ricky to my side. I playfully poked him in the tummy and he giggled and grabbed himself around his waist. He inched closer to me. I had to admit I liked this little guy; there was something about him.

Alice interrupted our playfulness, "Take a seat, Ricky. Therapy is going fine. He doesn't want to do his homework though."

"What homework would that be?"

"Ricky is supposed to cut out pictures and tell me what each picture is. He gives up quickly when he can't properly pronounce a word," she said, looking at Ricky testily.

"How about we give it a try? Alice, where are the magazines and scissors?" I ignored her uptight grunt as she lifted herself from her seat and left the kitchen. "I've missed you, Ricky. How've things been going?"

Alice returned with the requested items before he could answer me. "Here we go," I said to Ricky. "Thank you, Alice," I offered, but I couldn't look the woman in the face even as I took the things from her. Paging through the magazine I stopped at a picture of a clown. "How's this?"

Ricky smiled as I handed him the scissors. Awkwardly and painstakingly, Ricky cut out the picture. "What is it?" I asked.

"A cwown."

Another grunt came from Alice's direction.

"Can you say clown?" I asked, enunciating each letter.

Ricky tried to mimic my tongue and lip movements. We kept practicing for about twenty minutes. "Now let's clean up our mess," I instructed Ricky as I handed the scissors to Alice. Ricky took both hands and swept the littered papers together into a neat pile. He walked to the garbage can and dragged it to the edge of the table. Carefully and slowly, he scooped every piece of paper into the trash.

"Very well done," I ruffled his hair and patted his shoulder. "I'm so proud of you."

Ricky beamed. Alice still looked put out.

"Well, I better get going. I just wanted to stop and say hi."

"While you're here, I have a few questions now," Alice stated.

Before I could respond she said, "I was told there would be money for clothes and such. He needs more things. Here's a list of what I want to buy him."

I perused the list. "I'll check on the money for the clothes. Will tomorrow be all right to call you?"

"Yes," she said as she showed me out the door. I turned and waved to Ricky again. He waved back.

They received most of the money she wanted for clothes. As it turned out, those requests would be the first of many such requests.

Just before Thanksgiving, Alice and Dan called stating their desire to adopt Ricky. "Ricky is not available for adoption. That's why we placed him with you. We're hoping his mother will be able to take her children back into her home."

"She's only been to visit a few times in five months. It's not fair to the child. He should be able to stay here permanently."

"We can talk about this at a later date when we know more about his mother's situation. I hope you'll be patient with the process."

The next phone call was to inform me that Ricky had pneumonia. "He's been running a very high fever and I've taken him to the doctor. I also had to buy him medicine."

I went to visit Ricky immediately. He was so happy to see me despite his illness. I pulled up a chair to his bedside, but Ricky patted the bed beside his leg. I moved to join him. "Do you want me to read you a story?" Ricky seemed hungry for the attention.

With every visit I was feeling more and more uncomfortable with Ricky's living arrangements. Alice wasn't as kind as she seemed in the beginning.

Then at Christmastime, we made arrangements for all the kids to spend time with their mother. Alice called me nearly hysterical. "She didn't come to get him. What's going on?"

"I'll call and find out." I started to say more, but Alice hung up on me.

Now it was my turn to be angry. I found out information I knew Alice didn't want to hear, but I called her anyway. "His mother won't be coming. She's had some major setbacks and can't take any of the kids. Please explain this to Ricky. And Alice, try to understand it isn't Ricky's fault."

"But she said she was coming. Dan and I have plans. We've made reservations."

"His mother would like to deliver some presents tonight, however. What would be a good time?" I asked.

"We have plans tonight. We won't be here. Ricky will be with a sitter." She hung up again.

The first of the year brought changes for everybody, especially Ricky. I had nearly made up my mind that Alice and Dan were not the right foster parents for Ricky. He had a special need for emotional security they weren't able to meet. I decided to make another home visit. I called first and when I arrived, I was greeted cordially and asked to have a seat in the living room.

"Where's Ricky?" I asked.

"He'll be here shortly. He's cleaning up after playing outside. Would you like something to drink?" Alice offered.

"No, thanks."

Finally Ricky came to the living room doorway. "You may come in," Alice said, using her head to indicate where Ricky was to sit.

"Come here, young man," I said playfully. Hesitantly, Ricky looked at Alice and then shyly approached me. I ruffled his hair as had become habit. It was just one little way to touch him and let him know I cared about him.

I watched Ricky watch Alice. He didn't seem happy anymore. Agitated, I crossed my arms and my legs only to have Ricky uncross my legs and crawl into my lap.

Alice spoke first. "My husband and I are beginning to think we made a mistake in taking Ricky into our home."

Appalled at her insensitivity to Ricky's presence, I urged him, "Ricky, please go to your room while I talk with Aunt Alice."

He left obediently as I thought, *I made a big mistake too.* "Go on."

"Well, he's becoming increasingly disobedient." I let Alice talk but I didn't listen to her. It was obvious she was lying and I didn't understand the change. Ricky was a fine child and obedient to a fault.

"I'm going to take Ricky for a ride," I stated.

It was during the ride that I made my final decision to remove Ricky. I hated to uproot a child but I hated more to keep him in an environment that was harsh. This child was in need of nurturing. It was so hard to know what a five-year-old would be thinking. "I think there is another family who would like you to live with them. They have other children. Would you like that?"

Ricky's only word was, "Yes."

I had already called another family, so we drove over for a visit. I watched Ricky's face glow with excitement as the two boys in the house gave Ricky immediate attention. One was just a year older than Ricky but the other was nearly a teenager. The boys invited Ricky to go outside and play with them.

"Can I place him immediately?" I asked Mary, the new foster mom. "The current living arrangement isn't working."

Mary's eyes and smile said it all. She gave me a look that said, "He's already family." Offering me a cup of coffee, Mary went on to say, "He's very welcome here and the room is ready. He can move in anytime."

This second foster home was perfect. The older boy wrestled with Ricky on the living room floor. They laughed and teased each other. The younger boy was in Ricky's classroom, so they did homework together and shared a bedroom. They said their prayers together and became good friends. For one year, Ricky was in a home with a family that accepted him as their own.

The year was filled with TV watching in the evenings, a family vacation, love and discipline, and consistency. Meals were prepared at regular times and chores were assigned. Mary shared her suspicions that Ricky may have been abused in the last home. "I had to give a spanking to the boys one night and Ricky's response gave me the distinct impression he had suffered far worse," she explained. My heart burned at the thought he may have been abused.

Mary told me that her husband was being transferred for his job and they had to move out of state. That meant one thing . . . Ricky would have to move again. This would be his third move.

Ricky had matured a lot during that year. When I told him about the impending move, he had a request: "Could I live in the country?"

His request was granted and the transition to his fourth home went smoothly. Ricky was sad when Mary's family said good-bye, but his joy returned quickly enough at the sight of horses, cows, dogs, and chickens.

Ricky received valuable gifts at this home. There were children to play with, chickens to feed, and his own kitten to care for—he named her Tina. On one of my visits he told me, "Tina loves me very much and I love her and I take good care of her."

Over the years, I learned to love this little boy. And it was with this foster mother and father that Ricky was able to express his desire to be in a permanent home with a permanent family. I wanted to do what was best for him and I agreed this was necessary, so I officially initiated the adoption process. Ricky was now eight years old.

After investigating the current situations of each of his biological parents, I found nothing had changed with either parent. I petitioned the court to release custody of the children so each would be available for adoption. The courts approved the adoption petition.

After a year and a half, Ricky went again to an interim home and from there was placed in yet another home in the country. Although this was his fifth move since leaving his mother's house, thankfully it would be his last before his official adoption.

After five years of being separated from his own family, Ricky was reunited with one of his little sisters, Samantha, when she was moved into Ricky's foster home. This brought Ricky a deeper sense of belonging.

The two were very proud of each other and would brag to their friends about their "real" sibling. Ricky also took his responsibilities as a big brother seriously. He drew strength and courage from Samantha's presence. The two children were inseparable. They played together at school and at home.

Ricky formed a strong connection with this new foster family, particularly with the foster dad. They did typical father/son activities together. They worked on projects and fixed things around the house. They played catch and did farm chores together. He and Ricky had become "good pals." Sadly, one morning Ricky found the man in his chair—he had died.

Upon his foster father's death, Ricky was immediately concerned for the well-being of his foster mother. Despite his own sadness, he told me after the funeral, "I know I'm only nine and I can't do everything around the farm, but I can do a lot of work."

The pursuit of adoption continued. Both children were presented at the state placement meeting. I desperately wanted them placed together in the same home, but I knew there were other issues to be considered. Ricky had been in foster care for a long time. Plus, at his age he would require more one-on-one attention.

I felt that only mature and experienced parents would be able to handle Ricky. I wanted Ricky to have loving and dedicated parents. My heart ached at the thought that whoever took Ricky might not be able to accommodate two children.

I met with the children regularly, preparing them as best I could for the potential adoption. It was also my responsibility to explain to them that they might not be able to live together.

One of my saddest moments was telling Ricky that Samantha was being placed for adoption but he was not. Putting aside his own disappointment and sadness, Ricky asked, "Are her new parents nice? Where will she live?"

Would this be another loss in Ricky's life? How many monumental changes can one child endure? "Ricky, I'll keep working on finding parents for you too," I promised. I knew I wouldn't stop until he was settled and secure in a family.

When Samantha's adoption process was completed, Ricky's little sister moved to another part of the state with her new parents. About four months later, I received a call from Samantha's new mom. "Samantha told us she was living with her brother at the foster home. Is that true?" she inquired.

I explained the kids' past and brought her up-to-date on Ricky and Samantha.

"We had actually planned to adopt a boy and a girl," she explained. "And of course, we believe it's best to keep siblings together if it's possible. Can we adopt him?"

I took her request seriously but knew Ricky needed a special type of father. He would need to be caring but firm. He would need to be sensitive, not just physically strong in teaching Ricky. After much thought, I believed that Samantha's adoptive father could provide the warmth and affection and the type of outdoor activities that Ricky needed.

Ricky's adoption was finally being realized. It was a time of joy, but also sadness. Ricky was very concerned about leaving his foster mother. He knew she would miss him and continued to be concerned about how she would get along without him.

Many hugs and kisses passed between Ricky and his foster mother. The two had grown to love one another. The temporary living arrangement had lasted a long time and they were family. But the painful good-bye was a necessary part of closure if Ricky was to receive the gift of a permanent family through adoption.

After Ricky's placement, I made many home visits and was happy to report my satisfaction with the adoption of the two children. Ricky told me, "I'm learning to hunt and my dad and I go hiking in the woods."

Just like every father and son should.

Ricky and his sister, together finally, enjoyed a family with both a mother and father in the home. Originally from a home where Dad always traveled and was unavailable, the kids now had a father who prepared lunch every day before leaving for his swing shift job. "He's a good cook," the kids said in unison.

Ricky and Samantha settled into their environment with grace, accepting and appreciating their new family and friends. Ricky, his dad, and his grandpa became great friends. There was even a special place for Ricky as he was the only grandson to carry on the family name. With a maturity that continued to defy his age, Ricky worked with his grandpa in his store.

At one time, I would have said Ricky would grow up to be a man with many troubles. But I sigh with contentment as I reread the closing comments on Ricky's report: "The parents are very satisfied and happy with the children and . . . the children are very secure and happy in this home."

It took many years for the benefits of adoption to reach Ricky, but in the end, the system worked. I remember the little boy who couldn't speak clearly and was afraid to let go of my hand. Through God's grace, Ricky, now Rich, has grown to become a man of honor and compassion.

Forever Family

Michael and Veronica Poe

My husband and I married knowing we couldn't have any children together. I had two nearly grown children from a previous marriage and he readily accepted them as his own. We did discuss the possibility of adoption, however, and made the decision that we would discuss it further after we were married at least three years. We wanted to be sure our relationship was secure.

While driving through Texas on vacation, we were jumping from one conversation to another when my husband said, "You know, it's time for us to think about it."

I knew exactly what he was talking about. "Yeah, I guess we should think real seriously about it." Our travel time took on a whole new focus as we excitedly discussed the future of our family.

"What age do you want?" my husband asked me.

"I don't want a baby!"

"Why not?" came his surprised question.

"Because I'm not changing diapers and getting up at two o'clock in the morning. I've done that route, Buddy, and I'm not doing it again!"

Mike understood: "Yeah, an infant is a lot more responsibility. Besides, I already get up at all hours." His local truck driving job started early every morning. "But how young do you want to go?" He then suggested age twelve.

"I think that's too old, but I guess between two and nine would be good," I responded. We were both new to the adoption idea and had no idea what type of issues an older child might have.

We agreed we didn't care whether the child was a boy or a girl, feeling that if he were our birth child, God would make that choice anyway. Eagerness and peace filled us both for the remainder of the vacation.

When we returned home from our trip, we made the initial phone call. The county referred us to another organization and they sent the necessary paperwork and requirements. And so we officially started the process.

Our classes taught us valuable information for raising an older adopted child. We were aware that abuse, sexual abuse, and abandonment were just some of the potential issues we could be faced with. We gained tools to help children with attachment issues, and we were encouraged to remember that the instructors were there to help us with ongoing trials.

Since we were open to an older child and multiple children, it didn't take long for the adoption agency to call us. Our first call was for two little boys—brothers, just two and three years old. As it turned out, the foster family was actually pursuing adoption and had acquired an attorney. We discussed the possible outcomes. The foster family may be allowed to adopt, but then again they might get turned down. And what if we pursued adopting them and then had a huge court battle to contend with, all the while the boys needing a home and security? We felt it wasn't in their best interest for us to pursue adopting them.

Our next call was for Autumn. Autumn and two of her siblings were taken from their birth mother when Autumn was twenty-two months old. When Autumn was taken from her home she had been neglected. She had signs of malnutrition and wasn't thriving, and she had attachment disorder. Apparently, the older brother had already been in and out of foster care and exhibited evidence of abuse.

As part of the agency's way of preparing older children for adoption, we were asked to create a "Forever Book." In this book are photos of the adoptive family, their home, the child's new bedroom, grandparents, and other pertinent things that would help a child become familiar with their future environment. The counselor then presents the book to the child, saying, "We've found you a Forever Family." It makes the initial introduction less frightening.

I'll never forget when, prior to her adoption, we took Autumn to the park and played for about an hour. My husband and I acted like four-year-olds right along with Autumn. We had a great time. After a while she asked, "Are you going to be my mommy and daddy?"

We told her, "We'd like to be your mommy and daddy."

She got a real shy look and scrunched up her shoulders, giggled, and said, "OK, you can be my mommy and daddy."

My husband beamed like we had just given birth. We were so thankful Autumn was receptive to us and to the idea of being in our family. We wanted to be sensitive to her needs, so her question was affirming what we already felt in our hearts. We knew it would be a privilege to have Autumn as our daughter. After a few more visits she met my son Joseph. Much later she met my daughter, Annette, who is in the Coast Guard.

Our visits were always very positive, with the exception of the foster mother. She didn't want to relinquish Autumn to us. The foster mother said she loved Autumn, but the rest of her family didn't agree that they should adopt her. They already had a large family that included birth, foster, and adopted children. Unfortunately, the foster mother made the transition much more difficult than it needed to be.

For instance, both families were to meet with the agency and discuss the well-being of Autumn. The foster mother would never show up. That delayed the process.

On another occasion, we were to take Autumn for one week to see if Autumn would be comfortable with us and in our home. It was to be during a week that the foster family went on vacation. I arrived to pick up Autumn and the foster dad nearly shoved Autumn out the door. I had to ask for needed antibiotics and they sent Autumn with only the clothes on her back. The foster mother was sending such a mixed message. She said she loved Autumn but did not appear to put time into her personal welfare.

After that experience, I explained the situation to the agency and they were very upset with the foster family's behavior. Because of the foster family's actions, Autumn was immediately released to live with us. We did agree on one more meeting so Autumn could say good-bye to the foster family. We felt it was important for Autumn to have that closure.

Even at the last meeting, the foster mother made it uncomfortable. She was not prepared for the family photos she wanted to take and so she requested we come back that night. We accommodated her but it was difficult.

At that final visit, the foster mom gave us multiple bags of Autumn's belongings. But she never really said good-bye to Autumn. Instead, she gave the impression that we were stealing Autumn from them. We ended up in counseling for Autumn and our family after that situation.

The most challenging part of Autumn's transition was getting her to let us love her. At first Autumn wouldn't let us hold her. She threw huge fits, complete with kicking, pinching, spitting, scratching, and biting. Many nights I'd just hold her tight and be with her while she was angry. Eventually, after constant reassurance that we loved her, she seemed to start believing us. We just kept holding her. Even now she'll wake up my husband in the middle of the night to sit with her until she sleeps. Sometimes we let her sleep with us just so she knows we are here for her.

Another challenge we face is Autumn reverting to baby behavior. She wants to be rocked for hours. She wants me to stroke her hair and pamper her. These are things parents do from birth, but she never had those opportunities. She's catching up with her bonding needs. It takes consistency and per-severance on our part. I'm thankful for our adoption classes because they helped us anticipate this behavior. Autumn has come far, but I know it's not over yet.

We realize there is no magic age when her fear and insecu-rity will stop. At the same time, we're dealing with a four-year-old who is developing her own personality. She rebels against discipline and doesn't understand why she shouldn't have a bad attitude. We explain the importance of respect and doing what is right.

Because she's had three mommies in her short life, it took almost a year for Autumn to realize that I was the mommy who would be here forever. I'm learning that adopting an older child comes with problems that can be overwhelming. But, they can be overcome. I suppose a lot depends on the individual child. Autumn wanted a mommy and a daddy.

Autumn knows she is adopted and it's a topic we are very proud of. We tell people we adopted her and she proudly states it herself. She is everything we expected *and more*.

Part 13

Incredible!

Remarkable Adoptions

Precious Gifts Come in Small Packages

Patricia K. Layton

Surreal is the best word to describe the scene as I walked down the long white hospital corridor leading into the Neonatal Intensive Care Unit of Tampa's largest women's hospital. My husband and I walked the seemingly endless hallway together, just as we had so many years before. The white walls, white ceilings, and bare windows were in stark contrast to the emotional battle that raged in my heart and head. This time, we were here to meet our soon-to-be new baby daughter.

Both of our hearts were drawn to meeting her—but my head was stuck in memories of another time. Twelve years ago we had taken a similar walk in this same hospital to undergo an abortion. The circumstances behind each event were amazing to me. It all seemed so bizarre.

As Mike and I rounded the corner of the NICU into the open nursery area, we were both trembling, tightly gripping each other's hand. The room was filled with babies. Most were inside clear plastic bassinets that had two little "portholes" for the doctors and nurses to slip their hands through when caring for the sick and tiny babies. Some babies lay naked, tiny arms and legs flailing wildly, tubes and wires attached to them to monitor their every body function. Each one lay on a chest high, podium-like table covered with soft, white sheepskin.

That is how we first saw her. A tiny baby girl. The nurses had named her Julianna; Juli for the month of her birth and Anna for the prophetic beauty of the name. Julianna had been born to a sixteen-year-old girl approximately twenty-three weeks along in her pregnancy. Her birth weight was a mere one-and-one-half pounds and she was just ten inches long. She fit in my hand.

The day we met Julianna, she had recently undergone surgery and had dropped to only one pound. As we looked upon her for the first time, doctors and nurses gathered around to see for themselves the couple that had come to adopt Julianna. They were very protective and concerned for this little child.

I was in a trance. Without question, Julianna was the most incredible and beautiful thing I had ever seen. It took all that I had to maintain my balance. I feared I would collapse to the floor as I heard the sweet voice of God speak to my heart: "This, Pat, is what I create in a mother's womb. This is why I have called you to do the work you do." I felt, with overwhelming surety, God had literally placed a "preborn" child in my presence.

As I looked upon Julianna, my mind reeled. Drastic changes were occurring in our lives lately and now we were to be the parents of this precious gift. Again, I strained to hold onto consciousness. Only a few months prior God had given me "his call."

Not only were we the parents of two sons, an eighteen-year-old senior in high school and a ten-year-old, but my professional life was already a nonstop wave of activity. Amidst my professional responsibilities of running an insurance agency full-time, God had made it clear that I was to open Tampa's first Crisis Pregnancy Center (CPC).

As I stood beside this tiny baby lying on the white sheepskin, a large group of my closest friends were hard at work painting, wallpapering, and preparing the space that would house the CPC. After sharing with them the vision God had given me, they had eagerly joined my team of volunteers. I was running my own insurance business out of the front office and preparing the back for ministry.

We were set to open in just a few months and God was clearly leading the way. His favor preceded every move we made. Donations of all types were coming from various directions—paint, wallpaper, office supplies, pregnancy tests, furniture—on and on the blessings flowed.

My mind drifted farther back to a time hidden in the recesses of my mind. It was 1984 and I had asked Christ into my heart. I wasn't prepared for the mercy, love, and provisions he would lavish upon me after I humbly admitted my need for him. Christ moved into my life in a mighty way after that day.

Immediately, I was surrounded by mature Christian mentors who were committed to helping me learn as much as I could about God and his ways. They taught me to love the Word of God and how to pray. They were relentless in their unconditional love for me.

The Lord knew how important these friends would be to me as I struggled to believe that he could truly forgive a past as sinful as mine. God was giving me new direction for my life, but towering walls of pain had to be destroyed first. Eventually the walls did crumble.

I will never forget the day that he gently revealed the truth about abortion to me. I was saddened, again, by the choice I had made. By that choice a life was ended. But with conviction comes grace. I was immediately bathed by a wave of mercy, love, and forgiveness.

Back in the NICU, Julianna's mere presence drew attention from every adult entering the room. She was so beautiful and so, so fragile. My arms ached to hold her to my breast and comfort and nurture her. Oh, what I *almost* missed. Just a few mornings prior, my husband woke up and announced, "I think we should adopt a baby girl!" Right out of the blue—no recent conversations, sermons, or radio programs had even hinted about adoption. Nothing had prepared me for this revelation of his.

I responded emphatically, "Are you crazy? Can't you see how busy my life is? Does it look like I have time for a baby? A baby—we have a senior in high school!"

Needless to say, I was shocked and a bit miffed. We had discussed the possibility of adoption on several occasions in the past. We'd had our two sons, but for many years I had longed for a daughter. In fact, I had always believed in my heart that my aborted child was a little girl. But adoption was too expensive and there was too much red tape. Time passed and it never happened.

Fortunately, with God nothing is impossible. Thankfully, his ways are not our ways.

Mike arrived home from work that very afternoon looking frazzled and pale. He had taken the liberty of asking an attorney friend about the possibilities of adopting a child, maybe a toddler.

"Do you believe in divine intervention?" the friend asked Mike.

"Absolutely. Why?" Mike asked.

Our friend proceeded to tell Mike that he had just hung up from a conversation with someone at the hospital: "A birth mother has put up for adoption a little baby girl in the NICU. I know sixty or more families wanting to adopt, but most will be skeptical about this one." He continued, "This little girl was born three months early. She weighs just one pound. She is likely to have serious lifelong health challenges. She'll possibly be blind, unable to hear, and she could be retarded. It's difficult to determine right now and probably will be for a long time. In fact, Mike, we're not even certain how long she will live."

"I'll talk to my wife tonight," Mike said with a heavy heart, "but I don't think she'll consider it. Especially after the conversation we had this morning."

We sat on our bedside as my husband relayed the remarkable story to me that evening. We were both overwhelmed with emotion. In my typical fashion, I got right to work. I decided to call everyone I knew who was interested in adopting a child.

The first call was to one of my very dear "God friends." Elaine and I had become friends through a ministry we founded together called Sisters of Rachel, a healing ministry for women who have had abortions.

Elaine had an abortion in her late teens. That aborted child turned out to be the only child she would ever conceive. She was unable to become pregnant again and longed for a child. She listened intently to Julianna's story. Then there was a long silence on the other end of the telephone.

"What do you think, Elaine?" I asked her.

"I think I would absolutely love to have that little girl—but I can't."

"Why not, Elaine? God will work this out. He can bring this child through. I know he can," I pleaded with her to believe as I believed.

"Oh, I am certain that he will bring her through, Pat," she sighed.

"I don't understand then." I wanted more from her.

"This baby is not for me. God planned this little girl for you and Mike." She said it as if she was delivering a message. I heard her message and knew it to be true.

"She is for me," I whispered. *A tiny baby I've never seen is going to be my daughter. Mine and Mike's.* "Julianna is for us," I whispered again, this time with praise and thanksgiving.

I called Mike at work and we agreed to meet at the hospital to see our daughter for the first time.

So here we were, looking at this precious gift. It was love at first sight for both of us. We knew immediately and without doubt that God had delivered Julianna to us.

Mike and I spent the next three months going back and forth to the hospital. Each time I went to see Julianna, I would lay my hands upon her in her hospital bassinet and pray Psalm 139 and Jeremiah 1 over her. "Julianna," I said to my daughter, "God knit you together in your mother's womb. You are fearfully and wonderfully made. God knows the plans he has for you, Julianna. They are plans for good and not for evil. You will live. You will not die."

All of our friends and family stood together with Mike and me in agreement with those prayers. Our faith believed God would give our baby girl complete and perfect health. It wasn't an effortless or faultless faith. Sometimes, I would cry all the way home from the hospital and ask Mike, "What if she dies?"

He would gently remind me, "God brought this together, Pat. I know it's sad to think about, but if Julianna does die, I know it's God's plan for us to be her mommy and daddy. She needs us."

Our friends, our family, and Mike and I each took turns wondering just what we were getting into. But faith kept us all going. We became very close to Julianna's doctor and her main nurse, Jayne. As we drew closer to them we learned many miraculous details of her birth and her rescue from death at such a premature point in life. Not a single NICU team member denies the miracle of her life or her undefeatable spirit.

Julianna came home with us on an October day in 1988. She was three months old. Her beautifully shaped head was full of blond hair. Her perfect tiny rosy lips complemented her soft, sweet baby-scented pink skin. She was a healthy four pounds. So far there have been no complications, no health problems, nothing missing, and nothing broken.

Soon after we brought Julianna home from the hospital, a wonderful older lady who was a friend and volunteer for the CPC announced to me that God had instructed her to make herself available to help me with Julianna so that the CPC could open as planned. "Grandma Wooley" stood by my side and helped me with Julianna whenever I needed her until Julianna went into the first grade. Grandma Wooley is still a huge part of our lives and Julianna adores her.

The story of Julianna's miraculous life and her presence with me in the ministry has been a blessing to many considering the life-changing decision of adoption. She is now twelve years old and God continues to use her in the lives of others, especially mine. Mike and I will never forget the honor and privilege we have been given. It is said God moves in mysterious ways. Our experience is that God moves in remarkable ways and Julianna is our proof.

My Daughter's Eyes
Marcy Hukill

Despite great personal struggle, I never regretted our quest to adopt the little girl waiting for us. I had had a vision of her eyes, and it was her eyes that kept me faithful to the end.

My husband and I had two children by birth. It was during their adolescence that we knew we still wanted more children. I had undergone a tubal ligation years before, so we understood our limitations up front. After counseling with a specialist, we decided to have my tubal reversed. After two surgeries, we had to face the fact that scarring would prohibit the ovulation of my eggs and that we couldn't have any more children.

Still, the deep desire to have another child would not be quieted. After determining that it was impossible for my eggs to get through my fallopian tubes, we took the next step: in vitro fertilization (IVF). My husband and I were healthy, and our eggs and sperm were too, so IVF seemed a viable option.

Our doctor was working with another woman at the same time he was working with us. Many times the three of us would meet and discuss issues pertaining to IVF. The doctor had explained to each of us that I was the perfect candidate for this procedure—I had already given birth and had had healthy pregnancies. Everything was working just fine for me, except that the eggs couldn't get to where they needed to go. The other woman, however, had a slim chance of carrying the embryos for multiple reasons. Not only did her husband have a low sperm count, but also she suffered severe problems in her uterus, and her fallopian tubes didn't function properly. By all the evidence, it seemed impossible for her to carry the embryos.

Two weeks after we each underwent the IVF procedure, we both showed up for our pregnancy tests. The nurses drew the blood, and we waited for the results. I prayed for her because I knew her chances were so slim. She had no children, and everything appeared to be against her. However, when our tests came back, hers was positive and mine negative. She was pregnant and I wasn't. I was devastated. There was no explanation for my test results.

I went through IVF three times—each with a negative result. The first time was not only depressing, but I felt like the breath was squeezed out of me. And each time after that, more breath was squeezed out of me until I didn't want to breathe anymore. I was almost unable to function in any area of my life. I questioned God too. Why would he put the desire in my heart and then lead me to a dead end?

One evening, around eight o'clock, I was running on the treadmill in my family room. In the full-length mirror in front of the treadmill, I was watching myself run. I had gotten to the point where I couldn't think of anything else except having a baby. I was so depressed. As I ran, I listened to music through my headphones. I suppose I had been running about forty minutes, watching myself in the mirror, lost in my own world. Suddenly the brown eyes of a little girl appeared in the mirror. It stunned me. I was catapulted off the treadmill. Everything around me seemed to stand still in time.

I believe God deliberately stopped everything around me so I would hear him and sense his presence. He didn't tell me anything audibly, but I knew those brown eyes belonged to the baby girl I would someday have. I didn't see her face or anything else—just her eyes. Before that moment, I hadn't believed in visions.

Now the problem was how to convince my family I saw this baby. I didn't tell my husband about it for a long time. Finally one morning when I was praying in my dining room, I felt like I was supposed to take action. I knew I was supposed to get off my knees and start the search. I finally approached my husband. We agreed our only opportunity to have another child was through adoption. When I told him about the brown-eyed baby girl, he didn't really believe me. His spiritual experiences were very different from mine, so he couldn't understand.

We discussed adoption off and on. But every time I would talk about "the eyes," it led to an argument between us. He thought I was losing my mind, and he wanted me to go to a psychiatrist. Eventually our marriage started falling apart.

Every day my eyes were bloodshot from crying. As time passed, the kids stopped asking me what was wrong because they knew I was crying about *the* baby girl. My sorrow was so deep that the kids started feeling like they weren't enough for me. I tried to explain, but nobody seemed to understand this hunger in my soul.

For over a year, our family struggled. My husband and I couldn't even talk about a baby anymore.

One day I decided I must not have been praying for the right thing. God had already shown me the baby girl, yet everything else I loved was collapsing around me. So I started praying for my husband and family. I quit talking about a baby. It hurt deeply to deny a part of my being, but I found a Bible verse that helped me: "With man this is impossible, but with God all things are possible" (Matt. 19:26). I reminded myself constantly of this. I was the first to admit we were in an impossible situation. I couldn't have children physically, and my husband was now fine with not having more children at all. Because we already had two kids, we were put on a very long waiting list. Everything seemed impossible.

I was depressed and felt so hopeless that I was even starting to think that perhaps I was psychotic. Maybe I should have taken antidepressants, but I just kept thinking about that Scripture passage, believing it was up to God to find a solution to this insurmountable problem. If God had really shown me those eyes—and I still believed he had—then he would have to change my husband's heart so we could move ahead with adopting.

One night while lying in bed, my husband asked out of the blue, "Did you call the adoption agency?" I was astounded. The question shocked me because we'd had no real communication between us for quite a while. After that, we started talking more.

Eventually, we did our home study, one part of the adoption application process. We wanted to adopt any child as long as it was a girl—a brown-eyed girl. I had to go with my heart. I had seen her eyes and I knew they were brown.

The social worker questioned some of the answers on our application. She made me feel selfish and guilty for writing my desire for a brown-eyed girl. But I stood my ground, and even my husband supported me.

Finally, we received a telephone call from an attorney. "No promises," he told us, "but we have a mother who might give up her baby girl."

At the time I felt certain this must be the baby. The mother lived in another state, and we found out she was a drug addict. We made the trip to go see her, but everything fell through. The state told her if she would keep her baby, the government would pay for her to go to college and help her in other ways. We had hit yet another brick wall, and we returned home empty-handed.

We later received another telephone call from the attorney, but this time about a baby boy. Reluctantly, I met with the birth mom and that potential adoption also fell through.

Just before Thanksgiving, a social worker called us. She explained there was a birth mom wanting to relinquish her baby at birth. Apparently, other families weren't interested in this adoption because it was considered a special-needs adoption. We were definitely interested.

A month of anxiety went by before we heard anything. Then on December 23, the phone rang. It was the birth mom calling. Without small talk or introduction she simply asked, "You were going to take my baby?"

I nearly collapsed from the shock of the phone call. She continued talking: "I always dreamed of living on a farm. I always wanted the things you wrote about on the application."

When I finally regained my composure, we talked about her due date, how she was doing, and some other matters as well, and then we hung up. I didn't even know where she had called from or where she lived. The social worker was upset because the birth mom hadn't followed protocol. Clients are supposed to go through the proper channels and not speak to each other.

After Christmas the birth mom called us again, speaking to us from a McDonald's in Texas. "I think I'm going to have the baby," she told me. "I've got a pain," she said with a moan. Then the telephone went dead.

I called the operator and asked for a hospital in the area of Texas from which the birth mom had called. I realized I was looking for a needle in a haystack because there were so many hospitals in that metropolitan area. But I picked one and called it anyway. I asked for the emergency room and explained I was looking for a woman who was having a baby. I could only tell them the mother's first name, and I knew nothing about the father. The nurse rang another room and asked around for the birth mom. Miraculously, I had called the right hospital. The nurse got back on the telephone and exclaimed, "Oh, she just delivered a baby girl."

I almost dropped the receiver. My whole family was standing around when I heard the cry of a newborn baby. The nurse delivered the news that we had our new little girl. I cried out in joy. Immediately, my husband handed me the credit card and said, "Go."

Without asking her, I purchased an airline ticket for my sister and me. I called her at work and told her I was coming to get her immediately. She stammered and said something about clothes.

With only eight hours having passed since learning of the baby's birth, we flew to Texas. My sister and I ran into the hospital, arguing over who would see the newborn first. The door was shut when we reached the birth mother's room. I looked at my sister and she said, "You go first."

"I can't." I think I remember her saying she'd open the door for me. I was so weak she had to hold me up.

When I finally pushed open the door, I saw the birth mother in her bed, and the newborn Hannah was in a bassinet near her. I learned later that the mom had not even held her yet. When the mom saw me, she asked who I was. When I told her, she got out of bed and pushed the bassinet toward me and said, "Here's your baby."

I looked at my new baby daughter, staring into her face. These were the eyes I had seen so long before in the mirror. I held her and soaked up her essence, her sweetness. I knew God had given her to me.

It took nine days to complete the adoption of little Hannah. With paperwork, car seat, and other essential baby items in hand, we were prepared to return home.

The airline attendants treated us like royalty. The flight captain even made an announcement to the passengers as we showed off our new family member. Crew members and passengers rejoiced with us the entire flight home.

As expected, our entire family was waiting for us at the airport. And at the front of the crowd were my husband and two children, standing with a bouquet of balloons. As I moved to place Hannah in my husband's arms, I wondered if he would love her like I did. Inside, I struggled with what I would do if he didn't see her like I did. But when I handed her to him, he started to cry. His tears showed me that his love was sincere.

As I reflect on how Hannah came to be a member of our family, I marvel at God. I used to question if he really knew me, if he really saw *me*. Now I know without doubt that he had a little girl in mind specifically for me. My will would have been to have the IVFs work. But his will turned out so much better. I can't imagine my life without my daughter—little, brown-eyed Hannah.

A Child Just like Me

Sue McMillin

> He reached down from on high and took hold of me; he drew me out of deep waters. . . . He brought me out into a spacious place; he rescued me because he delighted in me.
>
> Psalm 18:16, 19

My mother chose her husband over me, her child, and gave me up moments after birth. I was placed in a foster home where my foster mother took full advantage of the system, as well as the money intended for food and nurturing. At eight months old, I and ten other children were rescued by authorities. At that time, I weighed ten pounds. I didn't know how to eat and was emotionally and physically starving.

That was many years ago. If authorities had not rescued me, I wouldn't have survived. If I hadn't been adopted by Smiley McMillin, I might not have understood that the power of a mother's love can nurture a neglected, unloved little girl back to health.

I am blessed because I was placed in the arms of a wonderful, beautiful woman who was once abandoned herself—a woman who had been praying for a very long time to love a child just like me.

Smiley McMillin was raised in the Louisville Jefferson County Children's Home. Margaret Louise—as she had been named at birth—lost her father when she was one year old. Margaret's mother later married William Smiley, and life seemed good again. But at the age of eleven, her mother entered the hospital for a simple operation and never left.

Margaret, nicknamed Smiley, reeled from the unexpected death of her mother, but the worst shock was yet to come. Unable to cope with his loss, William Smiley sent his daughter away to Louisville Jefferson County Children's Home. There, a woman who worked at the home, Elizabeth Broker, took young Smiley under her wing. Miss Elizabeth remained Smiley's primary caregiver until she left for college several years later.

Elizabeth left such an imprint on Smiley that she returned to the home after college to work part-time. As she worked with the children, she dreamed of one day having her own family and children to love. Elizabeth encouraged her to not give up, that one day she would have that opportunity.

When Smiley married Frazier McMillin, she was determined to have a family right away. She was devastated when she found out she couldn't bear children. Years passed as she prayed for a child.

None came.

One day, by chance, Smiley ran into Elizabeth Broker. They caught up on old times, and after they spoke for a long time, Smiley shared with Elizabeth her heartbreak at not being able to conceive a child. The older woman asked Smiley a blunt question, "When are you and Frazier going to adopt?"

Adoption had occupied Smiley's thoughts a great deal and she was excited to share her hopes with Elizabeth. Gently joking with Smiley, Elizabeth asked, "So tell me, do you want a pretty child or a very intelligent child?"

Without hesitation, Smiley answered in a soft voice, "Elizabeth, I want a child that's like me." Elizabeth understood.

Smiley, who knew what it meant to be abandoned, was not asking God for a normal baby. She was opening her arms and heart, praying for a child who was left behind just as she had been years before.

Eight months later I was placed in Smiley McMillin's arms. I was so scrawny and sick that I had to be carried on a pillow to avoid bruises. I was emotionally starved. I didn't know how to receive caresses or touch. Health-care workers had predicted possible retardation, but no one really knew what lay ahead. They simply couldn't predict the long-term effects of my grim beginning.

Smiley was undaunted by the challenges and welcomed them with a new mother's bliss. She began to concoct milkshakes out of eggs, chocolate, butter, milk, cream, cheese, potatoes—anything containing nourishment.

It wasn't easy. Months of starvation had deprived me not only of food but also of the desire and ability to eat. It took seventeen tries the first time she attempted to teach me to swallow. But Smiley was committed.

Feeding was a full-time job. From the blender to the bottle to the baby, my mother delivered food with lullabies and caresses, until I began to respond. With each inch of progress, my mother celebrated and thanked God.

Today our lives have come full circle. I now live with my beautiful, elderly mother and can't help being thankful that God "reached down from on high and took hold of me [and] drew me out of deep waters." I can never repay the love of Smiley McMillin, an orphan who reclaimed the life of a discarded infant.

Today, as president of *With Time to Spare*, I lead seminars for Fortune 500 clients and businesses across the country. My job is to bring organization to chaos. That is what God did for me as a tiny, abused baby. He brought order to chaos. As I share my organizational skills, I pray for opportunities to share how God can bring order into our personal lives as well. When I speak to women's groups, I cannot help but share my humble beginnings.

I will always be thankful for a heavenly Father who placed me in the arms of a woman who was asking for a little girl just like her.

A Family Thing

Kelly Fordyce Martindale

I'll never forget the day my youngest daughter realized the true meaning of adoption. On multiple occasions while she was growing up we had talked about my husband being adopted. Then one day I said, as I often had before, "I'm so glad Mike was adopted."

She looked shocked. "Mike was adopted?" she asked me. I nodded my head yes. As tears formed in her eyes, she breathed, "I'm so glad he wasn't aborted."

My family is full of adoptees, blendeds, steps, ex's, you name it. But one thing remains firm in all our minds: We are family. As I piece together all the different dynamics in our immediate and extended family, I've realized adoption is a family thing.

Adoption doesn't affect only the child and the parents but also those who live with and around them. My husband of ten years was adopted as an infant. This would be the first significant experience I had with the subject of adoption. His parents have 8mm films of bringing Mike home. You can't ignore the obvious joy on his mother's face and in her walk as she proceeds from the building to the car, all the while being recorded by the daddy of the new baby boy.

Then, a couple years later, they repeated the process when they adopted my wonderful sister-in-law, Lori. She, too, was an infant when adopted. My father-in-law shared that when he and his wife realized they couldn't have children, it was a natural and easy decision to pursue adoption. Forty-three years ago, the adoption process was much like it is today—lots of paperwork, home studies, and investigations. The only significant difference was that most adoptions were completely closed, which is the case with my husband and Lori.

Neither Mike nor Lori feel compelled to search for their biological parents; however, Lori says, "If I were to meet my mom, I'd have one thing to say: Thank you. Thank you for caring enough about me to let me have a secure, loving family."

Because of extenuating circumstances my husband allowed his three-year-old son to be adopted by his stepdad. It was a difficult decision and one he wouldn't repeat, but Mike did it knowing his son would be cared for and loved. Mike and his son have a good relationship today and, in fact, work for the same company.

Adoption first affected my family years ago when my great-grandpa's mom died. At the time he was just two years old. After seven years with his mean father, another family adopted my grandpa. He was nine. By the time he was sixteen, he moved out on his own and settled in Callaway, Nebraska. There, he was hired by my great-great-grandpa and at age twenty-one, he married my great-grandma, the mother of my grandma.

If that adoption had not occurred, only God knows if I'd even be alive. Adoption is a wonderful decision. I have adopted aunts, cousins, second cousins, nieces, uncles, grandparents, and the list goes on. Because of the loving choice made by one person, I am alive today. I am eternally grateful for the love of one family for another human being. That love changed history and continues to do so.

Part 14

Photo in the Locket

Adoption Reunions

Loved, and Loved Again

as told to Naydean Julch by Marlene Eaton

"Tell me again, Mommy, about the best Christmas you ever had."

"You mean the Christmas when we adopted you, honey?"

"Yes."

"Well," she said, pulling me into a warm embrace. "Once upon a time there was a mommy and a daddy who had two sons, but they couldn't have any more children and they wanted a little girl, so God gave them a special Christmas present . . ."

Thus my mother would tell how God had chosen me to be their daughter three days before Christmas in 1968. My parents told me the story year after year, so I always knew I was adopted. Richard and Lillian Rivera loved me from the moment they held me; there was no doubt about it.

I loved my parents and my brothers and knew they loved me. I was no different than any other child, adopted or otherwise. Sometimes when I argued with my mom, I would say things like "I hate you" or "I'm going to find my real mother." Fortunately, my mom never responded to my angry outbursts with anything but love and understanding.

I would often study my features in the mirror, knowing they were unlike those of my mom and dad. I wondered what my birth parents looked like and if I resembled them. I was intensely curious, but at the same time I feared a search for them would hurt my adoptive parents. I loved them with all my heart and did not want them to think I didn't want to live with them.

When I was twenty, I met my husband-to-be, Brian, at a Christian camp. We both agree that when we met, it was love at first sight. We were married in June 1990.

In 1993 I became pregnant. As I began to feel movement in my womb, I thought of my birth mother. I envisioned another woman who looked somewhat like me. I could see her caressing her tummy and hear her singing lullabies, and I would be reduced to tears as I wondered about the mother who carried me under her heart for nine months. Instinctively I knew she would want to know I was happy and well. It was time to begin my search.

In August of 1993, I went into labor and delivered my beautiful daughter, Megan. I kept thinking of my birth mother. What had her labor been like? Had she felt the same overwhelming love for me that I now felt for my daughter? The haunting questions demanded answers. I wanted her to know I had a good life, and placing me for adoption had been a brave and wonderful thing for her to do.

I talked at length with my husband, and he supported my desire to find my birth mother. I also called my mom, and she said, "I always knew there would come a day when you would want to know, and I have no problem with you trying to find her. I love you, and you will always be my daughter no matter what you find." Such a loving and supportive response, typical of my mom, was the blessing I needed to proceed.

One day, when Megan was about eight months old, a friend called and said, "Marlene, hurry. Turn on Oprah. She's talking about adoption." I turned on the television in time to get the telephone number of Operation Identity.

I always thought that finding my birth parents would be a long, drawn-out process. But I underestimated God.

I called Operation Identity, and they put me in touch with an agency in the state I was born. A woman told me I needed to hire a lawyer because that state had sealed records. I would need the help of an attorney to present my case, and I should have a good reason for needing to know, like medical history. My heart sank at the thought of hiring a lawyer. Here I was with a tiny baby, committed to not working outside the home, and our income was insufficient for that expense. I prayed, "Lord, you've led me this far. Please lead me the rest of the way."

The woman gave me the name of the adoption consultant for that state and said we could talk about the legal issues later. I called the adoption consultant, and he said, "Tell me your story; I'll take some notes." He never asked if my motive was to learn more about medical history, and it never occurred to me to mention it. I merely told him that my life had turned out great, and I wanted to let my birth mother know because I sensed she might be worried about me. Our conversation was brief, and he said he would get back to me.

I had started the ball rolling and now had the sinking feeling there was nothing I could do to stop it. Was I doing the right thing? My instincts said yes, though at times an unreasonable fear would come over me, and I'd worry about lawyer fees.

About a month later, the adoption consultant called back and asked, "Do you have a pencil and paper?"

"Sure," I answered, grabbing both.

"Here's your birth mother's name," he replied matter-of-factly. I nearly fell off the chair. I began crying as he gave me the information, fumbling with paper and pencil, and then interrupting him with, "But I thought I needed a lawyer."

"Just keep writing," he answered gently, and I did. He gave me her first and maiden names and a physical description from the 1968 interview when I was placed for adoption. She was a real flesh-and-blood person—her name was Pat.

We said good-bye, and with trembling hands I hung up the phone. My daughter was taking a nap, my husband was at work, and I was alone with God. I poured my heart out, thanking him, through tears, for the precious piece of paper I held in my hand. I kept staring at the words, halfway expecting them to disappear, as if written with disappearing ink. I was so overwhelmed I could hardly think straight.

Two days later, when we returned home from church on Sunday afternoon, two messages were on the answering machine.

The first was from the woman I spoke with at Operation Identity. She said, "Marlene, we've found your birth mother and she wants to meet you."

The second was from my birth mother. "This is Pat." She was crying. "I'm your birth mom. I would love to meet you. I have waited so long for this moment to come. Please call me." She left her number.

What I thought would take years had taken weeks. My husband and I looked at each other in amazement. In our wildest dreams we hadn't expected it to happen so quickly. I tried to think rationally but couldn't put two thoughts together, let alone two words. I still couldn't get over the fact that all of this had been accomplished without an attorney. God had bypassed the red tape.

I dialed the number of the woman who had been on my heart and mind throughout my pregnancy and especially at the birth of my daughter. Though that first conversation lasted about thirty minutes, we could manage only a few words, for we were both weeping.

"Thank you for not aborting me," I blurted out. "Thank you for loving me enough to place me for adoption."

"I've waited so long for this moment," she repeated.

We were amazed to find out how close she lived to my mom and dad. They were about twenty minutes apart and had even shopped at the same stores.

"Can I call them?" she asked.

"Of course," I answered and gave her their number.

I was living in Denver. We agreed that she would first meet my parents, and then she and I would meet. The next day Pat called my parents and was invited to their home. On a Saturday morning, right before Pat was to leave for the prearranged visit, her mail carrier delivered the pictures I had sent of my family and me. Pat later shared how desperately she wanted to see a physical resemblance between mother and daughter and was disappointed she could see more of my birth father in me than of herself.

Pat's drive to meet my parents was a tearful one. The hurt and pain from so many years resurfaced, as the unknown loomed ahead. My parents warmly received Pat. They were as curious about her as she was about them. Mom brought out the family photo albums and Pat saw me as a baby, a child, and a teenager. My birth mother thanked my adoptive mother for loving me and raising me and doing such a wonderful job. Pat said the greatest emotion she felt while visiting my parents was gratitude. My mom was thrilled for me that I was finding my roots and that my birth mother wanted to meet me.

A few weeks later, in May of 1994, Pat and her husband traveled from New Mexico to my home in Colorado. She introduced her husband, and then he left so she and I could have some time alone. It was an emotional encounter.

We embraced, and she said, "I've longed all these years to hold you in my arms." We went inside, sat, cried, and continued to hold each other for a long time. Pat brought me a gift, a necklace with my birthstone in it. I took her into the bedroom to meet her granddaughter, who was full of baby smiles and wiggles for the grandmother she had never seen before. Together, we savored the moment. Though there wasn't a great deal of physical resemblance between us, the little girl who had studied herself in the mirror was observing gestures and body language that were remarkably similar to her own. It was enough; the missing pieces of my life were falling into place.

Pat began her story. At twenty-two, she and my birth father were going together, and she was very much in love with him. But when she told him she was pregnant, he didn't want to get married. The day she decided to tell her mother of the pregnancy, her little sister confided in Pat that she was pregnant. That evening Pat's sister and her fiancé told her mother she was pregnant and of their wedding plans. Pat lay on her bed crying as she listened to her mother yell and scream obscenities at her younger sister in the other room. During those agonizing moments, Pat made the decision to keep her own pregnancy a secret from her family.

She was sure my father would change his mind about marriage as the pregnancy progressed, but when she was about six months along and unable to conceal it any longer, she realized that marriage was not in the picture. When she told him she was going to place the baby for adoption, he didn't discourage her and seemed somewhat relieved.

Pat moved to a town a couple of hours away and lived in a small mobile home. My birth father came to check on her a few times, but she had no other contact with friends or family except by phone and letters. Then he was sent to Korea with the Air National Guard, and, except for some kindly neighbors, she was completely alone.

Her sister, who had married and moved to another state, wrote to Pat, sharing her pregnancy experiences, but Pat was unable to share her own similar experiences. She struggled with lone-liness and anger. The father of her child had let her down, and she attributed her final decision to place her child for adoption to her mother's reaction toward her younger sister's pregnancy.

The terms of the adoption agreement required that she nei-ther see nor hold her baby after the birth. After a difficult and lengthy labor, she knew only that she had given birth to a daugh-ter. Within two weeks after my birth, she returned to her par-ents' home, empty-handed and empty-hearted.

The day she got back, they received news that her sister had given birth to twin girls. The family decided that since Pat wasn't working at the time, she should accompany their mother to visit the sister and help with the babies.

One of the newborns was not as strong and healthy as the other. At the hospital, as Pat held the stronger one, she began to weep uncontrollably. Family members, puzzled at her reac-tion, tried to reassure her. "Don't worry," they said, patting her. "The baby will be fine." All Pat could think of was how unfair life was that her sister had two babies, and she had none.

She and her mother returned home, and Pat tried to resume a normal life, but the painful secret in her heart was almost more than she could bear. When my birth father returned from Korea, they resumed their relationship and became engaged, but it didn't last, and her heart was broken again as they had a final parting.

Later Pat married. Four years after my birth, and within a week of my birthday, she had another daughter and felt as if God had given her a second chance at motherhood. Every year as she celebrated my half sister's birthday, she wondered about me and prayed that I was in a good family and not being abused. Not until eight or nine years later did she finally tell her fam-ily about the daughter she had placed for adoption. Pat's own mother was horrified that Pat had not told her; they exchanged harsh words and didn't speak to each other for five years. But after Pat and I met, she went to her mother and said, "If God and my own daughter can forgive me, why can't you?" Recon-ciling, they cried and embraced and are now at peace with each other.

When my half sister was fifteen years old, Pat told her about me. She let her daughter know that if she ever became pregnant, she would not have to go through it alone; her mother would be there for her.

The Christmas after I met my birth mother, she had a "Welcome to the Family" party for Brian, Megan, and me. I met all of her family, and it was a wonderful time of reunion.

Pat and I visit each other occasionally and especially enjoy calling and e-mailing each other. When I was pregnant with Andrew, my second child, Pat and my mom gave me a baby shower at my mom's house.

I am thrilled to know my birth mother and my half sister. My husband and I and our two children are thankful they are a part of our lives. For many years Pat lived with overwhelming guilt for placing me for adoption, and I always felt as if a piece of me was missing. When we met, she thought she deserved anger or hatred. She did not expect my love and acceptance. Pat feels she will never be able to recapture what she calls the lost years, but together we are building a future that includes each other.

I have also met my birth father, and we contact each other from time to time. But I am so thankful for the father and mother who raised me, and always let me know how much they cherished their 1968 Christmas present.

This I know—I was loved when I was born; I was loved again when I was adopted. And knowing this, I wouldn't change a thing about my life.

Precious in His Sight

Robin Barrett

When I think of the words "Jesus loves the little children, all the children of the world," my heart aches. As an adult, I now believe he does love me. But throughout my childhood I saw the way people treated each other and my brothers and me. They caused so much heartache that it was impossible for me to believe Jesus loved me. One of my most vivid memories happened more than thirty years ago.

My two little brothers and I watched in horror as our father, a giant of a man, flogged the air with a pair of his heavy denim overalls. The two straps, weighted at the ends by the metal clasps, wrapped around my mother's bare skinny arms as she tried to protect herself. Blood oozed from multiple lacerations and then my mother slumped to the floor when a buckle caught her in the head, leaving a horrible gash and releasing more warm red liquid.

That scene was just one of many we witnessed until we were permanently taken from our home. I was eight, Michael was six, and Kevin was just four years old. We were the youngest of seven children. When my parents married, my dad had three children and my mom had one. We three were born to the both of them.

Until we were permanently removed from our home, we had been in and out of foster care all our lives. My alcoholic parents would get extremely violent with each other, somebody would call social services, and we were taken from our home. Then our parents would get their acts together and we would be returned. It was a torturous cycle filled with insecurity and fear. Our parents didn't physically abuse us, but they were neglectful in every other sense.

The last time we were taken, my two oldest siblings, Ronny and Ann, had already moved out. My mom's daughter, Penny, was visiting an aunt in another state and ended up being raised there. For some reason, social services let my dad's daughter, Candy, stay with my parents. I suppose social services reasoned Candy was old enough to care for herself. Social services tried for some time to get one of our relatives to take the three of us, but it never happened.

My big sister Candy had to take me shopping for a dress because I had to go to court. We went to a huge store and I remember riding the elevator. We picked out a blue A-line dress.

It had a white belt and white collar and big navy blue buttons up the front. I had to testify at the court hearing about our living conditions. I could barely tie my own shoes and I had to go before the judge so he could ask me questions about our home life. My words might have been the determining factor for our adoption.

After that court hearing, we were placed in another foster home and our names were put on a list to be adopted.

Apparently, while Kevin, Michael, and I spent a year at that foster home doing chores far beyond our capabilities and fearing the "hell" we heard about at mandatory church revivals, our aunts were pondering who should raise us. They never made up their minds. Needless to say, my aunts and our foster parents were added to the list of those hindering my belief that Jesus loved me.

I tried desperately hard to care for and comfort my little brothers during that year. Even Kevin, at four years old, was forced to do farm chores. I suppose I spent most of my childhood protecting and nurturing them the best I could.

Eventually and thankfully, a family adopted the three of us. They had an older daughter named Patti. We spent the rest of our childhoods with them.

I was old enough to understand the things that happened to me. For example, I knew I had another family somewhere. Now I had this one and a seventh sibling. It seemed I had a huge family, but yet I always felt alone and very different from everyone else. I was an orphan and my heart wouldn't let me forget it.

I continued to feel like an orphan well into my adulthood. Being taken from my parents, as violent as they were, left a festering wound that infected my whole life. I married at a young age and had two children, but my past robbed me of all joy. At one point I finally realized it was time to lance the wound—I sought help from a counselor.

Counseling didn't solve everything, but it helped immensely. More importantly, it prepared me for what was to come.

It had been eighteen years since my brothers and I were taken from our family home. So I was quite shocked to answer the phone one day and hear Penny on the other end. She and my aunt had been searching for us. Because my adoptive family was in the military, we had moved frequently and that made it difficult to be found. But they hadn't given up.

I didn't know it then, but I was about to enter a phase of life that would answer many questions and bring healing and resolution to many heartaches.

The night my aunt and sister were to arrive at our home, I paced in front of the window of my tiny living room. I was separated from my husband and single parenting our two toddlers. Time seemed to stand still as I frequently glanced down the street in front of our duplex, anxiously awaiting the reunion. Penny's call a few weeks prior had opened the door of my wounded soul. *Was I ready? What will they think of me? What if they turn around and walk back out the door and make things harder than they already are?* Just as I was about to admit I couldn't do it, they pulled into the driveway. I watched them get out of the car. They looked at each other and then toward my door. I stepped back hoping they didn't see me spying on them.

My breath was labored and my heart nearly beat out of my chest as I opened the door. Immediately, we were all crying and hugging and crying more. It was minutes before we could talk. We'd hold each other close, then pull away to get a good look and hug again. It was a relief to find that my aunt truly had wanted to care for us but she just couldn't. We talked about that and we also talked about our parents and my life since the adoption.

They shared that most of my biological family suffered from alcoholism and other chemical dependencies. It seemed my parents and aunts and uncles on both sides had severe problems, and my parents had eventually divorced. Penny had stayed in touch with our mother, and Candy had lived with our dad until she was old enough to move out on her own.

Penny and my aunt stayed with me for several nights before driving back to their home state. It was a good visit and we made plans for another.

That night, alone again except for my kids, I lay in bed thinking about all the information I'd been given. *I really was wanted. I was loved, all this time.* Penny, even though she stayed close to my parents, had had a hard time also. She suffered the consequences of our parents' alcoholism as well. For so long I'd been jealous of her, but in reality I may have been the luckier one. We were taken from our family, but we were also taken from the disease and the violence and the fear. Penny still suffered from watching our mother walk in and out of her life. I cried for her, for my brothers, for myself.

That reunion was the first of several. Penny helped me get reunited with my mother also. We were to meet at my aunt's house. This time I drove to their state. I'm not sure if it was harder to wait for their arrival or anticipate arriving there. In both cases I was a nervous wreck. I finally arrived at my destination.

It was just about time to find the answers to the questions I'd been asking myself for hours during the drive and, of course, my whole life. *Will my mother like me? What will we talk about? Should I bring up the past or act like it didn't happen? Why hadn't she quit drinking and gotten us kids?* It was definitely more frightening to meet my mom than it had been to meet my sister.

The initial minutes were much like the first reunion—lots of hugging and crying. Looking at my mom, I could see alcoholism had taken its toll on her. She seemed fragile and in poorer health than I remembered. I wanted to be mad at my mom for all I'd been through because of her and my dad, but I couldn't. Somehow, deep inside me my spirit wouldn't let me. I felt sorry for her. She readily admitted she was an alcoholic and told me she would drink until the day she died. I didn't like the declaration, but I was thankful for her honesty.

I finally had the courage to ask her why she hadn't stopped drinking so we kids could come home. Her answer surprised me. I studied her face as a confused and tortured look came over her. Her distant gaze told me she was in another time.

She winced as she started: "I fell and hurt my back real bad. I couldn't get up, it hurt so bad. Your daddy hurt me more when he picked me up but he took me to the hospital." Tears fell slowly. Her cheek skin looked paper thin, smooth but translucent. "My back was broken. I was in so much pain. Your daddy brought me a drink and it helped some." She nervously fingered the wedding band she wore on her other hand. "They say

I went crazy," she started again. "I went back to the hospital but this time I told the doctor everything."

The memory of my mother collapsing on the floor right before me flashed in my mind. She had been clawing at her head and sobbing. She'd had a nervous breakdown. Her voice brought me back, "I told them everything . . . drinking, fighting, losing my kids. The doctor wanted to help me and I wanted his help. But it never worked. Your daddy knew just when to bring me a drink. I couldn't do it."

Talking with my mom helped me understand just how bad for each other she and my dad were. The reunion was not as I had dreamed, but it was what we both needed. We were honest with each other about our feelings and thoughts. I was able to tell her I loved her and wanted to continue to see her but on one condition. She accepted my condition that she had to be sober to visit with my children and me. And when she is sober, we are very close.

My mom helped me find my sister Candy. And Candy took me to see my father. He didn't know I was coming, but I could tell he recognized me instantly. After all, Candy and I looked much alike.

All the way to his hospital room I had convinced myself I was still mad at him. For years I had harbored anger at the huge man who wasn't bigger than his alcoholism. He was supposed to care for us and protect us. He was supposed to be the head of our household and make sure we stayed together as a family. Instead, we were a broken family, mentally, physically, and spiritually.

But I wasn't mad anymore. I couldn't speak either. I just stood there looking at the man who fathered me, frightened me, and failed to be a man of God.

My white knuckles gripped the side rail of the hospital bed as I stood there and cried. Trying not to think about the past, I looked upon the frail man before me. Tubes connected him to hanging bags and monitors beeped the sound of life, his life. *He doesn't look so big anymore.* His heart was giving up on him after all the years he had neglected everything but alcohol. My tears continued to fall.

"The gold dust twins," he spoke first and used the nickname he'd given Candy and me when we were still very young. It brought back a happy memory and I sobbed more. The last bit of hatred in my heart disappeared there in the hospital room. I felt at peace.

My father was in ICU so we could only visit for about ten minutes. I told him I'd come see him when he got out of the hospital, but I never did. He died a few years ago. I have no regrets, though, because those precious minutes were all I needed for resolution. I found I no longer had a place in his life, but I could tell I still had a place in his heart.

I was recently reunited with my older brother who is now in his fifties. He had always fussed over me when I was a little girl and I remember always bragging about my "big brother." He recognized and remembered me when we finally met again and he just sat in his chair and cried.

I haven't seen my oldest sister Ann, but I expect it's possible I will someday. I've stayed close with my little brothers. It's sad though. They have a lot of issues also and have dealt with them differently than I have.

I continue to be amazed at the instant connection I made with each family member. We bonded, but there is still a sense of self-protection. I imagine the walls will dissolve with time.

I look most like Candy. Our hair and face shape are exactly alike. I also laugh like her. My daughter looks like her Aunt Penny. My physique resembles my dad's side of the family. Ronny and I have the same eyes and even the same wrinkle across the bridges of our noses. My teeth are just like Penny's, Michael's, and Candy's. It did my heart good to find out these details.

I can't imagine how difficult it is to decide between parenting and adoption. But I know one thing from experience: It takes a loving parent to honestly admit, "I can't do it." A loving parent puts the needs of the child first. I also know that there are emotionally healthy, loving married couples who want nothing more than to raise children. But the only way they can is through the loving choice of adoption.

Over the years, I've often wanted my horrible life to be over. But one thing kept me going: "Jesus loves the little children, all the children of the world." I desperately wanted to believe he loved me. Once, I believed it enough to ask him into my heart. I now know Jesus was the one that kept me hanging on. Now my life, with Jesus at the center, feels complete.

In Everything There Is a Gift

Judy Sabah

I knew I was pregnant when I woke up that morning. It was a Sunday in December 1965.

The previous evening I had been on a date with Raymond. I had met him through my good friends Carol and Irvin. He and I had gone out together several times but what happened between us on that Saturday night wasn't planned.

Just divorced in November, I was single parenting three children ages two, three, and four and living in Kansas. When my inklings that I was pregnant were confirmed, my thoughts centered on how I would handle the situation. I felt it would be very hard to go through this experience in my small town.

So, I began making preparations for a move to Colorado since my father and some relatives lived there. My parents had divorced when I was five and I hardly knew my father, but I figured the move was the right decision under the circumstances.

I quit my job, stored the majority of my furniture with Carol and Irvin, and left for Colorado in March 1966 with my children. I put boxes on the floorboard of the backseat and covered the seat and boxes with quilts, blankets, and pillows so Jeff, Renee, and Harvey could sleep during the drive. I filled the trunk and the front passenger seat with as much as I could pack in. Besides our belongings, I had fifty dollars.

The only people who knew of my pregnancy were Carol and Irvin. When we got to Colorado I called my dad and told him our plans.

We arrived and that evening I told him the real reason I had moved to Colorado. The next morning we found a small furnished apartment, rented it, and put all my worldly possessions inside. Later that day, I went to see my former brother-in-law. I needed his help to find a job and he worked as a meat cutter at a local grocery store. He spoke with his manager about me becoming a checker and after an interview I was hired. Everything seemed to be going smoothly and quickly.

My children and I began settling into our new apartment. That Sunday after church, we went to visit my aunt and uncle. As we drove up in front of their house, my cousin came running out to tell me I had a phone call.

A cousin from Kansas was calling to tell me my mother had had serious complications from a routine operation. She was in a coma.

My uncle and I talked about what I should do. I was scheduled to start my new job the next morning. Another phone call revealed that my mother was seriously ill.

I quickly prepared to drive back to Kansas. My former in-laws kept my youngest son, Harvey. Taking Renee and Jeff with me, I drove most of the night, arriving there about four in the morning. We stopped at my aunt's house where several cousins were waiting for me. I was so happy to be off the road until they informed me my mother had passed away at 11:00.

The following several days were spent making preparations for the funeral. I thought about how hard it must have been on my mom to see me leave with her grandchildren. I was her only child and we meant so much to her. I had been the center of my mom's life ever since my parents' divorce. She hadn't even known I was pregnant.

After the funeral I returned to Colorado and started my new job the following morning. My life was a whirlwind and I hardly had time to think about my situation. So many changes had occurred in such a short time.

In early May the manager observed my changing shape and suspected I was pregnant. He asked my brother-in-law to ask me. I confirmed their suspicion and was released from my job. This was a time when women did not work while pregnant.

The next day I told my aunt about my situation. She worked at a nursing home and because I had worked in nursing homes in the past, she was able to help me get a job. My salary was cut in half.

In June a rather extraordinary thing happened. My former mother-in-law, Helen, who lived in Kansas, had a dream. In the dream she saw her daughter lying in a pool of blood. She felt strongly something was going on in Colorado, and she came to see what it was. It was then she found out about my pregnancy. We had always had a very close relationship and I was like a daughter to her. She felt the "daughter" she saw in the dream was me. She offered to take Jeff and Renee for the summer so I could take care of all the details for the baby's arrival, so Jeff and Renee returned to Kansas with her.

The doctor I was seeing was sympathetic to my circumstances. He told me as soon as he felt the baby was developed enough, he would induce labor. Three weeks before my due date, I gave birth to a beautiful baby girl. It was August 19, 1966.

Throughout my pregnancy I had thought about what I should do. As I considered my three children and this new baby, I knew the best decision was to give her up for adoption. The department of social services in Boulder County handled the adoption. In their policy, the birth mother wasn't allowed to see her baby. But when I begged my doctor to let me see her, he consented and the nurse held her up for me to see for about thirty seconds. That image of her is etched in my memory.

I knew this was the best decision I could make for myself, and for all my children.

I went on with my life.

Twenty-two years later, in January 1989, my daughter Renee came to me with a question: "Mom, I'd like to find my sister. What do you think?"

Finding my daughter had never occurred to me. In 1966, when I was working with social services in placing my baby, they made it very clear to me that my decision was one I could never change. I remember them telling me in a number of different ways that this was a final decision. I had never considered I might see my daughter again. I'm sure as time went on I might have realized the possibility since dramatic changes in adoption laws have occurred in recent years. Now birth parents being reunited with their children is a common experience.

I said to Renee, "I think it's a wonderful idea. I'm glad you want to do this."

She began her search. She didn't share many details with me, but she did tell me about her involvement with two groups—Adoptees In Search and Concerned United Birth Parents. In late April she told me she felt she was getting closer.

On May 16, the Monday following Mother's Day, Renee called: "Mom, I've found her. You'll love her. Her name is Calla and she wants to meet you. We'd like to come see you this afternoon at 4:00."

As the day passed, I wondered how I would greet the child I'd only seen for thirty seconds. But as Renee and Calla rode up the elevator of our high-rise apartment building, the answer came to me. When they stepped out of the elevator I stretched out my arms, and Calla came right into them. That moment is also etched in my memory.

We came into our apartment and talked. Some of the conversation was about the similarities Renee and Calla noticed about each other. What a gift this reunion was—a gift for everyone.

Calla had begun her own search the previous summer. She had placed an ad in the personal section of the newspaper in Longmont, Colorado, where she was born. Her plans were to join the group Adoptees In Search the following summer.

Calla also wanted to meet her birth father. We were able to get a message to him through Irvin in Kansas.

Raymond expressed a desire to meet Calla also, but when she didn't hear from Raymond, Calla again contacted Irvin. Three weeks after he expressed a desire to meet his birth daughter, Raymond had been working under his car when the car fell on him and he was killed.

Today I'm approaching my sixtieth birthday as well as the twelfth anniversary of my reunion with Calla.

Since then, both of Calla's families have been together for wonderful reunions and celebrations, including Calla's graduation from CU in Boulder and her marriage to Todd. We've also celebrated the birth of their first son, Tyler, born May 19, 1998.

Todd and I have a wonderful connection between us. We have spent lots of time talking and being together. I'm proud to say I have a wonderful son-in-law.

Amazing events have occurred in my life since 1965. Over those years, I have developed a philosophy I use in my life every day: In everything there is a gift. We must hold the thought that the gifts will eventually show themselves. As I look for the gifts in life, I find them. I am so grateful for all the ways in which my life has been blessed.

A Phone Call Away

Cindy Lambert

Is it really possible? I have two sisters? Both older than me? I'm thirty-seven years old and never knew I had sisters? How can that be? But there it was in black and white. That one piece of nonidentifying information alone was enough to make me want to pursue my search.

After the agency found my birth mother, she was very willing to share medical information and hear about me. But she didn't want to meet. However, she did agree to receive a letter from me. It was nine pages long. At first she told the agency she would respond. We gave her a long time to do so. Then she changed her mind and said she wouldn't be writing back. By then, several more months had passed. I had known for almost a year now that I had sisters and felt I couldn't quit now.

So I decided to pursue looking for my birth father. The first person I was working with from the agency had moved out of state, so I had to deal with a different intermediary. She wasn't as eager to help. However, at that same time, they were assisting a woman from Pennsylvania, also adopted through their agency. She had the same birth family name as I did. They thought that was strange since the name was so unusual.

The agency then realized we were first cousins who "just happened" to be looking for our birth families at the exact same time. Coincidence? I believe God had his hand in it. They put us in touch with each other—something they now probably wished they hadn't done. By doing so, over a period of a few short months, we were able to put the complete puzzle together—minus one piece. I still don't know the identity of my birth father.

My family and I went to Pennsylvania to visit my birth cousin and her family. I had known the location of my siblings for some time but had been afraid to contact them. My family kept trying to convince me to make the call. After much discussion, my cousin made the call for me. To say I was a nervous wreck would be an understatement. My heart was beating so hard and fast I could hardly breathe. Then my cousin said into the phone, "So you've been trying to find out for about ten years if you had another sibling?" I started to cry. She handed the phone to me. And for the first time in my life, I was saying hello to one of my sisters. It was Good Friday.

We both cried and laughed for the next hour or so. How could two people who didn't know each other talk so much? Believe me, we didn't have a problem. Before we hung up, we had agreed to meet sometime after I got back home. All this time my sisters had been living only an hour from my home.

Later that night, my other sister called me. The tears started all over again. By the end of that conversation, we had decided to meet on Sunday at 5:00 P.M. It would be Easter. How appropriate.

The anticipation was maddening. I wanted it to be 5:00 P.M. on Easter Sunday right now! On the plane ride back home to Philadelphia, my mind was a whirlwind. It bounced between fear and excitement, fear and happiness, fear and shock. Did I mention fear? What if they didn't like me? What if they changed their minds? What if, after meeting me, they decided they didn't want to pursue a relationship? What if? What if? What if? The unknown is always hard to deal with.

The day finally came! I arrived at the restaurant before they did. As I stood by the front door, my heart felt like it was in my throat. And then I saw them. They looked much different from the pictures I had found in their school yearbook while I was searching for them. But I knew it was them. One of them looked a lot like me. The other had my smile. What a strange feeling. These were my sisters!

They walked in and we threw our arms around each other and cried again! We talked and talked. We wanted to hear each other's whole story. Our birth mom had raised them, so they shared details about her and growing up. We shared photos of each of our families and we took new pictures. It was obvious none of us wanted the evening to end. The restaurant had closed long before we finally said our good-byes. But do you know the best part? It wasn't really good-bye.

It was "see you later . . . soon." What a happy Easter indeed!

Part 15

The Greatest Gift

Adopted Kids Say Thank You

Batter Up

Linda Cravens

How can one say thank you to a couple who took in a skinny, cross-eyed ragamuffin? Because my biological father was related to my adoptive mother, I always knew who he was. However, when anyone asks who my parents are, I reply without hesitation, "Mae and Bill Enlow." They are Mom and Dad to me. The person that I am today is largely a reflection of them, especially Mom.

Mom is one of those people who draw children like the Pied Piper. She has that magical quality of knowing what children want and need. She carries mints and gum in her purse as well as tissues and wet wipes, and no one gives warmer, more heartfelt hugs.

When I was younger, she never seemed to get flustered. She ruled her home with love and orderliness. Perhaps that's why I remember this incident so well, even though I was only four years old.

Mom answered the knock at the door expecting a salesman or the Avon lady. The man handed her a card stating that he was from the Child Welfare Department. Mom stared at the man in his dark business suit and conservative tie. She anxiously thought of my condition at that moment.

I sat on the polished kitchen floor with a large bath towel fastened around my neck with a clothespin. In my lap rested a bowl in which Mom had mixed chocolate cake batter. In my hand I held a large batter-laden spoon. Chocolate cake batter decorated the towel as well as my hands, face, and hair.

Mom wet a washcloth and began cleaning me up. As she scrubbed my face and hands, she apologized for my appearance. I saw no need for an apology and frowned at the man who had upset her.

"No need to apologize," the man replied. "If I had found her in a frilly dress sitting on the couch, I would be concerned. She looks very happy."

After an encouraging nod from Mom, I allowed him to take me to the living room without her. He asked me a lot of strange questions. I wondered how he could imagine I could be unhappy with a mom who let me lick the bowl as much as I wanted. I couldn't understand why he thought the milkman might have any reason to leave the kitchen. However, I eagerly showed him the toy the milkman gave me (a cardboard game provided by the dairy company). He seemed satisfied with my answers.

I noticed Mom hovering in the hallway between the kitchen and the living room. The man smiled at her and assured her that everything was fine. She must have met his expectations. When Mom and Dad adopted my brother and sister, Child Welfare didn't even bother to come to the house again.

These days, I am a mother myself. I don't bake chocolate cakes as often as Mom did. However, every time I mix a cake, I lick the spoon and remember that chocolate batter day with Mom.

My Tribute

William D. Watkins

The supreme happiness of life is the conviction that we are loved.

Victor Hugo

Adultery. Rejection. That's how my life began.

My biological mother had an affair while her husband was fighting in the Korean War. She got pregnant.

So she wrote to her husband overseas, confessed her adultery, and told him of me growing in her womb. He wrote her back, telling her that he would still accept her but not me. He didn't want a child not his own. Her options were stay wed or become a single mother.

What was she going to do now? Keep me and raise me on her own? Locate a doctor who would end my life in her womb? Take me to an orphanage or abandon me in a dumpster?

After heart-wrenching consideration, she decided to carry me to term and place me for adoption. She chose to give me life and an opportunity to live my life with people who wanted me and would love me. She, of course, wanted me too, but if she was going to save her marriage, she had to let me go.

In September 1952, Bill and Margaret Watkins had known for quite some time that they were unable to have children of their own. Margaret had already had two miscarriages, and the prospects of her carrying a child to term were bleak. Bill was in his last year of veterinary school at the University of California, Davis. A former WWII Air Force pilot, he was attending school with the help of the GI Bill and had a dedicated wife who worked full-time in the plant pathology labs on the university campus. They were deeply in love, and they wanted to raise a family. So, two years before I was born, they started the lengthy adoption process.

On September 22, they received a call from the adoption agency that a child—me—was now available to them. Bill and Margaret jumped at the opportunity. Margaret gave notice to her boss that she would be leaving her job to become a full-time mother. And Bill, now anticipating becoming a father, was more determined than ever to finish successfully the last several months of his education so he could secure a career that would support his family.

My parents tell me that when they saw me at the hospital in Sacramento for the very first time, they were speechless. They just stared at me, overwhelmed that they finally had a child they could call their own. After they left the hospital and stepped into their parked car, they remained in silence for a long time. Then my dad spoke: "Have you ever in your life seen such well-formed and sweet little hands?"

"No," my mom answered. "I thought his eyes were shaped beautifully. So were his bluish-tinted eyelids and tiny fingernails."

More silence went by, until Dad broke it again: "Did you happen to notice that he had a rather large nose?"

"Yes."

"But I have a large nose too," he observed.

Again they were silent.

My parents were hooked. Love had them in its grip, and their love for me would be demonstrated in countless ways daily from that moment on.

Only love could have seen them through the years that followed.

During my first year of postwomb life, I awoke on the hour every hour twenty-four hours a day and took one ounce of milk. I had all sorts of allergies and illnesses and required a good deal of medical care and parental attention. Even before my parents could bring me home from the hospital for the first time, my weight dropped considerably below my birth weight. I had to stay in the hospital a couple more days so doctors could get me to regain a pound.

When I asked my mom how she felt during what I would have regarded as a trying first year, her answer amazed me: "I loved every minute of it. Holding you, caring for you, feeding you . . . I rocked you and studied your every feature—your deep blue eyes, your cute nose, your tiny fingers, everything. You were God's answer to my prayers. One night when I was so despairing of not having a child, God gave me a peace about it, letting me know that it would be better than I could ever imagine. He was right. Almost a year later, he brought me you, and my life has been so much better than I ever dreamed it would."

Along with being a sick little kid, when I finally learned how to talk, most of my talk came in the form of what and why questions. I was curious about everything—colors and shapes, clothing and hairstyles, the ways people behaved and what they believed, television shows and movies, animals of all sorts and sizes, buildings and what people did in them, signs and colors and what they meant. Nothing escaped my hunger to learn. And my parents did everything they could to feed my craving, piling answers upon answers on top of my questions.

My growing-up years were full. My parents believed that idle hands were hands that would eventually find mischief. So they gave me plenty to do: swimming lessons, extra homework they would assign and grade, trips to some of the places I was studying in school (such as several of the old Spanish California missions and the La Brea tar pits and museum that display dinosaur remains), chores in our house and yard, music lessons, YMCA basketball, summer school, lots of visits to the local library, plenty of involvement in church activities, subscriptions to *National Geographic* and *Life* magazines, and an entire *World Book Encyclopedia* set so I could further expand my knowledge of the world. My parents also invited people over to the house who had interests I shared.

While growing up I always knew I was adopted. My parents never hid that fact from me. In fact, they used it to affirm that I was loved by choice. "Billy," they would tell me, "we asked God for you, and he answered our prayers. He loved you before we even knew you, and we loved you from the first moment we saw you. He brought you into our lives as a loving gift, and we have loved you ever since. You were put up for adoption—that makes you special. Your natural mother loved you enough to bring you into this world and make you available to us. You are our child, and we will always love you, no matter what."

They also told me that I could ask them anything I wanted to about my birth mother. Over the years, I have asked them several questions, and they have always answered without hesitation and to my satisfaction.

But I have never felt a need or desire to search out my natural mother. I harbor no ill will toward her. On the contrary, I'm deeply grateful that she gave me life when she could have ended it. I have lived nearly five decades now, and, though like all lives, mine has had its share of struggles and hurts, all in all it has been a life buoyed by grace and love. I could not have experienced any of it if my natural mother had not chosen life for me.

I'm even more grateful, however, that she opted for adoption, and that the Lord of life provided Bill and Margaret to be my parents. This is why I don't need to find my natural mother. I know who my mother and father are. They are the ones who adopted me, who raised me, who answered so many of my questions, who fed and clothed me, who nursed me back to health so often, who provided for my education, who taught me about God and his ways. They are also the ones who adopted two more children from birth while I was growing up: a brother named John and a sister named Carol. This adopted threesome played together, fought each other, and learned about family and the rest of life together. Most importantly, we experienced the riches of parental love lavished on us. Our parents—Dr. William Wallace Watkins, taken by cancer in 1990, and Martha Margaret Combs Watkins, my father's wife for forty-five years before his death, sacrificed for us and loved us, just as they promised, unconditionally and faithfully.

Mom still talks to me and looks at me as if she had received no greater gift during her lifetime. (She does the same with Carol and John.) As she told me, "Bill, never forget that you are not flesh of my flesh nor bone of my bone, but you are miraculously my own. You were not born under my heart but *in* my heart."

Thank you, Mom and Dad.

No child has been loved by choice more.

Orphan Train Rider

Stanley B. Cornell

My father fought in Europe during World War I. After being shell-shocked, gassed, and wounded they sent him home to Elmira, New York, in 1918. He could only work part-time at a General Motors assembly plant because every two months he would have to go to the Veterans' hospital to recuperate.

I don't know if my mother and daddy were sweethearts before he left for the war or if they met and married after his return. I was born in 1920, and sixteen months later my brother Victor came along.

We called our parents Daddy Floyd and Mother Lottie. I was four years old when Victor and I stood by Mother Lottie's bed and watched her die after giving birth to our baby sister.

In the 1920s New York had a state law that said if only one parent is left to take care of the children, he or she had to make a certain amount of money per child to raise them or the state would put them in the Orphans' Home. And since Daddy Floyd didn't make the required amount, he had to let the Children's Society come and take us to our "new home." Our baby sister was adopted by Daddy Floyd's sister.

I was only four and brother Vic was three, but I can still remember the big black limousine that came to pick us up. We were asked to sit in the backseat next to the lady supervisor. As we drove away I saw my Daddy Floyd holding on to the porch for support, crying into his handkerchief.

We were put in the New York Brace Farm School for Boys. About five hundred kids lived in three large barrack type buildings.

Victor and I were put in adjoining barracks with a wire fence separating us. The only way we could talk was to go to the fence and wait for the other one to show up at noon recess. We would talk and cry until the bell sounded. Vic would cry a lot because he was lonesome. It made me feel bad that I couldn't be closer to my brother.

One day he had a bloody scar above his eye and I asked him how that came about. He said, "Last night I got into a bully's sleeping spot and he kicked me." With several hundred children on both sides of the fence, I saw fights almost every day.

Our living conditions left a lot to be desired. We were so cold in the winter months and hungry every night when we went to sleep on the floor or, if we were lucky, on a cot. When we begged and cried for food, the attendants would tell us to shut up. If we didn't, we'd get whacked across the face, sometimes being knocked to the floor.

I have a lot of bad memories of being confined in that small area for two years with some mean-spirited workers. One time another boy and I spied some red apples in the back corner of the enclosed yard. The grass and weeds were at least two feet high, so we decided to crawl on our tummies out to the tree and eat some apples. We got to the tree, picked up five or six that had fallen to the ground, and started making our way back when one of the attendants spotted us. He picked us up by the seat of our britches and carried us to the front of the porch. There on the porch was a very large older man sitting in a rocking chair with a bullwhip, the kind that stagecoach drivers would use on their horses.

They drew a circle on the wall in chalk. We had to keep our nose in the circle by standing on our tiptoes. If we let down, we'd get whacked across the back and legs. From that punishment we both were quite bloody. I can still feel that awful pain to this day. After that I didn't care for apples for a long, long time.

After two years of living in the orphanage they put Victor and me on a train headed due west. We felt better being together on the train.

The train stopped about every hour to allow us to file off the coach and stand beside it. Men and women would walk by and look us over. The train would only stop at the smallest towns and usually at farming areas. Those of us who were not taken would get back on the train and off it would go to the next small town.

At noontime as we were marched back on the train, one of the attendants would hand us a sandwich and usually an apple to eat before we had to go through the same routine at the forthcoming town.

The soot coming from the engine was dirty and made it hard to breathe at times. I now know why we had to have so many face washings every day before we stepped down from the coach.

Vic and I were taken in by a Kansas family. It was wonderful to have the whole outdoors around us after being cooped up in the orphanage and the train. Our chore was to spend hours picking strawberries, although Vic ate more than he put in his bucket.

I can't say for sure why they decided to send us back after four months. It could have had something to do with those years where we had to fight for every crumb of food and inch of sleeping space. We were probably rough on their young children.

In December of 1927, Vic and I were put on another train together. This one had twice as many kids. On December 10, we found ourselves in Wellington, Texas. It was too cold for the farmers to "inspect" us by the side of the train, so we were marched about six blocks to the Wellington Hotel and formed circles in the lobby.

A farmer had come to town to buy groceries, heard about us orphan train riders, and walked over to check out the commotion.

He asked me, "How would you like to live with us? You'd have lots of room to run and play. Do you like horses, cows, and chickens? How about dogs?"

He only wanted to take one of us home, but we held onto each other and cried. Our chaperone asked if he could take the two of us as we had been through a lot of tough years. He said okay, took us to the table, and signed "Deger" across the dotted line.

Then he bought Vic and me a bag of jelly beans and put us in his Model T Ford. There was no heat in the Model T, so he threw a wool blanket over us and drove eighteen miles north to our new home on the farm.

He pulled the car in front of the house and went inside. While his wife and two daughters came outside to get the groceries, he watched through the window to see what would take place.

His wife was startled and jumped back because of our movement under the blanket. I was counting out the jelly beans, saying, "One you take and one for me."

They picked us up, carried us into the house, and warmed us by the potbellied stove. Our new sisters, Thelma age fourteen and Leona age eleven, talked us to shreds. Then they had us sing two or three songs, not because we were a good singing duet but because they liked to hear our New York Yankee brogue.

I was six and a half and Vic was five when we came to live with Mom and Dad Deger. We felt like we were in heaven with a bedroom all to ourselves, plenty of food, and clothes to wear. Mom was short and round in stature but long in the giving of love and understanding. She was very sensitive to everything around her. She gave us lots of love and a spanking once in a while when we needed it.

The summer I was eleven we started sleeping outside at night. It was too hot in the house with temps of 105 or more. We took our mattress and pillows outside and enjoyed the great outdoors.

Our sisters, Thel and Leona, would come out to our retreat and talk to us about our orphan days and tell us stories and jokes. After the girls went to the house to go to bed, I'd lie awake and look up at the diamond-studded sky, thinking how lucky Vic and I were to have a real family made of love.

On Saturday afternoons Dad would drive us to Wellington where he'd give Vic and me each fifteen cents to spend. Ten cents would go for a ticket to the movies and five cents would buy us a Coke or popcorn to munch on. It was always a treat and a day to look forward to—Saturdays!

Mom and Dad took us to Sunday school and church every week and also to Sunday night youth meetings. All was going along very well at our new home. Then about three years later people would say things such as, "Guess you know why the Degers took you and your brother—don't you? They only wanted you to work the farm and do the chores for them." But nothing could be farther from the truth. What they did was to open up their big hearts and allow us to come in. Vic and I put that idea out of our minds very quickly too.

Of course we did have to work, but so did my two sisters as well as Mom and Dad. In the thirties everybody worked to keep body and soul together. That's what made our home life so beautiful—we worked together.

When I was drafted into the army the only official paper that could be found was the one Dad Deger had signed when he took us off the train. Dad and Mom insisted that they had signed another paper making them our legal adoptive parents.

Since the paper could not be found the county clerk put my name down as Cornell instead of Deger and said we had never been legally adopted. I was willing to have my name changed to Deger, but the only judge around was on vacation and I had to report to Dallas in two days. I know having a different name hurt Mom and Dad a lot.

They wrote me letters when I was overseas, stressing they loved us just as much—no matter what our last name was.

During the war my captain helped me find my biological father by asking J. Edgar Hoover with the FBI to look into it. Because I had always called my father Daddy Floyd, they were able to locate him. We corresponded by letter and phone until our company boarded a ship for Africa. In 1942 we invaded North Africa, then Sicily, then Southern France, and across the Rhine River into Germany. After the war I met Daddy Floyd and we stayed in contact for years.

Mom and Dad Deger have always been my beloved parents, for they gave me a new beginning in life. They were always there for Vic and me when we needed clothing, shelter, food, and most of all love. They both have graduated from this earthly life to one much better, and I hope someday to be reunited with them.

"All is well," as I now have all the answers to my questions I had for these many years. In 2001, at age eighty-one, I learned the truth. Mom and Dad Deger did indeed legally adopt Vic and me on July 19, 1927.

Daddy's Little Girl

Christina Barrett

It has been almost a decade since my biological parents went through their divorce. In today's society, the word divorce is looked upon as a horrible epithet—something that tears families apart and causes pain and heartache. At the time of the divorce I was upset and sad, like most people, but as my life progressed, I realized God's plan for me had to be something very special.

I know it was hard on my mom to raise my brother and me. My mom, however, is a strong, courageous person who always taught my brother and me to look for the good things in life. Although that is true, I had a hard time thinking of positive things about being a girl without her father. I envied my friends who got to do things with their fathers because I wanted that so badly. I missed my dad and everything he had been before the divorce.

Finally, I worked up the courage to ask my mom if I could see my dad. I thought if I took the initiative and started going to his house that maybe we could have a relationship like my friends and their dads had. As I matured, however, I noticed something was missing. I became less and less eager to see him.

This entire ordeal was hard on my mom, but sometimes I think it was even harder on me. I would cry, thinking that it was my fault that things were the way they were. I would get angry with myself for allowing my heart and mind to project these fantasy images of a flawless family. Before long this burden became too much for me to handle. The emptiness I felt finally overwhelmed me. I thought that I would have to go through this time alone, but I didn't. God heard my prayers.

I remember when my mom told my brother and me she had met someone. We were so happy for her. She had done such a great job with us, but my prayer for her was that someone would take care of her for a change.

I answered the door the night of my mom's first date. I invited a tall, well-dressed man into our living room and I watched him sit down. Being curious about who he was, I sat in a chair across the room and looked him up and down. Looking back on this incident, I laugh, but at the time I was serious. I wanted to make sure he was good enough for my mom. The entire time he waited, I just stared at him. By the time my mom was ready, I had decided he would do.

This night would be the first of many happy nights for my mom and our family. My prayers were being answered. It wasn't long before I knew this man would complete our family and fill a void in each of our lives.

I was so happy and I liked him so much that, while they were still dating, I volunteered him to go on a field trip with my school class. We were going to the capitol building and my teacher informed us that we needed more chaperones. She also said that if we did not get enough chaperones, we might not get to go on the field trip. I didn't know about the rest of my classmates, but I was excited about going on this field trip and I didn't want something like this to ruin it. I figured that my mom's boyfriend, Brad, wouldn't mind walking around the capitol building with a bunch of fourth graders.

When I got home I was eager to tell my mom what I had done. She then told me that I shouldn't have done that and that I should have asked Brad first. I was very nervous to approach Brad after my mom had dampened my enthusiasm. But he agreed to go, and in that moment I realized he would make a great dad. After all, not many men would be excited to spend the day with thirty preteens.

After a few years of dating, Brad asked my mom to marry him and she said yes. I was so happy for her. Yet, even after this great event, there would also be another one.

I took it upon myself to ask Brad to adopt me. Many stories of adoption are quite different from mine. Usually the parents are the ones who choose to adopt, not the child. I however was given that chance. It's been a smooth and natural transition for our family, and more so since I learned my own mom was also adopted.

To start the process, I wrote a letter to Brad and told him why I wanted him to adopt me. In the letter I shared my definition of a dad. To me, a dad is a man who takes responsibility for a child, loves them, cares for them, *and* goes on field trips with them. For a long time now, he had been providing for me and loving me as if I were his own. Because of that, I wanted to make it official. I had thought of him as a dad ever since that field trip and now I was being blessed with having it authorized.

During this time, my mom and Brad met with lawyers and made court appearances. I also had to go before the judge to be questioned. I wasn't scared though, because this was a true blessing. My parents worked together to accomplish what they thought was best for me.

Once again, I am 100 percent "daddy's little girl." We do all the stuff I had longed for when I was younger. The emptiness I had once felt is gone and it's replaced with happy experiences and new memories.

My life has not been easy. But if someone would give me the opportunity to go back and change the tough times, I wouldn't. I am who I am today because of the events and challenges in my life. I have a family that most people can only wish for.

I am a living example of a successful adoption. Besides unconditional love as obvious evidence, my adoption proves successful because nobody would guess he isn't my biological dad. In our home and outside it, he is my dad and I am his daughter. But I'm very proud of one important fact—he didn't adopt me; I adopted him!

Doubly Grateful

Donna Davidsen

I don't remember ever not knowing I was adopted. My siblings and I grew up with this knowledge and it was just a part of who we all were. I do remember when one of my brothers figured out what it meant to be adopted. I'll always admire my parents for the explanation they gave to my brother and for the affirmation each explanation gave me.

Sitting us all down, our parents explained to my brother about his adoption: "Your birth mother loved you so much she realized she could not take care of you the way you deserved to be cared for. It took a lot of courage for her to admit that to herself. She felt there must be a loving family who could give you a happy and stable home. It must have been the most difficult decision she ever had to make. We are grateful to her and so blessed to have you as part of our family."

My parents loved being a mom and dad and they let each of us know that they were ecstatic to be our parents. They showed it in the big things and the little things—family vacations, Sunday Mass followed by a family brunch, a day on the boat, a kiss good night.

From an early age, I felt I was special, wanted, and loved. My life has been blessed with many relationships that allow me to still feel that way today. For all of this I have my birth mother to thank—she gave me life, thereby allowing me to receive all these gifts.

Now, as an adult, adoption has touched my life again. After a struggle with infertility, my husband and I also turned to adoption to have children of our own. I resisted making the leap from infertility to adoption because, for the first time in my life, I realized I would never see anyone who looked like me.

That was important to me, at first. But with time, a large amount of support from my husband, family, and friends, and a lot of prayer, I realized only God could make a perfect family. I knew he knew what child was meant to be with us.

Through open adoption, we have been blessed with the most beautiful boy I could ever imagine. I feel so incredibly privileged to be his mom. My husband feels lucky to be his dad, and we both know that our son was meant to be with us. Our prayer is that his birth mother will understand that we see him as a treasured gift.

The circle of our family is not yet closed; we are waiting to adopt our second child. Again, I am struggling with God's will and timing. We've been close to receiving a baby only to have the birth mom change her mind. But we trust God knows what is best for those children and we wouldn't want it any other way. We know from experience, when we do get to hold our baby in our arms, it will all make sense.

My hope for our children is that they will love their birth stories as much as I have loved mine. I have wonderful role models for sharing the special meaning of adoption. I can only hope to express it as lovingly as my parents did. Every opportunity I get I will share with my children about their special start in life. And I know, as our children grow, they will cultivate their own stories. We will do everything we can to provide the children with joy so their stories will be happy ones. We make that promise to their birth moms—thank you for your precious gift.

Full Circle

Leisa Krueger

Our home was a fun place to grow up. My parents had a way of making us feel excited about packing another foster child into our three-bedroom home. They taught us at an early age to think of others more than ourselves. I learned this lesson best by observing how unselfishly Mom and Dad served others.

My parents cared for many foster children throughout my entire childhood. My little brother even tried to convince me that babies came from social workers. At times we begged our parents to adopt them too. One Christmas three young siblings unexpectedly ended up in our home. It was my best Christmas ever because Mom and Dad encouraged us to focus on blessing them in every way we could.

As much as my parents loved us, there were times I felt inferior when children laughed at my siblings and me, and told us we weren't wanted because we were adopted. Adults could be just as insensitive. I hated hearing people say, "Is this your adopted daughter?" My mother and father loved me and took care of me, so that makes me their child. No extra adjectives are needed to describe our relationship.

When I was twenty-seven the laws changed and I was able to find more information about my adoption. I was content with being adopted, but had always been curious. When I was young I would look at people and wonder if they were my birth father or mother, imagining what they might look like.

Looking back I could have been more sensitive to my parents in how I handled my curiosity and search for my birth mother. At times they were hurt by my obsessing about where I came from. But they never interfered with my pursuits. They patiently waited for me to work through all the heart issues that overtook my affections during that season of my life.

When I met my birth mother it was an emotional reunion. After we became more familiar with one another she asked me to call her "Mother," but I can't do it. I feel it would be a betrayal of my mom, because she is the only one who deserves that title. Not long after the reunion, I had a great talk with my mom, and asked her forgiveness for not being more sensitive to her own insecurities.

My relationship with my birth mother is confusing. She seems to have unreal expectations of me. I am glad we did not meet until after I was an older adult. Whenever I tell Mom and Dad about another upsetting visit with my birth mother they encourage me to respond to her with kindness. They continually remind me that God allowed us to be reunited so I can demonstrate Christ's love and forgiveness to her.

Although my parents would be the first to admit they are not perfect in their parenting skills, I see in them a solid and secure reflection of our heavenly Father. They have always loved me unconditionally and more than I deserve.

God took me out of a situation I would not have wanted to be raised in, and placed me in their loving capable hands. I have been through all the things most adoptive children face—questions, uncertainties, and finally finding my birth parents, and have come full circle back to my loving parents.

Adoption Terms

adoption agreement—A document in which birth and adoptive parents agree to a plan of communication between them.

adoption party—A party thrown three or four times each year where families interested in adoption and children who are waiting to be adopted can get acquainted.

adoption plan—The birth parents' decision to allow their child to grow up in an adoptive family.

adoption triad—Birth parents, adoptive parents, and adopted child or children.

adoptive parents—Person or persons who adopt a child.

at-risk placement (or legal-risk placement)—The placement of a child into a family when birth parents' rights have not yet been legally severed or when rights have been severed but the appeal period has not expired.

birth parents, birth mother, or birth father—Biological or genetic parent or parents of a child or children.

confidential adoption (or closed adoption)—An adoption plan where birth and adoptive parents do not meet, do not share identifying information, and do not keep in contact.

designated adoption (or private adoption, identified adoption)—An adoption where birth parents identify a family without the help of a facilitator.

direct consent adoption—An adoption where rights are transferred directly from the birth parents to the adoptive parents.

direct placement—When waiting families receive the infant immediately after discharge from the hospital.

disrupted adoption—An adoption that fails before or after finalization.

domestic adoption—The adoption of a child who is born in the United States.

facilitator—A private or public agency or attorney who helps to arrange an adoption.

family assessment (or home study)—A series of interviews, both joint and individual, and a home visit or visits that are part of the preadoption process for adoptive families.

finalization—The legal process that makes the adoption permanent and binding.

foster care for infants—A temporary, loving home for an infant while the birth parents make a final decision regarding adoption or parenting.

identifying information—Information about members of the adoption triad, such as full names and addresses.

independent adoption—An adoption where the child is placed directly with the adoptive couple, usually through an attorney or intermediary, without preadoption counseling for the birth parents or the adoptive couple.

intake—When the adoptive family provides information to Bethany Christian Services in order to start the adoption process.

interstate compact—A law that requires written notice of the intention to place a child from one state for adoption or foster care with a family in another state.

networking—A process by which waiting families use a variety of techniques to make birth parents aware of their desire to adopt a child.

nonidentifying information—Information that allows the members of the adoption triad to know something about each other, but does not directly identify them to each other, such as first names, physical descriptions, occupation, education, personality characteristics, hobbies, interests, and religious affiliation.

open adoption—An adoption plan where identifying information about birth and adoptive families is openly shared and ongoing contact after placement occurs.

post-placement (or post-adoption) counseling—Counseling offered for adoptive families and birth parents after a child is placed for adoption.

post-placement (or post-adoption) reports—Report submitted by a social worker following a post-placement visit.

post-placement (or post-adoption) support services—Any assistance provided to the adoptive family and birth parents after placement. It always includes visits in order to prepare post-placement reports. Other services are provided as necessary.

pre-placement counseling—Counseling provided to prepare birth parents for the release of their child and to prepare adoptive couples for parenthood.

profile—Pictures and information that introduce a prospective adoptive family to birth parents.

relinquishment of parental rights—*See* voluntary termination of parental rights.

semi-open adoption—An adoption plan where planned communication spelled out in a written agreement takes place between the adoptive and birth parents while the child is growing up. This agreement and communication is arranged through a third party, called a mediator, who is sensitive to issues of both families.

social worker—A trained professional who counsels birth and adoptive parents regarding adoption and parenting.

special-needs adoption (or children with special placement needs)—An adoption involving children who have physical or emotional challenges, who are older children, or who are members of a sibling group or a racial minority, as defined by the federal government.

traditional agency adoption—An adoption where an agency identifies and brings together birth parents, children, and adoptive parents.

voluntary termination of rights (or surrenders)—A situation where birth parents have chosen to legally relinquish their parental rights.

waiting families—Families waiting to adopt a child.

Adoption Resources

The authors found the following resources helpful in their adoption research.

Adoption Exchange
e-mail: kids@adoptex.org
http://adoptex.org

Colorado
14232 E. Evans Avenue
Aurora, CO 80014
1-800-5246 or 303-755-4756

Missouri
100 N. Euclid Ave.
Ste. 910
St. Louis, MO 63108
1-877-ADOPT1 or 314-367-3343

New Mexico
3411 Candelaria NE
Ste. A
Albuquerque, NM 87107
505-247-1769

Nevada
3930 E. Patrick Lane
Ste. 120
Las Vegas, NV 89120
702-436-6335

Utah
1065 s 3300 E.
Salt Lake City, UT 84106
801-412-0200

Adoptive Breastfeeding Resources

LaLeche League International, Carol Bussel, IBCLC
http://www.LaLeche.org
1-800-LaLeche and 1-847-519-7730

http://www.breastfeedinghelp.com

e-mail: adoptivebreastfeeding@yahoogroups.com

Bethany Christian Services (Adoption Counseling and
Unplanned Pregnancy Support)
http://www.bethany.org
http://www.bethany.org/A55798/bethanyWWW.nsf/BCS/loca-
tions (to find pregnancy support near you)
1-800-BETHANY (24/7 Confidential Support)

Birthmothers Answerline
www.birthmother.org

CareNet (Adoption Resources and Unplanned Pregnancy Support and Resources)
109 Carpenter Drive
Ste. 100
Sterling, VA 20164
703-478-5661
1-800-395-HELP
Fax: 703-478-5668
e-mail: carenet@erols.com
http://www.care-net.org/homeframeset.html (to find pregnancy
support near you)

Christian Family Services (Adoption Counseling and
Unplanned Pregnancy Support)
Adoption services, pre-and post-adoption counseling for birth
parents, parenting classes, and more.
Executive Director Pam Fincher
1399 S. Havanna
Aurora, CO 80012
303-337-6747

Dave Thomas Foundation for Adoption
P.O. Box 7164
4288 W. Dublin-Granville Rd.
Dublin, OH 43017
614-764-3009
Fax: 614-764-6707
http://www.davethomasfoundationforadoption.org

Dave Thomas Center for Adoption Law
Capital University Law School
303 East Broad Street
Columbus, OH 43215-3200
614-236-6730
Fax: 614-236-6956

Child Diagnostics, Inc. Dianne Craft, president, has twenty-
five years experience and a master's degree in special education. She works with bright, but struggling children in Little-
ton, Colorado. She is a Certified Natural Health Practitioner
and uses natural supplements to help children feel, learn, and
behave better. She has worked successfully with adopted children with fetal alcohol syndrome, ADD, hyperactivity, mild
autism, learning disabilities, dyslexia, and anger and behavior problems. She urges parents to become partners with God
in working with their children by spending a day in prayer
and fasting. She trains parents to work with their children at
home, using brain integration exercises, right brain strate-
gies, and research-based nutritional therapies. For more infor-

mation and articles about children and learning, visit her web site: http://www.diannecraft.com

Other Resources
http://www.cpclink.com/pages/start.shtml
http://ww.pregnancycenters.org
http://www.teenmoms.ourfamily.com/whats_new.html

Stepping Stones (Offering Christian Support for Those Facing Infertility)
P.O. Box 294
Grand Rapids, MI 49501-0294
616-224-7488
Fax: 616-224-7593
e-mail: step@bethany.org
http://www.bethany.org

National Adoption Center
1500 Walnut Street
Suite 701
Philadelphia, PA 19102
215-735-9988
Fax: 215-735-9410
http://www.adopt.org

National Adoption Information Clearinghouse
330 C Street SW
Washington, DC 20447
1-888-251-0075 or 703-352-3488
Fax: 703-385-3206
e-mail: naic@calib.com
http://www.calib.com/naic

National Council for Adoption
1930 17th Street NW
Washington, DC 20009-6207
202-328-1200
Fax: 202-332-0935

e-mail: ncfa@ncfa-usa.org
http://www.ncfa-usa.org/home.html

North American Council on Adoptable Children
970 Raymond Avenue
Suite 106
St. Paul, MN 55114
651-644-3036
Fax: 651-644-9848
http://www.nacac.org

Contributors

Jeff Adams has written more than twenty plays and hundreds of articles. He is the author of two Bible study series: "Benchmarks of Christianity" and "Principles for Living." For speaking engagements, fax Benchmark Ministries at 520-753-2534 or e-mail adopted@ctaz.com.

Christina Barrett is sixteen and lives in Florida. She is a fulltime student who likes spending time with her family. She also enjoys volleyball, softball, horseback riding, and writing.

Robin Barrett is a full-time mother of two, a wife, and a medical administrative professional. She has gotten involved with her children's activities, such as baseball, coaching her daughters' T-ball team, karate, tap and jazz dancing, volleyball, and art exhibits.

Ann Brandt, a retired English teacher, is a mother of four and grandmother of seven. She writes for Christian and secular publications and is working on a book inspired by Genesis 50:20—how good can come from evil. It is based on her experience with a rare disease. Ann feels that long-distance grandparenting, while challenging, can be done effectively and lovingly.

Anne Calahan is the mother of three children whose activities keep her busy. Anne also enjoys gardening, bicycling, and cross-country skiing.

Jennifer Ciminski volunteered at a pregnancy center, counseling other young women with unplanned pregnancies after her own adoption decision. She got her master's degree and is now a special education teacher working with children with severe emotional disabilities.

Tanya Corn owned and managed her own hair salon for the past six years. Tanya recently sold her salon and is excited about spending more time with her husband and two toddlers.

Stanley B. Cornell owns two cafes with his wife and two sons—both adopted forty-seven years ago. The Children's Aid Society in Springdale, Arkansas, helped Mr. Cornell find the answers to the questions he had for the past seventy-five years. "My many thanks to Mary Ellen Johnson of C.A.S. for her interest in my years of searching. Mr. Vic Remer, Archivist of C.A.S. of New York City, searched the many boxes of stored papers and did find my brother Victor's and my papers that proved Mom and Dad Deger did adopt us. 'All is well' as now I have all the answers to my many questions!"

Linda Cravens is a wife, mother, and freelance writer. She serves as treasurer for the Fellowship of Christian Writers. "Everything I am today," she says, "I owe to Mae and Bill Enlow, who took in a cross-eyed ragamuffin and loved her as their own." You can read other articles by Linda Cravens at http:www.angelfire.com/ok3/literarylegacy.

Donna Davidsen lives in San Ramon, California with her husband, Erik, and son, Danny. They have an active and busy lifestyle, enjoying all sorts of outdoor sports. She was born in Rockford, Illinois and is the second oldest of six children. The five oldest were also adopted. She and her husband adopted their son at birth and are hoping to be blessed with another baby.

Janna Graber lives with her family in Colorado. She is a full-time writer and columnist working for newspapers and is a regular contributor to national magazines such as *Reader's Digest* and *McCalls*.

Lauren Gray is an adoptive mother to one beautiful girl (now 14), was a foster mother to two teen boys, and has been a teacher to hundreds of grade school students. She and her mom coauthored a book on motherhood without a single spat! Contact: klvs2write@aol.com.

Alice and Willie Gregory live in Seattle, Washington, where Willie practices law. They call Thaddaeus a blessing from God.

Susan Horner compiled, edited, and wrote many of the stories for *Loved by Choice*. She has writted for Focus on the Family Club House Jr., Club House, *Breakaway,* and the *Focus on the Family* magazine.

Marcy Hukill lives in Idaho with her husband and three children. They own their own business where she drives a diesel construction truck when needed.

Naydean Julch is a freelance writer who resides in Aurora, Colorado, with her husband, Albert. She is a personal friend of the young woman whose story she tells in "Loved, and Loved Again." When she first heard the story, she knew it was one that needed to be told and that it would bless and encourage others as much as it did her.

Leisa Krueger actively serves in her local church and has a heart for evangelism. She also enjoys entertaining and loves to travel.

Cindy Lambert resides in West Michigan. She is the mother of three children and works as an administrative assistant to the chief of police at a local law enforcement agency. She enjoys spending time with her family and friends, singing, playing her new keyboard, and reading.

Kathryn Lay lives in Texas with her husband and daughter. She writes frequently on parenting, marriage, and humor, as well as stories for children. Her writings have appeared in

Women's Day, Guideposts, Chicken Soup for the Mother's Soul, God Allows U-Turns Vol. 1, and hundreds more. She can be reached at rlay15@aol.com.

Patricia K. Layton is founder and president of A Woman's Place Ministries, a crisis pregnancy center based in Tampa, Florida. She is a busy speaker and writer as well as a wife of twenty-five years, mother of three and grandmother of two. Pat's desire is to write inspirational romance in her "spare" time. Pat can be reached at playton@allocated.com or (813) 931-1804.

Beth Louis has three adopted children. She home-schooled her two youngest children through junior high. Stacey, Beth's youngest child, is now attending college. Beth enjoys playing golf and making creative memory books of her family.

Kelly Fordyce Martindale is a freelance writer and a publisher of a monthly consumer paper. She has written for *Woman's Day, Today's Christian Woman,* and many other women's magazines and newspapers. She has contributed stories to other compilations and is working on a parenting book. You can reach her through www.lovedbychoice.com. She lives in Frederick, Colorado, with her husband and two of her four children.

Ann Cooper McCauley is the author of the historical fiction series *Golden Mountain!* Book one entitled *Gold Seekers* revolves around a Cantonese peasant girl and an American pioneer-missionary. The two are caught in a clash of action, religious persecution, and a flood of romantic emotion that swells into a three-book saga of cultural exchange.

Sue McMillin is president of With Time to Spare, www.withtimetospare.com. She has been featured in the *Washington Post, Changing Times, Brio,* and other publications. She is the author of four books including *Taken by Surprise* and *The Organized Woman.* Sue can be reached at organize@withtimetospare.com.

Anne McNamara has been married for seventeen years and is a mother of two beautiful daughters. She enjoyed a career in the medical field for over twelve years. She currently spends all her time raising her daughters and keeping the house under control. She spends a lot of time doing volunteer work for the schools, MOPS (Mothers of Preschoolers), and her church. Her hobbies include photography, sewing and crafts, and spending a lot of free time outdoors playing with the kids, hiking, camping, skiing, and playing tennis.

Jean M. Olsen and her husband, Dan, retired from missionary service in Africa in 1985 and settled in southern New Jersey. Their daughters, sons-in-law, and grandchildren live near enough to visit them often. When Jean isn't baking fresh cinnamon buns, she teaches piano and Sunday school and does freelance writing.

Greg Patchell and his wife, Donna, and their three kids (Artyom, 6; Vladislav, 5; and Kristina, 3) currently reside in Highlands Ranch, Colorado. Greg and Donna adopted their children from St. Petersburg, Russia, in December of 2000 after being married seven and a half years. Greg is employed in the Denver area and serves in the Army Reserves. The Patchells are members of Community Life Church of South Denver.

Nancy Petty lives in Denver with her husband and four children. She enjoys reading, gardening, and volunteer work involving children.

Michael and Veronica Poe were married in 1997. She has two children from a previous marriage but Michael did not have any until they decided to adopt after three years of marriage. At that time they knew they were ready to share their lives and their love with another child.

Shirley A. Reynolds is a freelance writer with a passion to write and touch hearts through stories of victory and overcoming life's hardships. Through her job as a federal probation clerk, work in her local church, and volunteer outreach to the homeless, Shirley has opportunities for a never ending supply of stories.

Wanda Lee Robb, a minister, mother, and pastor's wife, writes fiction centering around love, tragedy, and God's redeeming power. She is working on a novel about Christians persecuted in South America. She has one book and a three-book series under consideration. She lives in southeast Pennsylvania with her husband, daughter, two dogs, and a cockatiel. She enjoys reading and riding Sarah, her quarter horse.

Amy Roos is an active high school student who loves to play volleyball and soccer. Her friendships are very important to her, and she enjoys teaching Sunday school at her church.

Becky Roos is an athletic high school student who loves volleyball. She enjoys her friendships and the social activities involved in high school as well as teaching Sunday school at her church.

Janie Roos is a registered nurse who now is enjoying staying at home with her three children. She is a Sunday school teacher as well as vice president of the PTCO. She loves hiking and white-water rafting.

Judy Sabah is a professional speaker, author, and business/personal coach. A mother of four and a grandmother of four, she lives in Denver. Her favorite activities are dancing—the polka or waltz—and driving her yellow Saab convertible. Personal and spiritual growth are where she spends much of her time. She may be reached at 303-777-1765 or Sabah-coach@aol.com.

Mary Jo Sattler is a wife, mother, and grandmother. She volunteers for Special Olympics on a regular basis. Mary Jo keeps busy with all the things she manages to say yes to.

Jesika Sorenson is the ninth adopted daughter of missionary parents. She grew up in a biracial family with an international flavor—she has Jewish, Arab, and European siblings. Growing up, it was just Jesika and her parents because her sisters had all moved out on their own. "Though I felt like an only child, I was close to my parents. Their love and concern helped me through the trials of growing up." Jesika and her husband, Rick, are a biracial couple living in Boise, Idaho. She and Rick hope to adopt in the future. If anyone would like to contact Jesika to share their experiences with biracial adoption or receive encouragement or advice, she can be reached at e-mail address: rsorenson@rmci.com.

Cindy Sweeney, single mother of three and grandmother of eight, lives in Vermont and writes in her spare time. Bethany lived with Cindy for almost two years while she finished high school and saved money for college. Bethany is now married and recently gave birth to a son.

Emily Trisdale is currently a junior in high school. She enjoys baby-sitting and traveling with her family. Emily plans on going to college to become a teacher.

William D. Watkins is president of William Pens, a literary agency, and an award-winning writer. Among his own works are seven books, including *The New Absolute*, twenty-five study guides, and about two hundred other pieces of writing. He speaks and teaches nationwide at retreats, conferences, seminars, and educational institutions.

Diane York is a freelance writer of fiction short stories and nonfiction essays. She is a member of the Pens of Fire, a Christian critique and support group for writers. She lives in Kent, Washington, where she works with elderly and disabled clients, helping them with housework tasks.